WORKER BENEFITS

INDUSTRIAL WELFARE
IN AMERICA
1900-1935

An Annotated Bibliography

By MARTHA JANE SOLTOW
And SUSAN GRAVELLE

The Scarecrow Press, Inc.
Metuchen, N.J., and London 1983

016.33125
S 691

Library of Congress Cataloging in Publication Data

Soltow, Martha Jane.
  Worker benefits, industrial welfare in America,
1900-1935.

  Bibliography: p.
  Includes index.
  1. Welfare work in industry--United States--History--
20th century. I. Gravelle, Susan. II. Title.
Z7164.F8S66 1983 [HD7654]   016.33125'5   82-25494
ISBN 0-8108-1614-8

"It does not matter that the head of
some great corporation may be generous, that
he may desire to improve the conditions of the
working people. The working people are not
satisfied with these gifts and benefactions
which are given them by their employers.
What they want is not gifts; they want independence; they want security in their jobs -
the reasonable security that makes them feel
that they may not be dismissed from their employment without good cause and that they
cannot have in the absence of united action."

John Mitchell, President
of the United Mine
Workers, 1914

The above quotation was
part of an exhibit, The
Workers' World; the Indus-
trial Village and the
Company Town, produced
by the Hagley Museum,
Greenville, Wilmington,
Delaware. (1982)

FOREWORD

An article in the New York Times of July 2, 1981,
related how some companies are aiding their employees in
obtaining housing through financing mortgages at lower than
normal interest rates in order to attract a competent labor
force. The early textile industry was also concerned with
securing a qualified labor force. When the necessary water
power for the mills was located in isolated areas, the owners
frequently provided housing for their workers for a nominal
rent.

Workers' housing was only one aspect of employer
welfare programs. For the purpose of this bibliography,
industrial welfare is basically defined as any measure which
provides for the physical and general well-being of the employee, over and above direct wages paid and those programs
required by law.

Welfare work has been called by different names:
"industrial welfare", "industrial betterment", "paternalism",
"welfare capitalism", etc. I have chosen to use the term
"industrial welfare" in the title in order to differentiate
between those programs advanced by private philanthropic organizations, those required by law, and those initiated and
supported by industry.

Literature in this bibliography will primarily cover

the period from the late 19th Century through the 1920's.
The earliest measures were generally concerned with human and
social services while the early Twenties saw a burgeoning of
economic security programs and joint labor-management endeav-
ors. Numerous motives or reasons have been attributed to the
phenomenon of industrial welfare: paternalism, philanthropy,
moral responsibility, social consciousness, pragmatism, anti-
unionism, etc. Likely all of these have come into play at one
time or another. No matter what the motive -- the end result
was an increasing awareness that workers had needs as individ-
uals, that they were not just a means to an end.

The thrust of many employer welfare measures in the
Twenties was toward employee representation plans, or company
unions. These programs were both financially feasible and
useful in combatting trade unionism, at least until the onset
of the Great Depression which made it difficult for companies
to expand or even maintain welfare programs. Section 8(a) of
the National Labor Relations Act (1935) essentially put an end
to such plans by making employer-dominated unions illegal.

For all practical purposes, employer welfare programs are assumed to have ended in the Twenties. This is
questionable -- if anything they expanded. Only the termi-
nology and the stimulus for them changed. Many of the elements
of "employer welfare programs" of the late 19th and early 20th
Centuries are now called "employee benefits". One has only to
look at Employee Benefits, 1981, by the U.S. Chamber of
Commerce to realize that there is not much new in this field;
in 1980 an estimated amount equivalent to 37.1% of U.S. employers' payrolls go for employee benefits. A substantial
number of these benefits are the same as in years gone by:
group insurance, pensions, profit sharing, improved working
conditions, vacations, educational assistance, recreational

facilities, etc.

   The primary difference is that now many of the benefits are regulated by federal and state law and collective
bargaining rather than unilateral voluntary action on the part
of the employer. Another important difference is the change
in the philosophical concept of obligation owed the worker.
In any event, historically the "welfare capitalism" movement
was one step in the process of industrialization in America --
and a very vital one.

TABLE OF CONTENTS

INTRODUCTION

The majority of literature surveyed in this bibliography falls into 1) surveys of existing industrial welfare
programs, 2) descriptions of specific industry programs, 3)
descriptions of specific company programs, 4) descriptions of a
particular benefit, 5) biographies of leaders in the field,
and 6) scholarly works of an analytical nature. A section has
been added on labor's response to welfare capitalism; most of
this material was extracted from parts of larger works.
Sources included are secondary and are comprised of books;
special surveys and reports of industry and private organizations; government and state documents; publications of the
American Federation of Labor; pamphlet material; and above
all -- periodical literature. Relative to the latter -- two
particularly useful journals which contain a plethora of rele-
vant articles are 1) <u>Law and Labor</u> (1919-1932), and 2) <u>Engi-
neering Magazine</u> which became <u>Factory and Industrial Manage-
ment</u> (1891-1933).

This bibliography is selective in nature. On several occasions when we were not able to locate a particular
title and if the citation sounded useful it was included --
when this occurs no annotation follows. But more often than
not titles were left out when they were not able to be located
through inter-library loan.

Entries have not been duplicated except for one or

two exceptions. Because there is actually so little visable
material on labor's response to industrial welfare, these
sources were sometimes included in more than one section. A
few classic works in the field will also be found in two
places. The bibliography is arranged by categories to enable
researchers to easily locate materials on a particular topic.
However, many works do not readily fall under one heading exclusively; in this case we arbitrarily assigned sections.
Separate indexes include 1) Company Index and 2) Miscellaneous
Index.

        We wish to acknowledge the encouragement and con-
tinued support of Dr. Jack Stieber, Director of the School of
Labor and Industrial Relations. We also would like to express
our appreciation to Nancy Barkey Young, on whose shoulders
fell extra duties during the final stages of the preparation
of the manuscript. We are particularly grateful for Cynthia
Bullock's assistance in re-reading and proofreading the
manuscript. Her critical acumen and conscientious attention
to details has contributed immeasurably to the finalization
of the manuscript.

        As always in a bibliography of this kind, there will
be certain works which might or should have been included
depending on the approach of the user and/or ones depth of
knowledge. But it is hoped that this work will prove useful
for labor history scholars and that not too many major omis-
sions have occurred.

                Martha Jane Soltow

                Librarian
                School of Labor and Industrial Relations
                Michigan State University

Susan Gravelle

Graduate Assistant
School of Labor and Industrial Relations
Michigan State University

October 1982

DEVELOPMENT OF INDUSTRIAL WELFARE

Works in this section are primarily philosophical overviews
of industrial welfare. They examine the theoretical basis,
historical development, and reasons for the adoption of certain measures as well as theoretical analyses of the relationship of the worker to his company and job. Some works
discuss welfare as an anti-union tactic while others cite
business reasons or social responsibility as justifications
for the programs. They consider benefits of welfare to both
employees and employers and include advantages and shortcomings. Some works examine the relationship of industrial
welfare to other personnel ventures such as scientific
management and the efficiency movement. The role in industrial welfare of such organizations as the National Civic
Federation is discussed in this section.

1 Beeks, Gertrude. "Employees' welfare work." Independent,
     55:2864, October 22, 1903, 2515-2518.
        A philosophical overview of employer welfare by the
     welfare secretary of the International Harvester Com-
     pany and head of the Welfare Department of the National
     Civic Federation. Believes employers have a duty to
     care for the needs of employees. Suggests programs
     should be individually tailored to the needs of each
     company and discusses the advantages of a variety of
     programs. "Honesty of purpose" is necessary to devel-
     op workers' confidence in welfare programs.

2 Bendix, Reinhard. Work and authority in industry: ideol-
     ogies of management in the course of industrialization.
     New York, Harper and Row, 1963. 464 p.
        Pages 281-287 examine the emphasis on cooperation
     between labor and management that developed after
     World War I in the form of employee representation
     plans. Discusses philosophical implications of the

partnership of labor, management, and capital. Page
273 suggests that companies adopted welfare as part of
an open shop drive to keep unions out. Workers could
only expect to receive benefits if their output was
high and they did not join unions.

3   Berkowitz, Edward and Kim McQuaid. Creating the welfare
     state: the political economy of 20th century reform.
     New York, Praeger Publishers, 1980. 185 p.
        Chapter I centers around the contributions of three
     early proponents of industrial welfare: Nelson Olsen
     Nelson, Edward A. Filene, and Henry S. Dennison. Chap-
     ter III is concerned with the rise of welfare capital-
     ism, 1910-1930. Discusses General Electric's indus-
     trial relations policies. Each chapter contains exten-
     sive footnotes.

4   Bernstein, Irving. The Lean years: a history of the Amer-
     ican worker, 1920-1933. Baltimore, Penguin Books,
     1960. 577 p.
        Chapter 3 discusses employers' dealings with their
     workers, including the introduction of employer wel-
     fare programs. Traces the evolution from the use of
     hostile anti-union tactics to the subtler weapon of
     industrial welfare. Describes the development of the
     "Rockefeller Plan" for employee representation and
     welfare in the Colorado Fuel and Iron Company and dis-
     cusses a variety of programs of other companies. Pre-
     sents an overview of group life insurance, pensions,
     housing assistance, and stock ownership programs. Wel-
     fare was doomed to eventual failure because workers
     wouldn't put up with paternalism indefinitely.

5   Boettiger, Louis A. Employer welfare work. New York, Ron-
     ald Press Company, 1923. 301 p.
        Traces employer welfare programs from the medieval
     manor and guild up to American and European factories
     of 1920s. In addition to describing a wide variety of
     welfare programs, this work investigates theories and
     motives that impelled employers to institute these pro-
     grams. In this context, the programs of a variety of
     major corporations are briefly outlined and the ef-
     forts of welfare pioneers, including Americans Francis
     Cabot Lowell and Nathan Appleton, are discussed.

6   Bonnett, Clarence E. <u>Employers associations in the U.S.</u>
    New York, Macmillan Company, 1922. 594 p.
        Chapter 11 presents an overview of the National Civ-
    ic Federation, which included large employers, labor
    unions, and prominent citizens. Its purposes were "to
    promote industrial peace and prosperity" and to serve
    as an agent of "industrial conciliation and arbitra-
    tion." Believed employers had an obligation to pro-
    vide for employees' welfare. Claimed the chief rea-
    son for labor trouble is lack of communication between
    workers and the company. Welfare efforts focused on
    sanitary work places, recreation, education, housing,
    savings and loans funds, and industrial insurance.
    Outlines work of the Welfare Department and the Depart-
    ment of Pensions. Includes extensive bibliography.

7   Brandes, Stuart D. <u>American welfare capitalism: 1880-</u>
    <u>1940</u>. Chicago, University of Chicago Press, 1976.
    210 p.
        Traces the historical development of industrial wel-
    fare and outlines a wide variety of programs in several
    companies. Considers reasons for growth of welfarism,
    such as benevolence, union avoidance, enhancement of
    public image, and encouragement of loyalty and produc-
    tivity. The last chapter deals with the reasons for
    the decline of welfare capitalism which include worker
    resentment of paternalism, the Depression, labor legis-
    lation, and general prosperity.

8   Brody, David. "The rise and decline of welfare capita-
    lism." In <u>Change and continuity in 20th Century Amer-</u>
    <u>ica: the 1920s</u>. Edited by John Braeman, et al. Col-
    umbus, Ohio State University Press, 1968. 147-178 p.
        A little under half of this article is devoted to a
    general overview of industrial welfare, the remainder
    analyzes the reasons for its failure. Coverage ends
    with the early 1930s.

9   Brooks, John Graham. <u>Labor's challenge to the social or-</u>
    <u>der</u>. New York, Macmillan Company, 1920. 441 p.
        Chapter 7 provides an overview of welfare programs
    of several companies. Suggests welfare developed out
    of the emerging philosophy that labor is not a commod-
    ity. Defends welfare, claiming labor's attacks on it
    fail to consider its effect on employers' attitudes

toward workers and its educational benefits for workers. Chapter 19 surveys the development and motives
of profit-sharing plans.

10 Brown, H.F. "Industrial relations activities survive a
    critical test." Personnel journal, 13, 1935, 258-
    262.
        Examines conflicting theories relating to the rea-
    sons for employer welfare. One theory suggests welfare
    is based on a "misplaced paternalistic idea of philan-
    thropy" of a "policy of trying to hood-wink employees
    and wean them away from ideas of class consciousness
    and class struggle" while the other theory contends
    welfare was introduced to develop cooperation between
    management and workers and to reward accomplishment and
    service. If the first theory were true, welfare would
    not survive the Depression while, under the second
    theory, since welfare is an integral part of management
    policy, employers would retain as many programs as pos-
    sible. Surveys welfare's survival record at 233 com-
    panies during the Depression and finds most programs
    were retained, thus supporting the cooperation and re-
    ward theory. Estimates company expenditures on wel-
    fare in 1933.

11 Chu, Paul. "The modern approach to industrial welfare."
    International labour review, 71:6, June 1955, 555-574.
        Examines the nature, scope, and objectives of var-
    ious types of industrial welfare. Suggests welfare
    programs should help workers take part in the social
    and economic life of modern society. Welfare should
    be tailored to the needs of workers and should be of-
    fered to workers rather than forced upon them. Work-
    ers should participate in the administration of welfare
    services.

12 Commons, John R. Industrial goodwill. New York, McGraw-
    Hill, 1919. 213 p.
        A philosophical treatise on the need for goodwill
    between employees and employers. Compares commodity
    and scientific theories of management to industrial
    welfare as means of motivating and retaining workers.
    Examines the potential for using theories of democracy
    in dealing with workers. Chapter 12 presents a model
    plan for industrial democracy through shop committees

and discusses problems and benefits of various types of
employee representation. Weighs the costs and benefits
of providing such welfare measures as insurance, health
care, and educational opportunities.

13 Cook, E. Wake. Betterment; individual, social, and indus-
    trial; or highest efficiency through the golden rules
    of right nutrition; welfare work; and the higher indus-
    trial developments. New York, F.A. Stokes Company,
    1906. 349 p.
        A philosophical examination of employers' welfare.
    Suggests that welfare work pays because it makes work-
    ers more productive. Education develops worker cap-
    abilities, health and medical care preserves worker ef-
    ficiency, and adequate housing encourages employees to
    stay with a company. Providing schools for workers'
    children decreases juvenile delinquency. The National
    Cash Register Company is used as an example of model
    welfare. The company sponsored major community im-
    provement projects and provided such welfare benefits
    as a dining room with low-cost meals, a cooking school,
    and recreational activities.

14 Derber, Milton. The American idea of industrial democ-
    racy, 1865-1965. Urbana, University of Illinois
    Press, 1970. 553 p.
        Chapter 8 surveys welfare capitalism in the 1920s.
    A major reason for the development of welfare and the
    personnel function in industry was to keep trade unions
    out. Traces the development of welfare and stresses
    the need to gain the confidence of employees before
    welfare will work. Outlines the history of employee
    representation plans and briefly describes plans of
    pioneering companies. Company unions were different
    from trade unions because they were employer controlled,
    they discussed nonvital issues, and they had no real
    authority.

15 Duncan, James P. "The aims of industrial welfare." The
    Modern hospital, 7:2, August 1916, 127-128.
        A brief outline of the goals and scope of industrial
    welfare. Welfare is viewed as a service employers
    should willingly provide in appreciation for hard work
    and faithful service. Companies are morally obligated
    to care for worn out, depreciated workers just as they

care for the depreciation of machinery.

16 Dunn, Robert W. The Americanization of labor: the em-
    ployers' offensive against trade unions. New York,
    International Publishers, 1927. 272 p.
        Chapters 9-11 survey a variety of welfare programs
    adopted both as a defensive move against unions and
    out of humanitarian motives. True company motives for
    introducing welfare were to increase productivity, to
    attract high quality labor, to reduce turnover, to de-
    velop loyalty in order to keep workers docile, and to
    provide an excuse to keep wages low. Describes pro-
    grams of specific companies. Programs included mutual
    benefit associations, lunch rooms, athletics, educa-
    tion, thrift plans, and medical care. Cost of welfare
    and personnel work is assessed.

17 Dunn, Robert W. "The industrial welfare offensive." In
    J.B.S. Hardman, American labor dynamics in the light of
    post-war developments. New York, Harcourt, Brace and
    Company, 1928. 213-225 p.
        Examines welfare as a means of combatting unions.
    Estimates the scope of welfare programs including com-
    pany unions, stock ownership, group insurance, and pen-
    sions. Purposes of welfare are to fix "the workers'
    loyalty to a specific plant or company," to give work-
    ers a vested interest in the company, to find out what
    workers are thinking, and to lower turnover. Manage-
    ment usually retains the right to eliminate benefits
    at any time. Claims many companies with extensive
    welfare programs are among the most vigorous in op-
    posing unions. Suggests trade unions should take over
    company unions and make them independent from manage-
    ment.

18 Eilburt, Henry. "The development of personnel management
    in the United States." Business history review, 33,
    Fall 1959, 345-364.
        Author theorizes that personnel management is the
    outgrowth of industrial welfare on the one hand and
    scientific management on the other. Historical over-
    view covers from approximately 1900 to early 1920s.

19 Epstein, Abraham. "American labor and social legislation."
    In J.B.S. Hardman, American labor dynamics in the light
    of post-war developments. New York, Harcourt, Brace and
    Company, 1928. 245-252 p.
        Claims "the spread of industrial welfare in the last
    decade has undermined the very basis of existing Amer-
    ican unions". Companies have improved conditions to
    the point that unions have nothing to bargain for.
    Shortcomings of welfare are that benefits are only pro-
    vided by large firms, employees must often work sever-
    al years for one company to receive benefits, and bene-
    fits are never guaranteed. Claims costs of welfare to
    employers are inconsequential. Suggests the role of
    unions in the future should be to negotiate benefits
    without the shortcomings of welfare.

20 Epstein, Abraham. "Industrial welfare movement sapping
    American trade unions." Current history, 24:4, July
    1926, 516-522.
        A survey of industrial welfare practices of over
    1500 of the largest companies in the United States.
    Article describes the scope, incidence, and reasons
    for the growth of popular welfare programs and dis-
    cusses the adverse effects of such programs on the
    trade union movement. It compares the declining fre-
    quency of labor disputes in industries that incorporate
    industrial welfare to the continuing high rates of
    conflict in industries without welfare programs.

21 Epstein, Abraham. "Outwitting American unionism." The
    New republic, 47, April 6, 1927, 190-193.
        Advocates need for social legislation to provide
    benefits to workers. Contends private welfare pro-
    grams make workers too dependent on companies and have
    only succeeded because unions have failed to provide
    these benefits. Blames decline of unionism on this
    factor. Defects of the company welfare movement are
    that only large companies can afford to provide bene-
    fits; workers must stay with one company a long time
    to collect benefits; benefits are not guaranteed; and
    not enough is spent on welfare programs.

22 Filene, A. Lincoln. A Merchant's horizon. Boston,
       Houghton Mifflin Company, 1924. 266 p.
          A philosophical justification of industrial welfare
       and democracy in Filene's department store in Boston.
       Written by one of the store's founders, book describes
       how employees were made partners through profit-sharing
       and stock ownership. A cooperative association, man-
       aged solely by workers to avoid paternalism, instituted
       a wide variety of work rules and welfare programs.
       Filene's opposed unions because adversarial relation-
       ships conflicted with the spirit of the cooperative
       association.

23 Filene, Edward A. The Way out: a forecast of coming
       changes in American business and industry. Garden
       City, NY, Doubleday, Page, and Company, 1925. 306 p.
          A theoretical analysis of the role of the worker in
       industry, written by the owner of Filene's department
       store, a leader in industrial welfare. Believes be-
       nevolence and paternalism are not the ways to solve
       business issues. Advocates business based on indus-
       trial democracy. Says business practices should pro-
       mote a better social order and employees should have
       a voice in determining their conditions of work. Con-
       tends industrial democracy is inevitable due to the
       increasing democracy in government and the political
       power of the masses.

24 Fleisher, Alexander. "Welfare service for employes."
       Annals of the American Academy of Political and Social
       Science, 69, January 1917, 51-57.
          Overview of industrial welfare. Explains the im-
       portance of welfare benefits such as good working con-
       ditions and vacations and examines reasons for in-
       stalling welfare programs. Positive reasons are the
       owner's personal interest in his employees and a real-
       ization of the value of the human factor in produc-
       tion. Welfare is used to encourage a loyal, stable
       work force. Negative reasons for welfare include
       using it as a means of combatting unionism and as an
       excuse to keep wages low.

25 Frankel, Lee K. and Alexander Fleisher. The Human factor
    in industry. New York, Macmillan Company, 1924.   366
    p.
        Traces historical roots of industrial welfare from
    medieval guilds and manors to the welfare system of the
    early 1920s. Investigates the relation of industrial
    welfare to the efficiency movement and scientific man-
    agement programs. Considers the value of industrial
    welfare to both employers and employees and examines
    the effects of outside factors such as trade unions
    and labor legislation.

26 Granger, Marshall Allen.   ... An Application of the
    teachings of Christ to the relation of the employer to
    his employees. Lawrence, University of Kansas, 1914.
    (University of Kansas News Bulletin, 15:9, November
    23, 1914)   29 p.
        Advocates applying the Golden Rule of "do unto
    others as you would have them do unto you" to relieve
    the conditions of workers. Lists successful welfare
    programs of several companies to show the variety of
    programs that may be undertaken. Recognizes that the
    average employer is not moved by charity and cannot
    afford to play the good Samaritan but says welfare is
    also good business since it increases productivity.
    Says the employers' greatest reward will be seeing
    his workers healthier and happier.

27 Green, Marguerite. The National Civic Federation and the
    American labor movement, 1900-1925. Washington, Cath-
    olic University of American Press, 1956.   537 p.
        Chapter 6 examines the relationship between organ-
    ized labor and the Welfare Department of the National
    Civic Federation. A dichotomy existed between the
    official attitude of the Federation's labor members
    and labor leaders in general. The Welfare Depart-
    ment's initial goal was the establishment of workers'
    compensation laws. It also tried to educate employers
    on the benefits of welfare activities. The Federa-
    tion's Woman's Department and Department of Pensions
    and Social Insurance also pushed for welfare advances.

28 Hagedorn, Homer J. "A note on the motivation of per-
    sonnel management: industrial welfare, 1885-1910."
    Explorations in entrepreneurial history, 10:3-4,

April 1958, 134-139.
   Authors basic premise is that industrial welfare
flourished because of the possibility of labor short-
ages. Secondary reasons given were: anti-union feel-
ing and desire to increase efficiency. The influence
of Josiah Strong and William Tolman is discussed.

29 Heald, Morrell. The Social responsibilities of business:
    company and community, 1900-1960. Cleveland, Press of
    Case Western Reserve University, 1970. 339 p.
       Chapter 1 traces the development of employers'
    "social responsibility" to care for the welfare of
    their employees. Discusses the growth and decline of
    company towns in the railroad, textile, and iron and
    steel industries. Describes Pullman, Illinois, a show-
    place company town in its face but "riddled with sus-
    picion and fear." Examines the employee welfare move-
    ment that developed through YMCAs in the railroad in-
    dustry. Chapter 2 discusses the involvement of busi-
    ness leaders in "social uplift, civic improvement,
    beautification, and cultural enrichment." Describes
    welfare programs of leading companies and philanthro-
    pists.

30 Henderson, Charles Richmond. Citizens in industry. New
    York, D. Appleton and Company, 1915. 342 p.
       A philosophical overview of industrial welfare.
    Contends that welfare should be undertaken out of a
    desire to provide workers the best conditions possible,
    not out of a desire to control their lives. Suggests
    introducing welfare for good business reasons so work-
    ers do not feel patronized. Examines employee atti-
    tudes toward welfare and outlines a wide variety of
    programs in several industries. Appendix lists com-
    panies known for welfare efforts.

31 Herring, Harriet L. Welfare work in mill villages; the
    story of extra-mill activities in North Carolina.
    Chapel Hill, University of North Carolina Press, 1929.
    406 p.
       A scholarly overview of industrial welfare in the
    textile industry, with chapters on the general history
    and philosophy of employer welfare programs. Although
    this work deals primarily with the textile industry,
    its depth of analysis of programs and welfare issues

make it a broadly comprehensive study of industrial
welfare in general. Examines a full range of benefits,
many of which developed out of necessity in villages
isolated from established towns. Discusses variations
in the type and scope of welfare offered.

32 Houser, J. David. What the employer thinks: executives'
    attitudes toward employees. Cambridge, Harvard Univer-
    sity Press, 1927. 226 p.
        A survey of executives' attitudes and policies to-
    ward their employees and employee reactions to those
    policies. Includes discussion of welfare programs and
    motives for providing them. Executives generally felt
    an obligation to provide for physical and financial
    needs of workers but few felt obligated to promote per-
    sonal development. Executives in companies with well-
    developed welfare programs felt the greatest respon-
    sibility for the overall well-being of workers.

33 Hubbard, Charles W. "Some practical principles of wel-
    fare work." Journal of social science, 42, September
    1904, 83-94.
        Examines employer welfare as a means of assimilat-
    ing immigrants and the poor into society. Believes
    working conditions should develop good citizens. Em-
    ployees should be asked to voluntarily contribute to
    welfare programs and should participate in the admin-
    istration of programs. Emphasizes the development of
    pleasant and sanitary working conditions and discusses
    problems of providing workers' housing. Advocates pro-
    viding education in practical skills, especially for
    workers' children, in order to develop responsible
    citizens.

34 "Industrial peace and progress by the committee of 36,
    National Civic Federation." American federationist,
    9:3, 1902, 93-113.
        Commentary by business, labor, and public opinion
    leaders on the creation of the National Civic Federa-
    tion Industrial Department. Many of the comments come
    from individuals selected to serve on the industrial
    committee. Comments outline philosophical purposes
    and aspirations of the Department, emphasizing the
    need for harmony between capital and labor.

35 Industrial-Railroad Conference on new ideals in industrial
       betterment. Chicago, YMCA College, 1916. 71 p.
       Addresses from a conference on industrial welfare.
    Includes addresses on general philosophies of welfare
    as well as addresses describing programs of the Western
    Electric Company, the International Harvester Company,
    Westinghouse Air Brake Company, M.K. and T. Railroad,
    the Cortescope Company, and Ward Baking Company. The
    general consensus of the conference was that employers
    have a responsibility to care for the needs of workers.
    Genuine welfare is motivated by a desire to help work-
    ers, not just a desire to increase their productivity.

36 Labor Research Association. Labor fact book, v. 1. New
       York, Oriole Editions, Inc., 1972. 222 p.
       Pages 144-150 briefly outline a number of employer
    welfare programs, claiming all of them were introduced
    to tie workers to companies in order to keep out
    unions, avoid strikes, and get rid of "reds." Company
    unions, employee stock ownership, pensions, and group
    insurance are discussed in this light. Attacks com-
    pany-sponsored employee magazines as devices "to mis-
    lead the workers" and "enhance loyalty."

37 Laidler, Harry W. New tactics in social conflict. New
       York, Vanguard Press, League for Industrial Democracy,
       1926. 230 p.
       Section 3 presents a panel discussion on the chang-
    ing tactics of employers toward workers. Examines wel-
    fare as a challenge to the trade union movement and as
    a means of reducing turnover, increasing productivity,
    and enhancing loyalty. One speaker lists firms with
    company unions and says they give workers control over
    insignificant issues. Organized labor argues company
    unions have no power because they lack the right to
    strike, they have no treasury, they deal only with
    nonvital matters, mass meetings of workers are not per-
    mitted, and management has the final say on all mat-
    ters. The benefits of stock ownership, group insur-
    ance, and unemployment protection are also discussed.
    Representatives of the Standard Oil and General Elec-
    tric Companies describe and defend welfare in their
    firms.

38 Lee, John. The Principles of industrial welfare. London,
      Sir Isaac Pitman and Sons, Ltd., 1924. 94 p.
        A philosophical overview of industrial welfare.
      Discusses the responsibility of employers to provide
      for the welfare of employees and puts employer welfare
      in historical perspective. Mutuality is necessary to
      a successful relationship since workers surrender free-
      doms in exchange for benefits.

39 Leiserson, William M. "Contributions of personnel manage-
      ment to improved labor relations." In Wertheim lec-
      tures on industrial relations. Cambridge, Harvard Uni-
      versity Press, 1929. 125-164 p.
        Discusses role of personnel management in industry.
      Includes welfare work as personnel function based on
      a belief that employers have a duty to care for work-
      ers. Enumerates welfare measures and describes their
      growth throughout industry. Also includes development
      of employee representation plans and company unions as
      a personnel function designed to give employees a de-
      gree of self determination while keeping them away
      from antagonistic independent unions.

40 Lenin, V.I. "The ideas of an advanced capitalist." In
      Collected works, v. 19. Moscow, Rabochaya Pravda No. 4,
      July 17, 1913. 275-276 p.
        Soviet leader V.I. Lenin attacks Edward A. Filene's
      refutation of Marxism. Filene, founder of William Fi-
      lene's Sons department store in Boston, agrees with
      Marx that the masses will control the world. However,
      unlike Marx, Filene believes the masses will be led by
      their employers, the merchants and industrialists.
      Lenin attacks Filene's industrial democracy and welfare
      programs, claiming Filene must think his employees are
      "simpletons" if he expects them to be satisfied and
      grateful under such paternalism.

41 Lescohier, Don D. History of labor in the United States,
      1896-1932, v. 3. New York, Macmillan, 1935. 778 p.
        Chapter 17 traces the history of welfare work.
      Considers reasons for introducing welfare and examines
      incongruities of some programs. For instance, expen-
      sive libraries were sometimes provided for a work
      force that could barely speak English. Discusses the
      success of welfare in improving loyalty and work per-

formance. Surveys a wide variety of welfare benefits,
using examples from specific companies. Reasons for
failure of welfare include combining welfare with low
wages, long hours, and speed ups and intruding into
workers' private lives. During World War I, welfare
became popular as a means of attracting and retaining
scarce labor supplies. Other chapters survey medical
benefits, profit-sharing, and pensions.

42 MacLean, Annie M. "Trade unionism versus welfare work
      for women." Popular science monthly, 87:1, July 1915,
      50-55.
         Examines efforts at fair treatment of women in in-
      dustry. Compares the success of trade unionism and
      welfare work in improving working conditions. Sug-
      gests that the ultimate goal of unions is to elevate
      the working class and make workers better citizens.
      However, while welfare work may make employers better
      citizens, all it does for workers is make them depen-
      dent. Welfare work should strive to develop character
      and values as well as better physical condition.

43 National Civic Federation. Welfare Department. Confer-
      ence on welfare work. New York, Press of Andrew C.
      Kellogg Company, 1904. 205 p.
         A collection of addresses on industrial welfare,
      including addresses by leaders of several companies
      noted for welfare work. To be successful, welfare
      should be structured to insure protection of workers'
      self respect. Employee representation plans should
      not be too democratic or employees will be overbur-
      dened by committee work. Employees' physical well-
      being is of the utmost importance.

44 National Industrial Conference Board. Effect of the De-
      pression on industrial relations programs. New York,
      1934. 17 p.
         Examines changes in welfare programs during the De-
      pression. Due to the surplus of labor, welfare was
      no longer needed to keep turnover low. Some employers
      dropped programs without proven financial value to the
      company but many programs were maintained because they
      had become regular and necessary features of company
      policy.

45   Nelson, Daniel. Frederick W. Taylor and the rise of sci-
       entific management. Madison, University of Wisconsin
       Press, 1980. 259 p.
         Pages 16-19 and 118-119 discuss and criticize wel-
       fare programs of the National Cash Register Company.
       In Frederick Taylor's opinion such programs are a
       paternalistic demanding attempt to avoid unions and
       labor unrest. Ironically, Taylor's scientific manage-
       ment theories escalated the welfare movement.

46   Nelson, Daniel and Stuart Campbell. "Taylorism versus
       welfare work in American industry: H.L. Gantt and the
       Bancrofts." Business history review, 46:1, Spring
       1972, 1-16.
         Discusses the competing philosophies of Taylorism
       and welfare work and outlines their similarities,
       differences, and reasons for antagonism. Both devel-
       oped "in response to the businessman's demand for a
       more systematic approach to labor problems." Techni-
       cally-oriented Taylorism developed mostly in machinery
       industries while socially motivated welfare was found
       in department stores, textile mills, mines, and steel
       mills. Discusses Joseph Bancroft and Sons Company,
       the first firm to introduce both Taylorism and wel-
       fare. Welfare included housing, schools, low cost
       meals, in-plant laundry service, an emergency room,
       a library, and sewing and cooking classes. Employees
       resisted the introduction of Taylorism because its
       tactics clashed with the spirit of welfare; Taylorism
       was discarded in favor of welfare.

47   Noble, David. America by design: science, technology,
       and the rise of corporate capitalism. New York, Al-
       fred A. Knopf, 1977. 384 p.
         Pages 265 and 287-288 briefly discuss welfare work
       as the forerunner of modern industrial relations.
       Considers workers' resentment of paternalism as the
       major reason for the decline of industrial welfare.

48   Person, H.S. "Welfare work, industrial." Encyclopedia of
       the social sciences, v. 15. New York, Macmillan Com-
       pany, 1935. 395-399 p.
         A brief overview of industrial welfare. Defines
       employer welfare, discusses paternalism and enumerates
       a variety of welfare programs. Lists motives for

16 Development

installing welfare and traces its historical roots.
Considers the influence of welfare work in social legislation.

49 "Personnel and employment problems." Monthly review of
    the U.S. Bureau of Labor Statistics (Monthly labor re-
    view) 3:2, August 1916, 21-26.
        Summarizes papers presented at a managers' conference
    on personnel and employment problems. Includes a dis-
    cussion of welfare programs as a means of dealing with
    the human element of industry. Analyzes the role of the
    employment manager in developing these and other person-
    nel programs. Welfare can help reduce turnover, elimi-
    nate waste, and make workers more productive.

50 Porter, H.F.J. "The higher law in the industrial world."
    Engineering magazine, 29:5, August 1905, 641-655.
        Suggests employers should treat all employees as if
    they were valued industrial experts. Advocates welfare
    as a means of bringing management and labor into closer
    touch. A spirit of cooperation is necessary if business
    is to succeed and welfare can help develop this spirit.
    Employers need to give employees a stake in the success
    of the company and a voice in management through em-
    ployee representation. Describes a number of welfare
    programs and explains their advantages.

51 Porter, H.F.J. "Industrial betterment." Cassier's maga-
    zine, 38:4, August 1910, 303-314.
        Overview of industrial betterment in the United
    States. Suggests employers should avoid paternalism
    by instituting programs for good business reasons such
    as improving workers' productivity. Contends that in-
    dustrial betterment and democracy will eliminate the
    need for unions and will replace antagonism with cooper-
    ation. Outlines a typical employee representation plan
    and advocates providing education, health care, comfort-
    able housing, and other benefits to build a better work
    force.

52 Pratt, Edward Ewing. "A new industrial democracy." Annals
    of the American Academy of Political and Social Science,
    44, November 1912, 28-38.
        Traces movement toward increased industrial welfare

and concern for the well-being of workers. Employers
espouse industrial welfare both for the sake of the
workers and to increase their efficiency. Discusses
loss of efficiency, vocational education, and personal
relationships under the factory system and examines
welfare work as a means of returning these elements to
industry. Describes workers' struggles for a voice in
management through industrial democracy and emphasizes
the importance of worker loyalty and good will.

53 Price, C.W. Working conditions, wages and profits. Chicago, A.W. Shaw Company, 1920. 254 p.
     Part I, "The well-being of employees," examines the
relationship between good working conditions and profit.
Discusses the effects of welfare on absenteeism and productivity and estimates costs of various welfare programs. Describes how employers can help workers help
themselves through programs such as savings incentive
plans. Stresses the importance of maintaining a healthy
work force by providing meals and medical care.

54 Price, George M. The Modern factory: safety, sanitation,
and welfare. New York, John Wiley, 1914. 287-346 p.
     Chapter 7 provides an overview of industrial welfare
programs tracing historical development and examining
employer motives for introducing it. Motives include
fear of unionism, benevolence, and a desire for improved
worker productivity. Workers sometimes opposed welfare
because it was paternalistic, they were suspicious of
employer motives, and they viewed it as an anti-union
weapon. A wide range of welfare programs is outlined
using specific companies as examples.

55 Redfield, William C. The New industrial day: a book for
men who employ men. New York, The Century Company,
1912. 213 p.
     Suggests that workers should be treated with as much
care as machines are treated since a happy work force
can be an employer's greatest asset. Welfare not only
makes workers healthier and happier but also more productive. Emphasizes need for medical care and sanitary
working conditions.

56 Simons, Algie M. Personnel relations in industry. New
       York, Ronald Press Company, 1921. 341 p.
          A philosophical discussion of how welfare work fits
       into an overall personnel program. Chapter 11 outlines
       various welfare programs, stressing that companies
       should improve working conditions before attempting
       betterment in other areas. Emphasizes the need for
       recreation and health programs to keep workers strong
       and productive. Chapters 16-18 examine industrial de-
       mocracy and evaluate the strengths and weaknesses of
       various employee representation plans.

57 Slichter, Sumner. "Current labor policies of American in-
       dustries." Quarterly journal of economics, 43, May
       1929, 393-435.
          Traces the growth of humanistic labor policies,
       which employers developed to combat labor unrest and
       to improve workers' morale and encourage greater effi-
       ciency. Outlines various types of welfare programs,
       with examples from specific companies. Results of
       employer welfare have been increased productivity, a
       drop in union membership, fewer strikes, and lower
       turnover. The major problem is paternalism because
       the worker is encouraged to rely on the company in-
       stead of himself.

58 Tarbell, Ida. New ideals in business: an account of
       their practice and their effects upon men and profits.
       New York, Macmillan Company, 1916. 339 p.
          Suggests employer should provide welfare as part of
       a spirit of cooperation between workers and management.
       Chapter 2 surveys programs of several companies, in-
       cluding tennis courts, playgrounds, and lunch rooms.
       Welfare is worthwhile if it makes the workers say, "Gee,
       but this is a fine place to work!" Says employer lead-
       ership should develop "such a spirit of happiness that
       men and women are again singing at their work." Chapter
       4 discusses benefits of providing medical care for work-
       ers. Says benefits to the company can be concretely
       measured in terms of days saved and product increased.
       Chapter 6 suggests turnover can be reduced by such bene-
       fits as profit-sharing, pensions, and stock ownership.

59 Taylor, Albion G. Labor policies of the National Associa-
       tion of Manufacturers. (University of Illinois,

Studies in the Social Sciences, 15:1) Urbana, University of Illinois Press, 1928. 184 p.
     Chapter 7 outlines industrial betterment projects
of the National Association of Manufacturers. The
Association attempted to teach workers that the interests of employees and employers are identical. To
care for the needs of workers, the National Association
of Manufacturers advocated health insurance, vocational
education, and employee representation. A brief over-
view of these programs is presented.

60 Todd, Arthur J. "The organization and promotion of in-
       dustrial welfare through voluntary efforts." Annals
       of the American Academy of Political and Social Science,
       105, January 1923, 76-82.
          Examines motives and merits of industrial welfare.
       Estimates the prevalence, cost, and ease of administer-
       ing various programs. Examines various views on the
       employers' responsibility to provide for the welfare of
       the worker and discusses the hostility of organized
       labor toward the motives and methods of welfare.
       Unions opposed welfare because it was paternalistic
       and made workers' dependent on the employers. Presents
       various opinions on whether welfare is compatible with
       collective bargaining. Concludes that wages are not
       lower when welfare is provided and welfare will not
       prevent labor trouble.

61 Todd, Arthur J. "Reaching the main springs of the wills
       of people." Annals of the American Academy of Politi-
       cal and Social Science, 91, September 1920, 26-35.
          Discusses employer welfare as one way to increase
       workers' "will-power" to produce. Employee represen-
       tation develops will power by giving employees a chan-
       nel to express problems and ideas. Companies should
       provide lunch rooms and medical facilities to safe-
       guard employees' health and maximize their physical
       and creative capacities. Welfare work should be con-
       sidered a minimum standard of decency, not a special
       privilege bestowed upon workers.

62 Weinstein, James. The Corporate ideal in the liberal
       state: 1900-1918. Boston, Beacon Press, 1968. 263 p.
          Chapter 1 describes the organization and growth of
       the National Civic Federation, formed during an era

of "social responsibility" to represent "socially con-
scious big businessmen" and top labor leaders. Its goal
was to establish "a relationship of mutual trust between
the laborer and the employer." The NCF Welfare Department did not include labor representatives and focused
on welfare in nonunion firms. The purpose of the Welfare Department was "to promote sympathy and a sense of
identity between the employer and his employees, by in-
tegrating the lives and leisure time of the workers with
the functioning of the corporation." It viewed welfare
as a substitute for unionization.

63 Whitney, Anice L. "Administration and costs of industrial
       betterment." Monthly labor review, 6:3, March 1918,
       199-206.
          Discusses various aspects of industrial welfare. Es-
       timates costs to employers in several industries and
       compares conditions before and after welfare work began.
       Surveys administration of programs, including an esti-
       mate of how many companies allow employees to partici-
       pate with an outside agency, such as the YMCA, to pro-
       vide welfare and considers the value of hiring a welfare
       secretary.

64 Wood, Norma J. "Industrial relations policies of American
       management, 1900-1933." Business history review, 34:4,
       Winter, 1960, 403-420.
          Discusses employer welfare as one of the factors that
       led to the evolution of modern industrial labor policy.
       Employers introduced welfare to share prosperity through
       unselfish benevolence, to combat unionism, to "sugar-
       coat scientific management," and to improve the com-
       pany's public image. Describes the development and ex-
       pansion of a variety of programs including pensions,
       profit-sharing, and employee representation.

65 Young, Owen D. "Dedication address...(at the) Harvard
       Graduate School of Business Administration, June 4,
       1927." Harvard business review, 5:4, July 1927, 385-
       394.
          Expresses the philosophy that businessmen have a duty
       to prevent abuses of their work force. Managers must
       insure workers' job security and salaries. The greatest
       challenge for business is to develop programs that pro-
       tect workers' investment of time and skill in the com-
       pany.

INDUSTRIAL DEMOCRACY

Most works in this section deal with employee representation
plans or company unions, including descriptions of plans of
specific companies and broad surveys of many companies. They
discuss reasons for introducing employee representation,
trace their history and development, and examine their strong
points and shortcomings. Responses of organized labor are
presented and differences between company unions and trade
unions are examined. The role of the National War Labor
Board and the Shipbuilding Adjustment Board in encouraging
employee representation during World War I is explained.
Other works describe companies that operated on an industrial
democracy basis through such programs as employee ownership
and cooperative management. The Columbia Conserve Company,
Dutchess Bleachery, and Filene's Department Store were leaders in this area. Of special note for the philosophical concept of industrial democracy are the two Presidential Industrial Conferences of 1919 and 1920.

66 Atkins, Willard E. "The personnel policies of the A.
       Nash Company." Journal of political economy, 30,
       April 1922, 212-228.
          Describes labor policies of the A. Nash Clothing
       Tailoring Company in Cincinnati, which operates on
       the principles of "The Golden Rule" and industrial
       democracy. Welfare programs have been minor, includ-
       ing sanitary working conditions and a baseball and
       bowling team. Workers voted down more ambitious wel-
       fare offers by the company because they preferred that
       the money be spent to increase wages.

67 Baker, Ray Stannard. The New industrial unrest: reasons
       and remedies. Garden City, NY, Doubleday, 1920.
       231 p.
          Chapters 12, 13, and 14 examine welfare as a solution to
       the problem of labor unrest. Traces the development

of employee representation plans in the United States
and says that the plans should be honest attempts at
cooperation, not just attempts to keep unions out.
Samuel Gompers and organized labor oppose employee representation and all other welfare because they want
higher wages, not charity; welfare has strings at-
tached and restricts employees from striking.

68 Benge, Eugene J. Standard practice in personnel work.
      New York, H.W. Wilson Company, 1920. 286 p.
        Chapter 13 discusses employee representation as a
      means of making workers feel their work is worthwhile
      and giving them a voice in management. Claims
      attempts to substitute welfare for the "destructive
      weapons" of trade unionism failed because workers re-
      sented paternalism. Suggests employee representation
      will work better because it gives workers a chance to
      participate. Outlines model employee representation
      plans and discusses selection of employee and manage-
      ment representatives.

69 Berman, Edward. "Paternalism and the wage earner."
      American federationist, 32:5, May 1925, 355-361.
        An exploration and condemnation of paternalism and
      company unions. Focusing on the company union of the
      Milwaukee Electric Railway and Light Company, this
      article examines company-sponsored employee represen-
      tation plans as a means of keeping out independent
      unions and restricting employee freedom.

70 Bridgeport Brass Company. Industrial cooperative rela-
      tion plan. 1918. 27 p.
        Describes the employee representation plan of the
      Bridgeport Brass Company, introduced to promote co-
      operation between the company and workers. Discusses
      election of representatives and the structure and
      function of joint committees. The committees make rec-
      ommendations on labor issues to the company Board of
      Directors. Decisions must be unanimous to be put into
      effect without consulting the Board of Directors.

71 Broderick, J.T. 40 years with General Electric. Albany,
      Fort Orange Press, 1929. 218 p.
        Chapter 24 describes the works council at the

Schenectady plant of the General Electric Company.
The council was introduced to give employees and management an opportunity to confer over labor issues. It
was used as a vehicle of information to unify workers
and management and to help make management policies
"consistent, valid and widely understood." Workers
decided what issues would be discussed. Welfare benefits provided by the company include medical care,
pensions, and free life insurance.

72 Bruere, Robert W. "West Lynn." Survey, 56, April 1,
       1926, 21-27.
       An exploration of the successful company union of
    the General Electric Company in West Lynn, Massachu-
    setts. Created under supervision of the War Labor
    Board, this plan of representation replaced indepen-
    dent unions. Workers were not required to relinquish
    union membership, but the plan was so successful they
    voluntarily sacrificed democratic representation. Em-
    phasizing constructive rather than adversary inter-
    action, the company shared budget, cost and earnings
    information with the workers. Company-initiated bene-
    fits were higher than any union could have hoped to
    negotiate. Benefits included pensions, death bene-
    fits, insurance, housing, a savings bond program, ed-
    ucation and employee newspapers.

73 Bureau of Industrial Research. American company shop
       committee plans. New York, 1919. 37 p.
       Survey of shop committee employee representation
    plans of 20 companies. Plans developed out of a
    tendency toward decentralization in industry to pro-
    vide a channel for orderly discussion of conflicting
    interests. Outlines various methods of electing em-
    ployee representatives, qualifications of represen-
    tatives, types of committees and their functions, man-
    agement representation, and details of administration.

74 Burton, Ernest Richmond. Employee representation. Bal-
       timore, Williams and Wilkins Company, 1926. 283 p.
       Overview of employee representation plans, insti-
    tuted as a means of educating and culturing workers
    and maximizing use of human resources. Traces history
    of employee representation plans, examines motives for

installing them, and discusses potential benefits and
obstacles to success. Suggests direction for future
development of plans and outlines plans of specific
companies. Discusses potential effects of such plans
on unionism, on employee morale and on production and
quality of work. Appendix A lists statistics on results of various plans.

75 Calder, John. "Experience with employees' representation
       during business depression." Industrial management,
       64:2, August 1922, 112-117.
          Explains the employee representation plan at Swift
       and Company. A 2/3 vote of a joint employee-manage-
       ment conference is required for implementation of
       labor policy. The company believes it can win work-
       ers' trust and loyalty by giving them as much infor-
       mation about company operations as possible. Giving
       employees a voice in management when times are hard
       shows genuine concern for treating workers fairly.
       Describes how the joint conference dealt with the
       necessity of a wage reduction. Warns that employee
       representation should never be used to discourage or
       combat trade unionism.

76 Caskie, J.J.K. "The Philadelphia Rapid Transit Plan."
       Annals of the American Academy of Political and Social
       Science, 85, September 1919, 189-204.
          Outlines a cooperative welfare plan between the
       Philadelphia Rapid Transit Company and its workers.
       Plan includes Cooperative Welfare Association, funded
       jointly by the company and employees. Employees who
       join the Association become eligible for life insur-
       ance, sick leave benefits, and pensions. Cooperative
       profit-sharing, another aspect of the plan, provides
       wage increases to workers in direct proportion to
       increased gross profits.

77 Commons, John R. et al. Industrial government. New
       York, Macmillan, 1921. 425 p.
          A series of philosophical essays examining various
       forms of industrial democracy in some of the nation's
       leading welfare companies. Includes discussion of
       cooperative management, shop committees, company
       unions, profit-sharing, and various forms of employee
       participation. Some chapters describe the program of

a specific company while others present general philosophical discussions.

78   "Company union." In Herbert O. Eby, The Labor Relations
     Act in the courts. New York, Harper and Brothers,
     1943. 250 p.
          Chapter 10 analyzes the effects of the National
     Labor Relations Act on company unions. The Act essen-
     tially bans company unions by prohibiting employers from
     financially supporting or otherwise dominating any labor
     organization. Before passage of the Act, employees
     were often intimidated into joining the company union
     instead of an outside union. Outlines the National
     Labor Relations Board's legal battles to disband com-
     pany unions of several firms. The Board ruled there
     should be no link between disestablished company
     unions and new unions that may subsequently be formed.

79   "Company unions." American federationist, 41:2, February
     1934, 130-132.
          An editorial by William Green tracing the history
     of company unions and criticizing employers for using
     them to keep unions out. Claims company unions vio-
     late the spirit of Section 7(b) of the National Recov-
     ery Act, which encouraged workers to unionize. Criti-
     cizes the U.S. Department of Commerce for supporting
     company unions.

80   "The cooperative plan of the Philadelphia Rapid Transit
     Company." In U.S. Commission on Industrial Relations.
     Report and Testimony, v. 3. Washington, G.P.O., 1915,
     2731-2816. (64th Congress, 1st Session, 1915-1916,
     Senate Documents, v. 21, 6931.)
          Text of a hearing of the Commission on Industrial
     Relations on the employee cooperation plan of the
     Philadelphia Rapid Transit Company. Describes intro-
     duction of the plan following violent strikes and juris-
     dictional disputes among unions. Unrest was calmed
     by the cooperative plan, which gave employees a
     voice in labor issues. Through cooperation, service
     to the public improved, profits rose, and wages in-
     creased proportionately. An employee committee de-
     cided hours of work and had some voice in wage deter-
     mination. The plan also included pensions, jointly
     funded sickness and death benefits, and cooperative

buying to lower workers' living expenses. Testimony
from the company's managers, workers, and union representatives is included.

81 Derber, Milton. "The idea of industrial democracy in
       America, 1898-1915." Labor History, 7:3, Fall 1966,
       259-268.
          An analysis of industrial democracy as studied by
       the two Industrial Commissions of 1898-1902 and 1913-
       1915. The hearings detail the divergent views toward
       industrial democracy of three labor groups: AFL,
       Industrial Workers of the World, and the Socialists,
       as well as those of the employer and of scholars.
       Three journals in particular reflect the changing
       attitude toward industrial democracy during this
       period: the Monthly review of the National Civic
       Federation, the Outlook, and the Survey.

82 Derber, Milton. "The idea of industrial democracy in
       America: 1915-1935." Labor History, 8:1, Winter,
       1967, 3-29.
          Traces the evolution and influence of employee rep-
       resentation and trade unionism from the establishment
       of the National War Labor Board to the National Labor
       Relations Act. Although both forms of industrial de-
       mocracy proved ineffective during the Depression, the
       struggle between them was renewed with the advent of
       Section 7(a) of the National Industrial Recovery Act.
       Examines seven criteria for industrial democracy and
       compares the contributions of both employee represen-
       tation and trade unions within this framework.

83 "Discussion of employees' representation at Eighth Annual
       Safety Congress." Monthly labor review, 9:5, November
       1919, 234-236.
          Brief synopsis of papers presented to the National
       Safety Council on employee representation plans. A
       representative from the International Harvester Com-
       pany described its company's plan and a member of the
       Philadelphia Independence Bureau reported results of
       a survey of 50 firms with employee representation
       plans. Clothing industry and American Federation of
       Labor representatives discussed the relation of rep-
       resentation plans to independent unions.

84 Douglas, Paul H. "Shop committees: substitute for, or
    supplement to, trade unions?" Journal of political
    economy, 29:2, February 1921, 89-107.
        Examines differences between shop committees and
    trade unions and considers whether the two can co-
    exist. Shop committee plans differ from trade unions
    because they represent employees of only one plant
    and management initiates and participates in the coun-
    cils. Flaws in shop committee plans are: 1) some
    employers control the election of representatives;
    2) functions are limited to trivial matters; 3) em-
    ployers often have superior voting power or veto
    power; 4) many employees don't qualify to vote or
    hold office; 5) representatives are intimidated by
    threat of discharge; and 6) they have no bargaining
    strength. Concludes that shop committees and trade
    unions should coexist since both an antagonistic
    and cooperative relationship with the employer is
    desirable.

85 Dunn, Robert W. The Americanization of labor: the
    employers' offensive against the trade unions. New
    York, International Publishers, 1927. 272 p.
        Chapter 6 attacks company unions, claiming they
    are introduced solely as a tactic to keep unions out.
    Discusses the growth of different types of plans and
    describes plans of the Western Union Telegraph Company
    and the meat packing industry. Many company unions
    did not permit employees to belong to trade unions.
    Company unions only went through the motions of
    collective bargaining but had no economic or politi-
    cal power. Employee representatives were often only
    allowed to meet in the presence of management. Sug-
    gests trade unions should attack company unions by
    challenging them to obtain substantial benefits for
    workers. The failure of company unions to meet this
    challenge would demonstrate their lack of power.

86 Dunn, Robert W. Company unions: employers' "industrial
    democracy". New York, Vanguard Press, 1927. 206 p.
        Examines the significance, purpose, and practices
    of company unions from organized labor's point of
    view. Stresses that company unions do not allow gen-
    uine collective bargaining. Traces their development
    in various industries and describes several types of
    plans. Employers introduced employee representation

to encourage cooperation with management, to ease ill-
will and friction, and to defeat trade unions. Describes plans of several companies with particular
emphasis on plans in the railroad industry. Considers
various methods of "selling" company unions to workers, including through threats and undercover operations of detective agencies. Chapters 12 and 13 sum-
marize organized labor's case against company unions
and tactics for replacing them with independent
unions.

87 Dunn, Robert W. "Westinghouse 'welfare'." Labor age,
        15:9, September 1926, 6-8.
        Attacks company unionism at the Westinghouse Elec-
    tric and Manufacturing Company. Describes the company
    union as a "velvet glove" covering the company's
    "iron hand." The purpose of the company union and
    other welfare programs was "to keep workers happy,
    dumb, carefree, and contented." Says trade unions
    are needed to make workers strong enough to deal with
    the company. Welfare benefits at Westinghouse include
    life insurance, a building and loan association, stock
    distribution, scholarships, a store, cafeterias, ath-
    letic facilities and activities, a band, a chorus, a
    night school, pensions, and vacations.

88 "Employee representation in the American Multigraph Com-
        pany." Monthly labor review, 13:1, July 1921, 18-21.
        Explains the Federal Shop Committee Plan of the
    American Multigraph Company. Employers formed a Cab-
    inet and Senate while Congress was comprised of em-
    ployee representatives. Through this system, workers
    were granted an 8-hour day without a reduction in pay
    and produced as much in 8 hours as they previously
    had in 10. During the Depression, wage and hour cuts
    and layoffs were more acceptable to workers because
    the Congress helped make the decisions.

89 "Employee representation in the United States." Monthly
        labor review, 9:3, September 1919, 123-125.
        List of companies with shop committee employee
    representation plans. Includes list of references
    on employee representation.

90 (Employee representation plans) <u>Industrial management</u>,
        59, 1920.
            Describes the employee representation plans of:
            Colorado Fuel and Iron Company
            February 1920, 123-125.

            Goodyear Tire and Rubber Company
            February 1920, 125-126.

            Standard Oil Company
            May-June 1920, 355-360, 496-501.

91 "Employees' councils in the United States Post Office
        Department." <u>Monthly labor review</u>, 13:2, August 1921,
        16.
            Outlines plan for a national council of postal
        employee representatives who would meet monthly with
        representatives of the welfare department to consider
        welfare issues affecting postal workers. Local coun-
        cils of employees and supervisors would also be organ-
        ized.

92 <u>Experience with works councils in the United States</u>. New
        York, National Industrial Conference Board, Research
        Report #50, May 1922. 191 p.
            A survey of all known employee representation plans
        in the United States in 1922. Some plans were set up
        by the National War Labor Board and the Shipbuilding
        Adjustment Board during World War I. Many of these
        ceased to function after the war. Voluntary plans
        were more successful because they were not forced on
        the parties by an outside agency. Examines the suc-
        cess of various councils in opening communications
        between workers and management and analyzes both
        beneficial and detrimental results of plans. Empha-
        sizes the need to educate foremen concerning their
        role and to make sure management plays an active part
        in the plans. Examines the opposition of organized
        labor to company unions and considers the ability of
        some trade unions to work in harmony with company
        unions. The Appendix lists companies with employee
        representation plans.

93 "Extent and characteristics of company unions: prelim-
        inary report." <u>Monthly labor review</u>, 41:4, October

1935, 865-876.
A survey of 593 firms with company unions. Lists
age, membership requirements, dues, and benefits provided. Discusses issues company unions are permitted
to negotiate and lists the number of company unions
with written agreements. Lists the number of companies
with both company unions and trade unions and estimates the number of company unions that are allowed to
communicate with company unions of other establishments. Employers often would not allow their company
unions to communicate with other company unions for
fear they would band together and form independent
unions.

94   Fairley, Lincoln. The Company union in plan and practice.
       New York, Affiliated Schools for Workers, 1936.   57 p.
       Describes typical company union plans. Employers
dominate company unions by initiating them, financing
them, and participating in their affairs. Defects in
company unions are that they are weak because of employer dominance, they do not strike, and they play
no real part in the labor movement. Traces the history of company unions and considers their future in
light of passage of the National Labor Relations Act.

95   Filene, Edward A. "Employees run our business." La
       Follete's magazine, 21, October 1919, 161-162.

96   French, Carroll E. The Shop committee in the United
       States. Baltimore, Johns Hopkins Press, 1923.   109 p.
       (Johns Hopkins University Studies in Historical and
       Political Science, Series 41, No. 2)
       Examines employee representation as an alternative
to unions. Traces the history of shop committees and
describes their establishment in various companies.
Discusses the role of the National War Labor Board
and the Shipbuilding Labor Adjustment Board in encouraging the formation of shop committees. Analyzes
the organization and structure of various types of
plans. Finds that management rarely gives up any
control to shop committees. Describes the opposition
of organized labor to employee representation. Labor
leaders called employee representation an attack on
unions, lacking economic and representational power.
They are used by employers to "dictate, manipulate,

and control the wishes of workers."

97   Goodyear Tire and Rubber Company. <u>Industrial representa-</u>
     <u>tion plan</u>. Akron, OH, 1919. 84 p.
          Describes the employee representation plan of the
     Goodyear Tire and Rubber Company. To be eligible to
     join, employees must be "industrians," which means
     they are at least 18 years old, understand English,
     are American citizens, and have been with the company
     at least 6 months. The text of the plan is included.

98   <u>Handbook of the Filene Cooperative Association</u>. Boston,
     Filene Cooperative Association Publicity Committee,
     1924. 52 p.
          Describes the Filene Cooperative Association, which
     was created to give employees a voice in the company.
     Outlines the development of a credit union, insurance
     plan, restaurant, clinic, educational programs, and
     recreational and athletic activities. A jointly funded
     mutual benefit association paid sick benefits. The
     text of the Charter, Constitution, and By-laws of the
     Cooperative Association are provided.

99   Hapgood, William Powers. <u>The Columbia Conserve Company</u>:
     <u>an experiment in workers' management and ownership</u>.
     Indianapolis, 1934. 187 p.
          Describes the "experiment in industrial democracy"
     of the Columbia Conserve Company. Employees owned a
     large portion of the company's stock and completely
     controlled the business. Employment and wages were
     guaranteed. Welfare benefits included sick pay, paid
     vacations, and pensions. During the Depression, em-
     ployees voluntarily cut their own salaries.

100 <u>Industrial representation experience of Standard Oil</u>
     <u>Company (New Jersey)</u>. 1919. 19 p.
          Examines the employee representation plan of the
     Standard Oil Company of New Jersey. Purposes of the
     plan were to dispense justice, "to provide a point of
     contact between employees and management," and to
     "create an opportunity for the expression of views by
     all." A joint employee/management committee discussed
     issues relating to labor. The number of joint confer-
     ences and issues discussed are listed. Employee and

management attitudes toward the plan are discussed.
The text of the plan is included.

101 Interborough Rapid Transit Company against William Green,
     et al, brief for defendants. New York, Workers Educa-
     tion Bureau Press, 1928. 479 p.
        Pages 63-88 compare company unions to independent
     trade unions. Says bona fide company unions should
     not discriminate against employees who are trade union
     members. Company unions should promote cooperation to
     improve services, give employees a voice in determining
     wages and working conditions, and provide a forum for
     airing grievances. However, only trade unions can be
     effective at stabilizing wage levels influencing labor
     legislation, and providing a genuine spirit of cooper-
     ation with management. Concludes that company unions
     are better than no unions but they have many limita-
     tions. They can successfully supplement, but not re-
     place, trade unions. If company unions prevail, trade
     unions "will be driven to secret association and
     destructive methods" and radicalism will prevail.

102 International Harvester Company. Harvester Industrial
     Council. March 1919. 22 p.
        Text of the employee representation plan of the
     International Harvester Company, introduced "to estab-
     lish closer relations between the employes and manage-
     ment." Guarantees employees the right to present sug-
     gestions, requests, and complaints, and have them fair-
     ly decided. Includes provision for impartial arbi-
     tration of unresolved disputes. Outlines eligibility
     requirements for representatives and rules for elec-
     tions.

103 International Railway Company. A Plan for collective
     bargaining and cooperative benefits. Buffalo, NY,
     1923. 24 p.
        A review of the accomplishments of the Philadelphia
     Rapid Transit Company's Mitten Cooperative Plan. The
     plan resulted in improved service to the public, in-
     creased wages, a grievance process, and such welfare
     benefits as sick pay, pensions, life insurance, a sav-
     ings fund, and a stock purchase program. Compares
     the cooperative program to "the destruction wrought in
     Buffalo during 10 years, under union domination."

Specifically, compares conditions of International
Railway in Buffalo, which was in shambles following a
strike. Proposes adoption of the Mitten Plan by the
International Railway and describes details of the
plan.

104 La Dame, Mary. The Filene store. New York, Russell Sage
     Foundation, 1930. 541 p.
          Investigates the experiment in industrial welfare
     and democracy in Filene's Department Store in Boston.
     An employee cooperative by workers provided a variety
     of welfare benefits; including a clinic, sick benefits,
     savings and loans, restaurants, clubs, education, a
     band, orchestra and choral club, and a weekly bulletin.
     Profit-sharing and employee stock ownership were unsuc-
     cessfully introduced on the theory that those who work
     for an organization should own it.

105 Leiserson, William Morris. Adjusting immigrant and in-
     dustry. New York, Harper and Brothers, 1924. 356 p.
          Chapter 8 surveys the extent of employee represen-
     tation plans in companies that hire immigrants. Dis-
     cusses the need to teach immigrants the principles
     of representative government and describes employee
     representation plans as "practical schools of citizen-
     ship." Presents opinions of various industrial leaders
     on the value of employee representation and describes
     various types of plans and their methods of operation.

106 Leiserson, William Morris. "...Employment management,
     employee representation, and industrial democracy."
     Address delivered before the National Association of
     Employment Managers, Cleveland, May 23, 1919. Wash-
     ington, G.P.O., 1919. 15 p.
          Examines forms of employee organization, including
     employee representation plans. Employee representation
     plans only provide industrial democracy if committees
     bargain over or have a voice in determining terms and
     conditions of employment. Analyzes the growth of
     employee representation as an attempt to control labor
     unrest. Cautions employers not to rush into introduc-
     ing employee representation without considering how it
     will fit into established personnel operations.

107 Leitch, John. Man to man: the story of industrial de-
     mocracy. New York, B.C. Forbes Company, 1919. 249 p.
         The creator of the Leitch Plan of employee repre-
     sentation explains how his plan was successfully im-
     plemented in several companies. He introduced employee
     representation and participation plans in companies
     with labor problems; productivity and worker morale
     improved. For example, labor unrest at the Packard
     Piano Company was transformed into a mutual belief
     that, "If there is no harmony in the factory, there
     will be none in the piano." The plan established a
     democratic governing structure comprised of employee
     representatives in a House of Representatives, super-
     vision and lower management in a Senate, and top
     management in a Cabinet. Cost savings from increased
     efficiency under that plan were shared with workers.

108 Lescohier, Don D. History of labor in the United States,
     1896-1932, v. 3. New York, Macmillan, 1935. 778 p.
         Chapter 18 examines the development of company
     unions. Considers the claim of organized labor that
     employee representation is "a definite device... to
     control and manipulate the labor force." Describes
     plans of specific companies and discusses the promo-
     tion of employee representation by the National War
     Labor Board during World War I. Other chapters sur-
     vey medical benefits, profit-sharing, and pensions.

109 Litchfield, Paul. The Industrial republic. Cleveland,
     Corday and Gross Company, 1946. 73 p.
         Book 2 describes the Industrial Assembly of the
     Goodyear Tire and Rubber Company, introduced to bring
     democracy to industry. Presents the text of that plan,
     which created a Constitutional System with a House of
     Representatives, a Senate, and an Executive Branch.
     Describes powers, duties, and rules for electing re-
     presentatives. Management retained veto power over
     all proposals. Representatives could not be discharged
     during their terms of office. Discusses success of the
     plan and examines employee losses in the Depression
     of the 1920s caused by their investment in the com-
     pany's stock ownership plan.

110   Luchek, Anthony, "Company union, F.O.B. Detroit." The
      Nation, 142:3680, January 15, 1936, 74-77.
         Traces the history of company unions in the auto
      industry. Installed to keep independent unions out,
      company unions were most active at General Motors,
      Chrysler, Hudson, Packard. Company unions made a pre-
      tense at democracy and gained only minor benefits.
      The Automobile Labor Board "bargaining agency" replaced
      company unions and provided a semblance of independent
      representation but was still largely controlled by the
      companies. Independent unions eventually took over
      after many struggles.

111   McClellan, W.F. "Employees' representation with reference
      to safety." Monthly labor review, 15:5, November 1922,
      22-26.
         Describes the structure and functions of Armour and
      Company's employee representation plan, with special
      emphasis on its safety function. Plan revolves around
      joint employee/management conference board which set-
      tles issues of wages, hours, and working conditions.

112   McQuaid, Kim. "An American Owenite: Edward A. Filene
      and the parameters of industrial reform, 1890-1937."
      American journal of economics and sociology, 35:1,
      January 1976, 77-94.
         Outlines industrial welfare practices at Filene's
      Department Store in Boston, one of the first U.S. com-
      panies to institute welfare measures. Edward A. Filene,
      the store's founder, combined his welfare efforts
      with a program of industrial democracy, under which
      employees established conditions and rules of employ-
      ment. Welfare measures included education, recreation,
      hygiene, bonuses, mutual insurance, and savings and
      loan programs.

113   McQuaid, Kim. "Industry and the cooperative commonwealth:
      William P. Hapgood and the Columbia Conserve Company,
      1917-1943." Labor history, 17:4, Fall 1976, 510-529.
         Analyzes the cooperative experiment in industrial
      democracy of the Columbia Conserve Company, under the
      leadership of William Powers Hapgood. A joint worker/
      management council decided issues concerning wages,
      working conditions, and problems of management. Hap-

good held veto power but his veto could be overriden
by two-thirds vote. Furthermore, the council held
the power to fire Hapgood. The council was open to
all employees who wanted to join. Workers were made
part owners in the company through profit-sharing and
stock ownership. The cooperative did not survive the
the financial pressure of the Depression.

114 McQuaid, Kim. "Young, Swope, and General Electric's 'new
     capitalism'... 1920-1933." American journal of eco-
     nomics and sociology, 36:3, July 1977, 323-334.
        Traces the history of welfare work at the General
     Electric Company and the development of employee works
     councils during World War I. Following a series of
     strikes, the works councils developed into comprehen-
     sive employee representation plans, giving employees a
     significant voice in company operations. Under the
     direction of Owen D. Young, and Gerard Swope, the pro-
     gram became a model of company unionism. The company
     union was not used to avoid labor unions. In fact,
     the company covertly supported industrial unionism,
     but did not want to deal with the confusion of several
     craft unions. Welfare programs introduced during this
     period include life insurance, pensions, stock options,
     and company guaranteed mortgages.

115 Meeker, Royal. "Employees' representation in management
     of industry." Monthly labor review, 10:2, February
     1920, 1-14.
        Traces growth of employee representation plans, de-
     veloped on the theory that employees will work harder
     and be happier on jobs they help plan. Describes shop
     committees and works councils as an "attempt to re-
     store some of the democracy lost through machine in-
     dustry and big business." Comments that managers do
     not have all the brains of an organization and worker
     insights should be considered. Workers should be given
     real voice and responsibility in management.

116 Meine, Franklyn J. "The introduction and development of
     the Works Committee in the Dennison Manufacturing Com-
     pany." Journal of personnel research, 3:4-5, August
     1924, 129-172.
        Comprehensive documentation of the development and
     operations of the works committee of the Dennison

Manufacturing Company. Provides minutes of meetings called to establish the works committee and discusses employee and employer recommendations on
powers of the committee, voting regulations and procedures, eligibility requirements of representatives.
and bylaws of the plan. Trades the growth of the
committee and lists its accomplishments, which included investigations of company pensions, lunch
rooms, and vacation and holiday pay policies. The
committee also developed a profit-sharing plan and
an unemployment fund.

117 Miller, Earl J. Workmen's representation in industrial
     government. (Studies in the Social Sciences, 10:3,4)
     Urbana, University of Illinois, 1924. 182 p.
        A survey of the employee representation movement,
     designed to gain "the cooperation of labor or to
     check the growth of unions." Describes plans of sev-
     eral companies and discusses their success in democ-
     ratizing industry, providing various benefits to
     workers, increasing workers' efficiency, reducing
     turnovers, and handling grievances. Opinions of sev-
     eral employers are presented. Describes different
     types of councils and compares plans that operate
     with unions to those in non-union firms. Suggests
     that employee representation has the potential for
     successfully stopping unions.

118 Miller, Frank B. and Mary Ann Coghill. The Historical
     sources of personnel work... Ithaca, New York State
     School of Industrial and Labor Relations, Cornell
     University, 1961. 110 p.
        Chapter 6 presents an annotated bibliography of
     employee representation plans. Includes brief anal-
     ysis of employer motivations for installing plans,
     such as anti-unionism and an ideological commitment
     to democracy.

119 "More sophisticated methods." American federationist,
     42:5, May 1935, 469-471.
        William Green attacks company unions as a "sophis-
     ticated method of opposing real unions." Traces the
     history of company unions and claims they are an at-
     tempt to circumvent the National Recovery Act, which

gives employees the right to unionize.

120 Myers, James. Representative government in industry.
     New York, George H. Doran Company, 1924. 249 p.
        Advocates industrial democracy as a means of re-
     placing the master-servant relationship with repre-
     sentative government in industry. Analyzes the de-
     gree of democracy employee representation actually
     brings to industry and finds most employee represent-
     atives have no real power and rarely challenge the
     judgement of management. Suggests employees should
     be allowed to discuss any issue and their agreements
     with management should be binding. Suggests democ-
     racy should be accompanied by the financial democ-
     racy of profit-sharing. Uses the example of indus-
     trial democracy at Dutchess Bleachery. Believes
     autocracy in industry "creates either the mind of the
     slave or the mind of the rebel."

121 National Industrial Conference
        There were two National Industrial Conferences
     convened by President Wilson, one in October 1919
     and the other in December of 1919. The purpose of
     these conferences was to develop machinery for the
     settlement of industrial disputes and the plan gen-
     erally dealt with the implementation of arbitration
     and collective bargaining measures. Much of the plan
     was devoted to industrial democratization measures
     such as shop committees, works councils, employee rep-
     resentation plans, etc.
        The following are but a few of the articles deal-
     ing with the National Industrial Conference(s).

        Atkins, Willard E. "The Industrial Conference,"
           Journal of political economy, 28, May 1920, 431.

        Best, Gary Dean. "President Wilson's Second
           Industrial Conference." Labor history, 16:4,
           Fall 1975, 505-520.

        Chenery, William L. "The President's Conference
           Report." Survey, 43, January 3, 1920, 328.

        Gompers, Samuel. "The President's Industrial Con-
           ference." American federationist, 26:12, Decem-

ber 1919, 1124.

Hurvitz, Haggai. "Ideology and industrial conflict: President Wilson's First Industrial Conference of October 1919." Labor history, 18:4,
Fall 1977, 509-524.

"National Industrial Conference, Washington, D.C."
Monthly labor review, 9:5, November 1919, 40-49.

"Preliminary statement of the President's Industrial Conference." Monthly labor review, 10:1,
January 1920, 60-68.

Report of the Industrial Conference called by the
President. (December 1, 1919) New York, Martin
B. Brown Company, 1920. 51 p.

"Report of the President's Industrial Conference."
Monthly labor review, 10:4, April 1920, 33-40.

122 National Industrial Conference Board. Collective bargaining through employee representation. New York,
1933. 81 p.
   A history of employee representation plans. Considers future of such plans in light of the National
Industrial Recovery Act which gave workers the right
to organize without employer interference. Discusses
various types of plans and compares them to independent unions. Appendix A lists companies with employee
representation plans and Appendix B provides texts of
plans of John Morrell and Company, the Bethlehem Steel
Corporation, and the Loyal Legion of Loggers and Lumbermen.

123 National Industrial Conference Board. Experience with
works councils in the United States. Research Report
#50. New York, Century Crofts, 1922. 191 p.
   A study of employee representation. Attributes the
failure of shop committees during World War I to the
fact that they were forced on employers and employees
by the War Labor Board. Surveys companies that
changed or abandoned plans. Examines the adequacy of
company plans in dealing with grievances and discusses
their ability to cope with recessions and wage reduc-

tions. Presents employer opinions on the character of
workers' representatives and the value of works councils. Organized labor claimed employee representation
did not really protect workers' rights. Appendix
lists companies with employee representation plans.

124 National Industrial Conference Board. Works councils in
     the United States. Research Report #21. Boston,
     1919. 135 p.
         A survey of companies ordered to have shop commit-
     tees by the National War Labor Board and the Ship-
     building Labor Adjustment Board and all other com-
     panies known to have employee representation plans.
     Traces the history of employee representation in the
     United States and describes programs in individual
     companies. Describes typical plans, including their
     structure, functions, and extent of authority. Appen-
     dix 1 lists companies with employee representation.

125 New York Telephone Company. Plan of employee representa-
     tion. New York, 1920. 35 p.
         The text of the New York Telephone Company employee
     representation plan, created to provide a forum for
     discussing labor problems. Outlines membership eligi-
     bility requirements, structure and functions of com-
     mittees, and the election of representatives.

126 Ozanne, Robert. A Century of labor-management relations
     at McCormick and International Harvester. Madison,
     University of Wisconsin Press, 1967. 300 p.
         Chapter 7 describes the employee representation
     plan of the McCormick-International Harvester Company.
     Established to keep independent unions out, this
     "Works Council" gave workers a voice but no real power
     in determining labor policy. Meetings of employee rep-
     resentatives were held in the presence of management
     but meetings of all employees were not allowed.

127 "The Pacific Mills Plan of employee representation." Law
     and labor, 5:9, September 1923, 263-264.
         Describes the introduction of the Pacific Mills em-
     ployee representation plan, including the election of
     representatives, outcomes of the first meeting, and
     rules of operation. The purpose of the plan was to

provide employees and management a means of consulting
with each other on matters of mutual concern.

128 Peterson, Florence et al. Characteristics of company
     unions, 1935. U.S. Department of Labor, Bureau of
     Labor Statistics, Bulletin 634. Washington, G.P.O.,
     1938. 313 p.
        A survey of company unions in 14,850 firms. Traces
     the historical development and estimates membership by
     industry, region, and size of establishment. Examines
     financing and dues, meetings, functions of committees
     and issues discussed, membership requirements, and
     election of representatives. Discusses the coexis-
     tence of company unions and trade unions in some
     firms. Concludes that most company unions are estab-
     lished by management in response to trade union ac-
     tivity. Most company unions are unable to bring any
     kind of pressure against the employer. Appendix 1
     discusses the legal status of company unions and Ap-
     pendices 2 and 3 contain case histories of specific
     company unions.

129 Peterson, Florence et al. "Characteristics of company
     unions." Monthly labor review, 46:4, April 1938,
     821-830.
        A survey of 126 company unions, most established in
     response to pressure of trade union activity. Company
     unions were almost always established with management
     assistance and financing and most included management
     in the association. They were most successful in ob-
     taining safety and health improvements and least suc-
     cessful in matters concerning wages and hours. Nego-
     tiating problems resulting from company unions status
     are discussed. Management participation in company
     unions decreased after passage of the National Indus-
     trial Recovery Act.

130 Philadelphia Rapid Transit Company. President Mitten's
     talk to combined membership of employee and employer
     committeemen in convention assembled. 1923. 13 p.
        Describes the development of the Cooperative Wel-
     fare Association of the Philadelphia Rapid Transit
     Company. The Association is jointly funded but the
     company raised wages so employees could afford their
     share. A savings fund, sick benefits, and pensions

are provided through the Association. The company
also offers stock purchase options.

131 "Report of the President's Industrial Conference."
     Monthly labor review, 10:4, April 1920, 33-40.
          Summarizes report of the President's Industrial
     Conference, which recommended employee representation
     plans as a means of combatting industrial unrest. Sug-
     gests regional boards set up to adjust disputes volun-
     tarily submitted by parties of employee representation
     plans.

132 Schacht, John N. "Toward industrial unionism: Bell
     Telephone workers and company unions, 1919-1937."
     Labor history, 16:1, Winter 1975, 5-36.
          Describes how company unions at Bell Telephone Com-
     pany were transformed into industrial labor unions.
     The company introduced company unions during a strike
     wave in an effort to keep independent unions out. The
     company unions had no real power but they put employ-
     ees from around the country in contact with each oth-
     er, they provided a means for sharing information
     about wages and working conditions, and they inadver-
     tently helped employees develop organizing skills.
     These factors facilitated the development of an in-
     dustrial union after the Wagner Act outlawed company
     unions.

133 Seager, Henry R. "Company unions vs. trade unions."
     American economic review, 13:1, March 1923, 1-13.
          Traces the development of company unions and com-
     pares their growth to declining trade union membership.
     ship. Examines advantages and disadvantages of trade
     unions in public service industries. Finds that trade
     unions are more successful in gaining improvements for
     workers. However, the power of trade unionism depends
     on the right to strike, a right which is inappropriate
     in public service industries because continuous serv-
     ice is vital to the public interest. Concludes that
     company unions are preferable if the employer treats
     workers in good faith but trade unions are necessary
     when employers exploit workers.

134 Shepard, George H. "Industrial representation and the
     fair deal." (2 parts) Industrial management, 63,
     February and March 1922, 81-85 and 185-188.
          Examines employee works councils as a means of
     giving workers a voice in management and preventing
     labor unrest. Works councils can be developed in
     conjuction with trade unions if antagonism and union
     reluctance to participate in management can be over-
     come. Lists necessary elements of successful works
     councils.

135 "The shop committee and the unions." In William L. Stod-
     dard's, The Shop committee; a handbook for employer
     and employee. New York, Macmillan, 1919. (Chapter 10,
     91-100 p.
          This Chapter deals with the relationship of the
     shop committee concept to unions and examines where
     they are alike and where they differ.

136 "Shop committees in Bridgeport: survey of employee rep-
     resentation plans installed by War Labor Board."
     Industrial relations, 8:1, September 3, 1921, 804-807.
          A study of 63 companies in Bridgeport, Connecticut,
     where 41 representation plans were installed with lit-
     tle success.

137 Simons, Algie M. Personnel relations in industry. New
     York, Ronald Press Company, 1921. 341 p.
          Chapters 16-18 trace the growth of industrial de-
     mocracy and outline various employee representation
     plans. Reasons for instituting such plans and their
     strengths and weaknesses are discussed. Plans of spe-
     cific companies are mentioned and their effects on
     workers, management, and production are evaluated.
     Includes discussion of role of unions in joint man-
     agement plans.

138 Spahr, Robert H. Employee representation or work coun-
     cils. Washington, Chamber of Commerce of the United
     States, 1927. 43 p.
          Traces the history of employee representation
     plans. Describes various types of plans and discusses
     favorable and unfavorable experiences with each
     type. Provides statistics on eligibility require-

ments, rules, details of administration and number of
plans in operation. Objectives of employee representation are to increase efficiency, loyalty, and goodwill, to prevent labor trouble, and to give employees
control over their own conditions of employment.

139 Standard Oil Company of New Jersey. A Job with Standard
     Oil Company (NJ). 1934. 36 p.
        Describes welfare programs of the Standard Oil
     Company of New Jersey. Focuses on the employee repre-
     sentation between workers and the company to discuss
     wages, hours, and working conditions. Other welfare
     programs include paid vacations, sick benefits, stock
     and insurance options, death and unemployment bene-
     fits, jointly funded pensions, and vocational educa-
     tion. A medical department was established to reduce
     illness and absense.

140 Stoddard, William Leavitt. The Shop committee; a handbook
     for employer and employee. New York, Macmillan, 1919.
     105 p.
        This small book, written by an administrator of the
     National War Labor Board, presents essential facts and
     principles of the shop committee movement. Chapter 10
     deals with shop committees and the trade unions. Ap-
     pended is a list of existing shop committee systems
     found in the United States.

141 Taussig, Frank W. "The opposition of interest between em-
     ployer and employee: difficulties and remedies." In
     Wertheim lectures on industrial relations. Cambridge,
     Harvard University Press, 1929. 197-229 p.
        A general discussion of employer/employee relations.
     Considers employee representation plans as a means of
     bringing workers and management closer together but
     criticizes them as paternalistic and a weapon for keep-
     ing out independent unions. Concludes that whatever
     means are used in employment relations, the key to suc-
     cess is the underlying spirit of employer and workers.

142 Tead, Ordway and Henry C. Metcalf. Personnel administra-
     tion; its principles and practice. New York, McGraw-
     Hill, 1920. 519 p.
        Chapters 27-29 discuss advantages to management of

employee representation plans. Plans help management
know and meet the needs of workers and reduce conflict by fostering a spirit of cooperation. Describes
types of plans, their functions, limitations, adminis-
trative procedures, and provisions of good plans.
Surveys employee and employer attitudes toward plans.

143   Thompson, Laura A. "Union-management cooperation: a
      list of references." Monthly labor review, 25:4,
      October 1927, 220-227.
         A number of these citations deal with representa-
      tion plans in the railroads as well as in some other
      industries.

144   Tipper, Harry. Human factors in industry. New York,
      Ronald Press, 1922. 280 p.
         Pages 136-140 describe the employee representation
      plan of the Bethlehem Steel Corporation. A joint em-
      ployee/management committee considers all matters re-
      lating to conditions of the workers. Rules for elec-
      tion of employee representatives are listed. Unre-
      solved disputes are sent to an appeals committee and
      may eventually be taken to arbitration.
         Pages 140-152 outline the employee representation
      plan of the International Harvester Company. A works
      council, equally represented by employee and manage-
      ment representatives, decided labor issues. Disputes
      could be taken to arbitration by mutual agreement.
      Details of council structure and the selection of rep-
      resentatives are listed.
         Pages 158-164 describe the employee representation
      plan of the American Multigraph Company. This Consti-
      tutional System included a Congress comprised of 12
      employee representatives elected by workers and 12 ap-
      pointed by management. A Senate included supervisory
      and technical staff. Suggestions approved by both
      houses were sent to a Cabinet of executives for con-
      sideration.

145   "Types of employer-employee dealing." Monthly labor re-
      view, 41:6, December 1935, 1441-1446.
         Analyzes types of employee-employer relations, in-
      cluding individual relations and dealings with trade
      or company unions, of 14,725 companies surveyed. Es-
      timates incidence of company unions compared to other
      types of employee-employer relations. Breaks data

down by industry and size of establishment.

146   Ulriksson, Vidkunn. The Telegraphers; their craft and
      their unions. Washington, Public Affairs Press,
        1953. 218 p.
           Chapter 10 describes company unionism for Western
      Union employees. Its purpose was to keep labor unions
      out. AFL members were excluded and preferential
      treatment was guaranteed for employees who were com-
      pany union members. Employees were pressured to join
      and those who opposed the company union risked losing
      their jobs.

147   Wander, Paul. "The challenge of company-made unionism."
      In J.B.S Hardman, American labor dynamics in the light
      of post-war developments. New York, Harcourt, Brace
      and Company, 1928. 226-244 p.
           Cites welfare and company unions as causes of the
      lack of organizing success of labor unions. Claims
      company unions gave employees voice in labor issues
      but no decision making power. Believes "the trade
      union is the only effective source of power to bal-
      ance that of the company." Company unions achieve
      only minor innovations but have no leverage to bargain
      for substantial gains because they do not have the
      right to strike. Advocates integrating company and
      trade unions to obtain both a spirit of cooperation
      with management and economic leverage.

148   Whitney, Anice L. "Development of shop committee sys-
      tems." Monthly labor review, 9:5, November 1919, 225-
        233.
           Examines movement toward shop committee employee
      representation plans, growing due to employer recog-
      nition of the importance of good relations with work-
      ers. Suggests employers and workers come to clear
      understanding of amount of control employees are to
      assume so misunderstanding will not cause problems.
      Discusses three types of representation plans: com-
      pany unions, welfare committees, dealing only with
      personnel questions, and agreements with trade unions.

149   Wolfe, A.B. Works committees and joint industrial coun-
      cils. Philadelphia, U.S. Shipping Board Emergency

Fleet Corporation, Industrial Relations Division,
1919.   254 p.
    Overview of employee representation through works
committees and joint industrial councils. Describes
features of various plans and discusses psychological
reasons for instituting them. Chapter 5 discusses
works committees in the United States and includes
views of the AFL and various government agencies.
Appendix IV describes a typical plan and Appendix V
presents texts of plans of specific companies. Includes opinions of companies without employee representation plans.

150 "Works councils and shop committees in the United
        States." Monthly labor review, 10:1, January 1920,
        191-194.
            Synopsis of a study of 176 companies with works
        councils. Lists industries with councils and esti-
        mates the proportion of companies with both works
        councils and trade unions. Evaluates the success of
        works councils in improving labor relations. A syn-
        opsis of a separate study of 13 companies considers
        the coexistence of shop committees and labor unions
        and the rivalry that may result.

DESCRIPTIVE SURVEYS AND BIBLIOGRAPHIES

This section includes surveys of welfare programs of a large
number of companies. Works provide statistics and analyses
of the prevalence and scope of various programs. Some works
describe programs of all the individual companies surveyed
but most discuss characteristics of programs in general,
sometimes with brief examples from specific companies. Includes surveys of programs in particular industries and geo-
graphic locations. Bibliographies on industrial welfare are
also contained in this section.

151 Baker, Helen. Personnel programs in department stores.
        Princeton, Princeton University, Industrial Rela-
        tions Section, 1935. 85 p.
            A survey of welfare benefits in 50 department
        stores. Discusses various types of benefits and
        describes programs of specific companies. Medical
        departments usually are a minor function since stores
        do not have many accidents. Mutual benefit associa-
        tions are usually jointly funded and provide group
        insurance and pensions. Cafeterias, vacations, and
        recreational facilities are common benefits in the
        retail industry.

152 Balderston, C. Canby. Executive guidance of industrial
        relations; an analysis of the experience of 25 com-
        panies. Philadelphia, University of Pennsylvania
        Press, 1935. 435 p.
            Leading industrial welfare practices are surveyed
        through case studies of 25 major firms well known for
        their industrial relations programs. From the case
        studies, a composite, model welfare program is postu-
        lated. Industrial characteristics affecting em-
        ployer willingness and ability to institute welfare
        programs are discussed and various approaches to em-
        ployer/employee relations are evaluated.

153 Conference on welfare work. (March 16, 1904, under the
     auspices of the Welfare Department of the National
     Civic Federation)   New York, Andrew H. Kellogg Com-
     pany, 1904. 205 p.
          A collection of addresses by welfare leaders in-
     cluding representatives of employers well-known for
     welfare efforts. Includes descriptions of numerous
     programs and debate over general philosophies of
     welfare.

154 The Department stores of New York City. U.S. Commission
     on Industrial Relations. Report and Testimony, v. 3,
     2213-2410. 64th Congress, 1st Session, Document 415.
     (Senate Document, 21:6931) 1914.
          Testimony before the U.S. Commission on Industrial
     Relations on labor conditions in New York City de-
     partment stores. Includes testimony by Gertrude
     Beeks, welfare director of the National Civic Feder-
     ation. She describes the NCF's investigation of
     working conditions and welfare programs in New York
     City department stores and explains the NCF's overall
     policy for working with employers to improve working
     conditions and develop welfare programs. Testimony
     of store managers and employees is also presented.

155 Detroit Public Library. Welfare work in industry.
     Selected list. Detroit, 1916. 4 p.
          A bibliography of works on employer welfare.
     Categories include industrial hygiene, safety meas-
     ures, social insurance, and welfare work.

156 (Employers who are reported to have established some
     form of welfare work.) Monthly review of U.S. Bureau
     of Labor Statistics (Monthly labor review), 4:2,
     February 1917, 315-334.
          This partial list of employers is arranged alpha-
     betically by state and within state, by city.

157 Epstein, Abraham. "Industrial welfare movement sapping
     American trade unions." Current history, 24:4, July
     1926, 516-522.
          A survey of industrial welfare practices of over
     1500 of the largest companies in the United States.

Article describes the scope, incidence, and reasons
for the growth of popular welfare programs and discusses the adverse effects of such programs on the
trade union movement. It compares the declining frequency of labor disputes in industries that incorpo-
rate industrial welfare to the continuing high rates
of conflict in industries without welfare programs.

158   Gilman, Nicholas Paine. A Dividend to labor: a study
      of employers' welfare institutions. Boston, Hough-
      ton, Mifflin and Company, 1899. 400 p.
          Overview of industrial welfare. Chapter 2 dis-
      cusses moral obligation of employers to provide for
      employees. Chapter 8 describes welfare programs of
      numerous companies and discusses reasons why some of
      the programs were instituted. Profit-sharing is
      discussed in Chapters 9 and 10, focusing on the pro-
      grams of Bourne Cotton Mills, Procter and Gamble
      Company, and Nelson Manufacturing Company. Appendix
      I examines dangers of paternalism. Pages 377 and
      378 of Appendix II list American companies with pro-
      fit-sharing plans and Appendix III lists companies
      that abandoned profit-sharing and discusses reasons
      for abandonment.

159   "Health and recreation activities in industrial estab-
      lishments." Monthly labor review, 26:4, April 1928,
      14-21.
          A Bureau of Labor Statistics survey of welfare
      work in 430 companies. Findings are compared to
      results of a similar survey in 1916-17. Discusses
      various types of programs and the number of companies
      providing them. Programs include medical and hospi-
      tal service, paid sick leaves, paid vacations, lunch
      rooms, recreational facilities, group life insurance
      and disability funds, education, libraries, savings
      and loan plans, and profit-sharing.

160   Holbrook, Chandler. "Journal: a business trip 70 years
      ago." New England magazine, 20, March 1899, 23-32.
          Extent of welfare activities in New England and
      Middle Atlantic states, 1827-1928.

161 Hyde, Elizabeth A. "Social betterment among employees'
     families." Monthly labor review, 6:1, January 1918,
     195-205.
         Description of welfare work aimed at helping work-
     er's families. Based on Bureau of Labor Statistics
     survey of 431 companies, 158 of which had family
     welfare programs. Programs include better housing
     and streets, sewerage, lighting, water, help with
     gardening, medical care, and educational, religious,
     and recreational facilities.

162 Meakin, Budgett. Model factories and villages; ideal
     conditions of labour and housing. London, T. Fisher
     Unwin, 1905. 480 p.
         Survey of major industrial welfare programs in the
     United States and Europe. Based on visits to factory
     sites, this work describes and compares a wide varie-
     ty of welfare activities. Includes photographs of
     model programs and a chapter on theory behind and
     problems of administering the programs. A section
     on American examples of model villages depicts indus-
     trial housing in several company towns and discusses
     problems of providing housing to workers.

163 Miller, Frank B. and Mary Ann Coghill. The Historical
     sources of personnel work. Ithaca, New York State
     School of Industrial and Labor Relations, Cornell
     University, 1961. 110 p.
         An annotated bibliography with chapters on indus-
     trial welfare. Chapter 2 deals with sources on a
     variety of welfare issues. Chapter 6 covers employee
     representation plans, Chapter 7 consists of sources
     on safety and hygiene, and Chapter 10 deals with pro-
     fit-sharing.

164 Monthly bulletin of the Free Public Library, New Bed-
     ford, Massachusetts. April 1909, 32-33.
         A bibliography of 37 books and periodical articles
     on industrial welfare.

165 National Civic Federation. Welfare Department. Welfare
     work in mercantile houses. New York, 1905. 32 p.
         A survey of welfare work in retail establishments.

Discusses programs and philosophies of seven major
companies. Goals of welfare were to make employees
"intelligent, loyal, happy, and progressive." Programs included education, lunch rooms, medical care,
sanitary and comfortable working conditions, and
various financial benefits.

166 National Civic Federation. Welfare Department. "Work-
     ing conditions in New York stores, a report upon
     welfare activities in 22 retail concerns..." Nation-
     al Civic Federation review, 4:1, July 15, 1913, 32.
         The National Civic Federation asks, "Are retail
     dealers meeting their full obligation, under modern
     conditions, to their employees?" The Federation be-
     lieves employers have a duty to care for the comfort,
     health, safety, and well-being of workers. Describes
     a variety of benefits including lunch rooms, loans,
     recreation, sanitary and pleasant working conditions,
     health care, and vacations. Refutes the popular con-
     ception that retail employees are poorly treated and
     concludes that working conditions are generally good.

167 National Civic Federation. Woman's Department. Commit-
     tee on Welfare Work for Industrial Employees. Wel-
     fare work, clothing, manufacturers, New York City...
     investigation, 1908-1909. New York, 1909. 31 p.
         An investigation of working conditions in the gar-
     ment industry. Compares spacious, clean, well-venti-
     lated factories to other factories where conditions
     are deplorable. Concludes that the companies with
     good working conditions are also likely to be the
     ones with welfare benefits, such as libraries, lunch
     rooms, and medical care.

168 National Industrial Conference Board. Industrial rela-
     tions: administration of policies and programs.
     New York, 1931. 114 p.
         Survey of industrial relations and welfare pro-
     grams in 302 companies. Discusses reasons for gradu-
     al growth of welfarism and enumerates a wide range
     of programs. Examines company justifications of the
     expense of welfare, including lower turnover, strike
     prevention, attracting better workers, improving
     public image and simple benevolence toward workers.
     Considers methods of administering benefits and

assesses their success in improving company operations.

169 National Industrial Conference Board. Industrial rela-
     tions programs in small plants. New York, 1929.
     60 p.
         A survey of welfare programs in 4,409 small plants.
     Describes programs and estimates prevalence of each
     program by industry. Examines the influence on wel-
     fare of such factors as a company's overall labor
     policy, the size of the community and characteristics
     of the industry. Discusses special problems of wel-
     fare for small employers, such as high per capita
     cost burden. Estimates companies expenditures on
     each type of welfare program.

170 National Industrial Conference Board. What employers
     are doing for employees: a survey of voluntary
     activities for improvement of working conditions in
     American business concerns. New York, 1936. 70 p.
         Describes the results of a survey of 2,452 American
     companies which were drawn from a broad cross section
     of American business, mostly in manufacturing indus-
     tries. The survey provides data on the scope and
     frequency of a variety of industrial welfare pro-
     grams. Data is broken down by specific program, by
     industry, by size of company, and by geographic
     region.

171 New Jersey. Bureau of Statistics of Labor and Industry.
     "Industrial betterment institutions in New Jersey
     manufacturing establishments." Twenty-seventh annual
     report, 1904. 153 p.
         Surveys welfare policies of New Jersey companies.
     Describes programs of specific companies and examines
     welfare work as an alternative to unions and strikes.
     Plans of the Celluloid Company, the Ferris Brothers
     Company, the Ingersoll-Sergeant Drill Company, the
     Sherwin-Williams Company, and the Weston Electrical
     Instrument Company are described in detail.

172 Olmsted, Victor H. The Betterment of industrial con-
     ditions. U.S. Department of Labor, Bureau of Labor
     Statistics, Bulletin 31. Washington, G.P.O., Novem-

ber 1900. 1117-1156 p.
    Short descriptions of industrial welfare measures
offered by various clubs, stores and factories in the
United States.

173 Otey, Elizabeth Lewis. Employers' welfare work. U.S.
     Department of Labor, Bureau of Labor Statistics,
     Bulletin 123. Washington, G.P.O., 1913. 80 p.
         A survey of welfare programs in approximately
     50 American companies. Based on personal visits to
     each company, this bulletin presents an industry-
     by-industry overview of welfare efforts. Includes
     companies from a variety of manufacturing industries,
     mercantile industries, and public utilities.

174 "Personnel plans of representative banks." Monthly
     labor review, 41:1, July 1935, 56-61.
         Analyzes personnel plans of 50 banks. Welfare
     programs focus on economic security on the theory
     that employees in debt cannot be trusted to handle
     large sums of money. Economic programs include sav-
     ings plans, stock ownership, group insurance, pen-
     sions, and sick pay. Medical care, paid vacations
     and lunch rooms are other common benefits. Many
     banks pay for vocational college courses and English
     classes.

175 Rhode Island. Commissioner of Industrial Statistics.
     "Welfare work of Rhode Island." 19th annual report,
     1905. Providence, 1906. 183-200 p.
         A survey of Rhode Island companies providing wel-
     fare to workers. Suggests that workers produce best
     when their health and comfort are looked after. De-
     scribes programs of several companies with special
     emphasis on the Gorham Manufacturing Company, a
     national leader in welfare. The company's programs
     included a cafeteria and recreation hall, a library,
     medical care, a bank, and pensions.

176 Russell Sage Foundation. Welfare work. New York,
     Russell Sage Foundation Library, 1915. (Bulletin
     #12, August 1915)
         An annotated bibliography of American and foreign
     works on industrial welfare.

177   Stevens, George A. and Leonard W. Hatch. "Employer
      welfare institutions." <u>3rd annual report of the U.S.
      Commissioner of Labor</u>. New York, Department of Labor,
      1903. Part 4, (In: New York Assembly Documents,
      1904, 22:61) Albany, 1904, 223-329 p.
          A survey of welfare practices in about 110 New
      York firms. Programs examined include healthy and
      pleasant working conditions, club rooms and assembly
      halls, paid vacations, educational and athletic
      facilities, housing, religious services, profit-
      sharing, savings and loan programs, medical care,
      pensions, and insurance. Briefly describes programs
      of all 110 companies, including discussion of the
      scope of the programs and costs to companies and
      workers.

178   Stevens, George A. and Leonard W. Hatch. <u>Typical
      employers' welfare institutions in New York</u>. (Mono-
      graphs on Social Economics) Albany, New York State
      Department of Labor, 1904. 30 p.
          A survey of welfare work in 108 New York firms.
      Lists companies providing welfare and describes the
      programs of J.H. Williams and Company, the Witherbee,
      Sherman Company, the Solvay Process Company, the
      Roycroft Shop, and the Natural Food Company. De-
      scribes a wide variety of programs and examines em-
      ployer motives for introducing welfare. Discusses
      the attitudes of employees toward welfare.

179   "A study of welfare work." <u>Monthly review of the U.S.
      Bureau of Labor Statistics</u> (Monthly labor review),
      3:1, July 1916, 18-23.
          Explanation of a Bureau of Labor Statistics ques-
      tionnaire mailed to employers known to be interested
      in welfare work. Questionnaire gives employers a
      list of welfare programs and asks them to indicate
      which programs their company has instituted. Also
      asks the employer to note which of his programs he
      considers most important and/or most satisfactory.
      A follow-up plan for a more intensive and detailed.
      survey of some firms is also described.

180   Timmons, Benjamin Finley. <u>Personnel practices among
      Ohio industries</u>. (Ohio State University Bureau of

Business Research Monographs #18) Columbus, Ohio
State University Press, 1931. 136 p.
   A survey of personnel practices, including welfare, in 189 Ohio firms. Discusses prevalence of
welfare by program, by industry, and by size of
establishment. Considers costs to employees and
employers of various types of plans. Includes discussion of such programs as medical service and
facilities, educational and recreational services,
vacations, pensions, and insurance.

181 Tolman, William Howe. Social engineering; a record of
     things done by American industrialists employing
     upwards of one and one-half million of people.
     Introduction by Andrew Carnegie. New York, McGraw-
     Hill, 1909. 384 p.
        This work, drawing its illustrations from over 200
     U.S. firms, surveys the following industrial welfare
     programs: efficiency promotion, hygiene, safety,
     mutuality, thrift, profit-sharing, housing, educa-
     tion, and recreation. The duties of a "social secre-
     tary" are analyzed in Chapter 2. The last chapter
     attempts to answer the question, "Does it pay?", by
     reprinting replys from industrialists who had first
     hand experience with industrial welfare programs.

182 U.S. Library of Congress. Division of Bibliography.
     Supplementary list of references on welfare work
     for laborers. October 18, 1915. 12 p.
        A bibliography of works on employer welfare. In-
     cludes foreign as well as American works.

183 "Welfare department." The National Civic Federation
     review, 4:3, March 1914, 23-24.
        Describes the past year's welfare projects, in-
     cluding a survey of welfare in New York City depart-
     ment stores. Outlines major obstacles to conducting
     the survey such as employer ignorance of the meaning
     of welfare. Discusses plans to begin a welfare edu-
     cation program for employers and training programs
     for welfare workers. Lists welfare aid given to
     various groups during the year.

184 Welfare work for employees in industrial establishments.
     U.S. Department of Labor, Bureau of Labor Statistics,
     Bulletin 250. Washington, G.P.O., 1919. 139 p.
          Overview of welfare practices in American indus-
     try. A survey of 431 companies in 31 states compares
     programs within and across industries. Includes dis-
     cussion of regional or industry roadblocks to indus-
     trial welfare efforts and examines costs of the pro-
     grams.

185 "What personnel activities cost." Industrial relations,
     2:14, April 17, 1920, 221.
          Results of a survey of personnel activities of
     57 companies. Lists types of services provided
     and average cost of each. Estimates the average
     number of benefits provided by each firm.

186 Whitney, Anice. Health and recreation activities in
     industrial establishments. U.S. Department of Labor,
     Bureau of Labor Statistics, Bulletin 458. Washing-
     ton, G.P.O., 1928. 94 p.
          Compares a 1926 survey of welfare programs of
     430 companies with a similar study ten years earlier.
     Presents account of the kinds of work carried on and
     estimates which programs have been most popular and
     successful. Greatest advances in the ten year pe-
     riod were in the areas of medical care, vacations, and
     group insurance. Other benefits examined are sick
     pay, lunch rooms and low cost meals, recreational and
     athletic facilities, social and cultural activities,
     education, and savings and loan plans. Includes
     chapter on welfare in company towns.

COMPREHENSIVE COMPANY AND INDUSTRY PROGRAMS

This section includes descriptions of entire welfare programs
of specific companies and general descriptions of several
types of welfare programs, including suggestions for establishing model overall welfare programs. Works that deal with
only one program of one or several companies are listed in
this bibliography under the program headings. The Company
Index should be particularly helpful in locating works in
this section.

187 Adams, Kate J. Humanizing a great industry. Chicago,
        Armour and Company, 1919. 32 p.
           Describes the policy of "big brotherhood between
        employer and employee" of Armour and Company of
        Chicago. The company believed it had a responsibility
        to care for its employees, especially since many
        employees were foreign and needed help due to the
        language barrier. Welfare benefits included shower-
        baths, free health and dental care, jointly funded
        pensions, and a library.

188 Allen, Hugh. The House of Goodyear: a story of rubber
        and the modern business. Cleveland, Corday and Gross
        Company, 1943. 416 p. (Chapter 10, "Personnel,"
        162-193 p.)
           Describes the development of industrial welfare at
        the Goodyear Tire and Rubber Company. Goodyear in-
        troduced the nation's second company hospital, a
        factory restaurant, an employee insurance coopera-
        tive, low cost purchase options on company housing,
        a pension plan, and educational and recreational
        programs.

58

189   American Cast Iron Pipe Company history: story of
        modern industrial relations, Birmingham, AL, Ameri-
        can Cast Iron Pipe Company, 1920. 76 p.
          Describes welfare programs of the American Cast
        Iron Pipe Company of Birmingham, Alabama, which em-
        phasized fraternalism, not paternalism. The company
        provided a wide variety of benefits including a bath
        house, housing, athletics, churches, schools, recrea-
        tion, pensions, and a Christmas bonus. Medical serv-
        ices and a disability, sickness and death benefit
        program were jointly funded. All programs and bene-
        fits were racially segregated. Data on labor turn-
        over and attendance before and after the institution
        of welfare measures are provided.

190   American Telephone and Telegraph Company. Welfare work
        in behalf of telephone operators. 1912? 16 p.
          Describes welfare benefits of the American Tele-
        phone and Telegraph Company. Welfare was provided to
        keep workers at peak efficiency. Programs included
        lunch rooms, rest rooms, gardens, and educational
        classes. The work environment provided sufficient
        heat, light, and fresh air.

191   Becker, O.M. "Square deal in management." Engineering
        magazine, 30, February 1906, 660–687.
          Presents guidelines for setting up industrial
        welfare departments. Focuses on on-the-job welfare.
        Benefits include adequate lighting, heat, cleanli-
        ness, and ventilation and shower and laundry facili-
        ties.

192   Boettiger, Louis A. Employer welfare work. New York,
        Ronald Press Company, 1923. 301 p.
          A general picture of industrial welfare through
        the early 1920s. A wide variety of programs are dis-
        cussed and costs and risks to employers are weighed
        against potential benefits. Work outlines welfare
        efforts of several corporations and of American wel-
        fare pioneers Francis Cabot Lowell and Nathan Apple-
        ton.

193   Brissenden, Paul F. "Employment policy and labor stabil-
        ity in a Pacific Coast department store." Part II,
        "Description of employment system and labor poli-
        cies." Monthly labor review, 9:5, November 1919,

122-127.

Describes welfare policies of a large Pacific
Coast department store whose policies are based "en-
tirely upon a sound business basis, instead of upon a
sentimental, charitable, or paternalistic basis."
Programs include a clinic, vocational education, a
library, sick pay, and paid vacations.

194   Brissenden, Paul F.   Employment system of the Lake Car-
        riers' Association.   U.S. Department of Labor, Bureau
        of Labor Statistics, Bulletin 235. Washington,
        G.P.O., January 1918. 58 p.

Investigates the "Welfare Plan" of the Lake Carriers' Association, an employer association of Great
Lakes shippers. Prior to introduction of the plan,
nearly all employees of the association were members
of the Lake Seamen's Union. The plan took effect at
the same time as announcement of an open shop policy.
Benefits included assembly rooms, libraries, death
benefits, and a savings plan. The plan required employees to carry log books of ship captains' recommendations. The union opposed the plan, claiming the
benefits were merely sugar coating the open shop policy and log book requirement. It claimed the log
book ratings would be used to blacklist union men and
crush unionism. After the plan began, turnover increased significantly and union membership dropped
sharply.

195   Cardullo, Forrest E.   "Industrial betterment; a study of
        safety and welfare work in manufacturing and selling
        organizations."   Machinery, 22:3, November 1915, 171-
        201.

Examines industrial betterment as a major social
movement to promote human welfare. Describes a di-
verse variety of programs, using examples from specific companies. Employers introduced welfare to keep
workers healthy and happy and thus more efficient,
to attract and maintain high quality workers, and for
reasons of humanitarianism and social responsibility.
Discusses the mixed attitudes of labor toward welfare. They appreciate the benefits but often resent
the paternalism and anti-unionism associated with
them. Predicts welfare will be a permanent feature
of industrial life.

196   Carleton, Frank T.   "The Golden Rule factory."   Arena,
         32:179, October 1904, 408-410.
            Built upon the belief that making men is more im-
         portant than making money, the S.M. Jones Company
         operated on principles of fair treatment and kind-
         ness. Company provided a profit-sharing/stock owner-
         ship program, a dining hall, a park and playground,
         and a variety of social activities.

197   Clothier, Robert C.   "The employment work of the Curtis
         Publishing Company."   Annals of the American Academy
         of Political and Social Science, 65, May 1916. 94-111.

            Describes the operations of the Curtis Publishing
         Company employment department, whose function is "the
         raising of the standard of efficiency of the working
         force" by making employees healthier and happier.
         Discusses a variety of company welfare programs in-
         cluding hospitals, pleasant and safe working condi-
         tions, a restaurant with low-cost meals, recreation
         and reading rooms, a savings fund, sick benefits, a
         boys' camp, and a country club with recreational fa-
         cilities and educational programs.

198   Commons, John R.   " 'Welfare work' in a great industrial
         plan."   Review of reviews, 28:1, July 1903, 79-81.
            Analyzes welfarism at the McCormick division of
         the International Harvester Company. In an effort to
         create a model factory, McCormick introduced benefits
         such as improved ventilation and sanitation, a low-
         cost lunch room, pianos, a dancing platform, a bank,
         an opera company, and care for the sick and injured.
         Article considers philosophical implications of wel-
         fare work and suggests reasons welfare may or may
         not succeed in a given instance.

199   Commonwealth Edison Company.   Employes' handbook. 1917.
         59 p.
            This handbook includes description of the welfare
         policies of the Commonwealth Edison Company. De-
         scribes eligibility requirements and benefit levels
         of the pension plans, savings fund, and stock owner-
         ship program. Other benefits include an educational
         program, athletic activities, a library, and music
         and drama clubs.

200 Cook, E. Wake. Betterment; individual, social, and in-
       dustrial; or highest efficiency through the golden
       rules of right nutrition, welfare work, and the high-
       er industrial developments. New York, F.H. Stokes
       Company, 1906. 349 p.
          Chapters 11, 12, and 15 describe the model fac-
       tory and welfare program of the National Cash Regis-
       ter Company. John H. Patterson, president of NCR,
       believed "Welfare work is practical religion." The
       company sponsored community improvement and beauti-
       fication programs by encouraging gardens and cleanli-
       ness. Welfare included a dining room with low cost
       food, a cooking school, and recreational activities.

201 Dunn, Robert W. The Americanization of labor: the em-
       ployers' offensive against trade unions. New York,
       International Publishers, 1927. 272 p.
          Chapters 9-11 survey a variety of welfare programs
       adopted both as a defensive move against unions and
       out of humanitarian motives. True company motives
       for introducing welfare were to increase productivi-
       ty, to attract high quality labor, to reduce turn-
       over, to develop loyalty in order to keep workers
       docile, and to provide an excuse to keep wages low.
       Describes programs of specific companies. Programs
       included mutual benefit associations, lunch rooms,
       athletics, education, thrift plans, and medical care.
       Cost of welfare and personnel work is assessed.

202 Eads, George W. "N.O. Nelson, practical cooperator, and
       the great work he is accomplishing for human uplift-
       ment." Arena, 36:204, November 1906, 463-480.
          Describes the philanthropic programs of the N.O.
       Nelson Manufacturing Company. Nelson believed "mak-
       ing men" was more important than making money and
       felt "there could be no industrial peace until the
       conflicting elements between capital and labor had
       been harmonized." He believed capital was overpaid
       at the expense of labor so he introduced a profit-
       sharing plan to overcome the inequity. He also
       built the model town of LeClaire, Illinois and sold
       houses to employees through a monthly payment plan.
       The company did not impose paternalistic rules on
       workers' lives. Other benefits provided include kin-
       dergartens, an industrial school, pleasant working
       conditions, a sick benefits fund, and a library.

Employees were encouraged to unionize.

203   Eastman Kodak Company. <u>Industrial relations</u>. Roches-
      ter, NY, (n.d.) 36p.
          Describes welfare programs of the Eastman Kodak
      Company, which included vocational education, a li-
      brary, sick and vacation benefits, recreation, lunch
      rooms, a savings and loan association, housing, and
      an employee representation program. Medical service
      included a visiting nurse and nutrition work.

204   Eaton, J.M. "Industrial welfare work a factor in modern
      management." <u>The Modern hospital</u>, 7:2, August 1916,
      104-109.
          A description of industrial welfare benefits at
      the Cadillac Motor Car Company, provided to improve
      the well-being of workers and make them happier and
      more productive on the job. Benefits include a low-
      cost restaurant and meal service, sanitation and hy-
      giene efforts, legal aid, and medical care. A joint-
      ly funded benefit society provides sick, accident and
      death benefits.

205   Ely, Richard T. "Industrial betterment." <u>Harper's
      monthly magazine</u>, 105:628, September 1902, 548-553.
          Compares welfare practices and industrial better-
      ment efforts of the isolated cotton mill town of Pelzer,
      South Carolina, with the programs of Cleveland,
      Ohio, a metropolitan industrial center. Welfare in
      Pelzer, owned and controlled by one company, is
      classified as patriarchal and paternalistic while
      Cleveland's welfare is characterized as democratic,
      based on what workers want rather than on what a
      company dictates. The Sherwin-Williams Paint Com-
      pany is presented as a model Cleveland welfare com-
      pany and its wide range of programs are discussed.
      Welfare practices in other companies across the coun-
      try are also briefly listed.

206   Emmet, Boris. <u>The California and Hawaiian Sugar Refin-
      ing Corporation</u>. Pasadena, CA, Stanford University,
      Graduate School of Business, 1928. (Stanford Busi-
      ness Series #2) 293 p.
          Pages 55-99 describe welfare programs of the
      California and Hawaiian Sugar Refining Corporation.
      Programs include paid vacations, Christmas bonuses,

educational programs, a library, parks, and playgrounds. Company housing is rented or sold to employees. A community club provides recreation and
athletic facilities. The jointly funded Employee
Mutual Benefit Association administers group insurance, disability and death benefits, and provides
medical care. Welfare programs have increased efficiency and productivity and lowered turnover.

207 Emmet, Boris and John E. Jeuck. Catalogues and count-
     ers: a history of Sears, Roebuck and Company. Chi-
     cago, University of Chicago Press, 1950. 788 p.
          Pages 279-292 describe welfare programs at Sears,
     Roebuck, and Company, which were designed to improve
     workers and build "esprit de corps." A jointly
     funded mutual benefit association provided sickness
     and disability benefits. Sears was one of the first
     companies to provide noncontributory sick pay.
     Profit-sharing was provided as a form of retirement
     security. Other benefits included medical services,
     a restaurant, a library, and athletic facilities.

208 Feis, Herbert. Labor relations, a study made in the
     Procter and Gamble Company. New York, Adelphi Com-
     pany, 1928. 170 p.
          An overview of labor relations at Procter and Gam-
     ble including a description of welfare programs. The
     profit-sharing plan took the form of a contributory
     stock purchase plan with dividends that increased
     with length of service. Pensions and sickness and
     death benefits were jointly funded. An employee
     representation committee was used mainly as a forum
     to make minor suggestions and air grievances. Em-
     ployees were afraid to make serious criticisms for
     fear of retaliation. The company guaranteed em-
     ployment for all employees with at least 6 months
     service who joined the profit-sharing plan.

209 Fleming, Robben W. and Edwin E. Witte. "Marathon Cor-
     poration and seven labor unions." In Causes of
     industrial peace under collective bargaining. Case
     Study #8. Washington, National Planning Association,
     1950. 63 p.
          Pages 12-22 describe welfare benefits at the
     Marathon Corporation, a Wisconsin paper company.

Welfare included company-owned housing, a company
store, a visiting nurse, group life and sickness insurance, pensions, a library, recreation programs,
and a magazine. In addition, mill councils provided
workers with a forum for making policy suggestions
to management. Programs were not used to fight
unionism.

210 Frankel, Lee K, and Alexander Fleisher. The Human
     factor in industry. New York, Macmillan Company,
     1924. 366 p.
          Traces the development and scope of welfare prac-
     tices in industry. Examines a wide range of welfare
     programs in light of their value to employees, at-
     titudes of communities, their effect on productivity,
     and other advantages of such programs. Examples are
     drawn from a variety of companies and industries.

211 Freeman, Albert T. "The labor system of the John B.
     Stetson Company." Annals of the American Academy
     of Political and Social Science, 22:3, November 1903,
     33-38.
          Describes industrial welfare efforts of the John
     B. Stetson Company. Benefits include a hospital,
     recreational facilities, pensions, an accident and
     illness fund, stock allotment and a savings fund.

212 Gardiner, Glenn Lion. Management in the factory. New
     York, McGraw-Hill Book Company, 1925. 225 p.
          Chapter 6 suggests that welfare programs should
     be developed to meet workers' needs in order to pro-
     mote contentment and stability in the work force.
     Worker health should be safeguarded through medical
     care, clean and healthy working conditions, and
     instruction in hygiene and sanitation. Other welfare
     programs include savings plans, legal aid, insurance,
     sickness and death benefits, pensions, education,
     housing, restaurants, and recreation.

213 Giddens, Paul H. Standard Oil Company (Indiana): oil
     pioneer of the Middle West. New York, Appleton-
     Century-Crofts, 1955. 741 p.
          Chapter 12 and various other sections of the book

describe the "humanizing" of the Standard Oil Company of Indiana. The company introduced several welfare programs including pensions, pleasant working conditions, paid vacations, sickness, disability and death benefits, and athletic and recreational facilities. Houses were erected and sold to employees and an overwhelmingly successful stock purchase plan was introduced. An employee representation plan gave workers a voice in labor affairs without infringing on the right to join unions.

214 Gilman, Nicholas Paine. A Dividend to labor: a study of employers' welfare institutions. Boston, Houghton, Mifflin and Company, 1899. 400 p.
     Pages 304-310 describe the profit-sharing plan of the Bourne Cotton Mills in Fall River, Massachusetts. Dividends are paid regularly in exchange for workers' pledges of loyalty to the company and promises to save part of their earnings. Pages 310-316 describe welfare programs of the Procter and Gamble Company. Programs include a pension fund, stock ownership, housing, a library, medical care, sick pay and two paid holidays. Special focus is on profit-sharing, introduced after a series of strikes to improve labor relations. Pages 323-333 outline welfare at the Nelson Manufacturing Company in LeClaire, Illinois. Benefits include profit-sharing, illness and disability pay, housing, schools, a library, entertainment and a cooperative store. The company avoids paternalism and does not forbid union membership.

215 Gilson, Mary Barnett. What's past is prologue; reflections on my industrial experience. New York, Harper and Brothers, 1940. 307 p.
     Chapters 10 and 13 describe personnel work at the Clothcraft Shops of Joseph and Feiss Company. Chapter 10 discusses the company union, which operated in a purely advisory capacity. Rules of elections and operations were unilaterally imposed by management and membership was a condition of employment. Employee representatives helped formulate a paid vacation plan. Chapter 12 describes efforts to care for off-the-job needs of workers. The company provided a visiting nurse, counseling on domestic problems, and a dispensary. Chapter 20 describes conditions on

Hawaiian sugar plantations, including such welfare
benefits as housing and hospitals.

216 Gilson, Mary Barnett. "Work of the Employment and Service Department of the Clothcraft Shops." Proceedings of the Employment Managers' Conference. U.S.
Department of Labor, Bureau of Labor Statistics, Bulletin 227. Washington, G.P.O., 1917. 139-152 p.
     Defends employer paternalism and describes welfare
programs of the Clothcraft Shops in Cleveland. Emphasizes mental development of the workers using
such educational tools as a library, English classes
for foreign-born workers, on-the-job vocational
training and home visits to teach hygiene, health
and homemaking. Other benefits include a bank, a
dispensary, and recreational activities.

217 Goodyear Tire and Rubber Company. The Work of the
Labor Division. Akron, OH, 1920. 97 p.
     Outlines welfare measures at the Goodyear Tire
and Rubber Company, where company policy states,
"The capitalist must be made to work and the workman
must be made a capitalist." Welfare programs included English and Americanization classes, a library, a lunch room, free legal advice, a hospital,
and athletic activities and facilities. Appendix A
is the text of the Industrial Representation Plan
which provided for joint conferences to discuss
labor issues. Appendices B, C, and D describe the
sick benefit, life insurance, and retirement plans

218 Goss, Mary L. Welfare work by corporations. Philadelphia, American Baptist Publication Society, 1911.
36 p.
     Reviews welfare programs of several companies and
suggests employers should recognize that the company
and the worker have inseparable interests. Describes
the pioneering welfare efforts of the National Cash
Register Company which provided gardens, lunch rooms,
education, and outings, and launched a massive community improvement project. Other companies discussed include the Colorado Fuel and Iron Company,
the Cleveland Cliffs Iron Company, the New York City
Railway Company, the Chicago Telephone Company and
the International Harvester Company.

219 Heath, C. "History of the Dennison Manufacturing Com-
     pany-II." Journal of economic and business history,
     2, November 1929, 163-202.
          A wide range of welfare programs are outlined in
     this company history. The company instituted a
     unique combination of profit-sharing, employee stock
     ownership, and sharing management functions with
     workers. Other welfare benefits included a clinic,
     lunch room, a library, savings fund, unemployment
     benefits and a housing fund.

220 Henderson, Charles Richmond. Citizens in industry. New
     York, D. Appleton and Company, 1915. 342 p.
          Pages 31-34 discuss welfare programs of the Mil-
     waukee Electric Railway and Light Company, considered
     a typical welfare company. The purpose of the Wel-
     fare Department was "to promote the well-being, the
     happiness, and the contentment of its employees."
     Benefits included a library, recreational and enter-
     tainment facilities, a pension fund and loans. An
     employee mutual benefit association provided medical
     benefits.
          Pages 34-43 outline welfare at the Illinois Steel
     Company where labor policy promised that "every man
     shall be guaranteed a square deal with the Company."
     Programs included educational efforts, visiting
     nurses, pensions, layoff avoidance, and stock options.

221 Hughes, Florence. Sociological work, the New Jersey
     Zinc Company. Palmerton, PA, New Jersey Zinc Company,
     1914. 59 p.
          Describes welfare programs of the New Jersey Zinc
     Company. Programs included a kindergarten with a
     playground, a library, a gymnasium and other athletic
     and recreational facilities, bands, medical staff and
     facilities, and low-rent housing. Night classes for
     employees included English classes to help foreign
     employees overcome the language barrier.

222 "Industrial relations in a large sugar refinery."
     Monthly labor review, 29:1, July 1929, 69-75.
          Outlines welfare programs of the California and
     Hawaiian Sugar Refining Corporation, instituted to
     promote high morale among workers. Programs include
     paid vacations, a nurse, shower and lunch rooms,

group insurance, aid in financing houses, parks, playgrounds, and clubs. A jointly funded mutual benefit association provided disability and death benefits. Welfare programs resulted in lower turn-over and higher productivity.

223 International Harvester Company. International Har-
     vester Company and its employees. Chicago, 1912.
     56 p.
         Advocates employer welfare in the belief that an employer must preserve his employees the same way he protects the rest of his business. Describes the company's programs including pensions, lunch rooms, rest rooms, athletic programs, sanitary and healthful working conditions, a school, and a hospital with a sanitorium. A jointly funded employee benefit asso-ciation provided disability, death, and illness bene-fits.

224 John B. Stetson Company. The Human element in the Stet-
     son business. Philadelphia, John B. Stetson Company,
     1921. 32 p.
         Outlines benefits at the John B. Stetson Company, where welfare was considered "an investment in good-will, health, skill, and efficiency." A profit-shar-ing plan based on employee merit, was provided in the form of a Christmas bonus. Low interest building loans help workers purchase their own homes. Pen-sions and stock bonuses were given at the discretion of the company. Other welfare included English and naturalization classes, a cooperative store, cafeteri-as, low cost dental care, a hospital, sick benefits, group insurance, and an athletic association.

225 Jones, Samuel M. Letters of labor and love. Indianap-
     olis, The Bobbs-Merrill Company Publishers, 1905.
     248 p.
         A series of philosophic letters by "Golden Rule Jones" to his employees in the machine shops of Acme Sucker Rod Works. Includes descriptions of company welfare programs, provided to raise living standards and promote equality for all. All workers who had been with the company six months received paid vaca-tions because employees who work long, hard hours

in a machine shop are at least as entitled to vacations as office workers. Other benefits include cooperative insurance, a Christmas bonus, the Golden
Rule Park and Playground, picnics, a band, and a
dining hall.

226 "Jordan-Marsh ninth floor heralds new era in personnel
     work." Dry goods economist, 74, March 13, 1920, 73+.
          Describes the "Fellow-workers floor" of the Jordan-
     Marsh store in Boston, designed to give workers a
     place to relax so they will be in a better frame of
     mind to serve customers. The floor provides an audi-
     torium, a library and reading room, a cafeteria,
     rest rooms, and a roof garden. Other company welfare
     includes athletic and educational activities, "health
     research," and a rest house outside the city where
     workers go for parties and paid vacations.

227 Korman, Gerd. Industrialization, immigrants and Ameri-
     canizers; the view from Milwaukee, 1866-1921. Madi-
     son, State Historical Society of Wisconsin, 1967.
     225 p.
          Chapter IV, "The Web of Welfare Work," deals with
     the history of the industrial welfare measures at
     International Harvester Company.

228 Leiserson, William M. Adjusting immigrant and industry.
     New York, Harper and Brothers, 1924. 356 p.
          Chapter 7 examines working conditions for immi-
     grants in America. Includes description of the
     extent and scope of such welfare benefits as medical
     care, lunch rooms, recreation, publications, and
     language lessons, with examples from several com-
     panies. Asserts that improved working conditions
     are a vital prerequisite to absorbing immigrants into
     "the common life of America."

229 Lief, Alfred. Family business: a century in the life
     and times of Strawbridge and Clothier. New York,
     McGraw-Hill Book Company, 1968. 343 p.
          Chapters 5 and 9 describe the early welfare pro-
     grams of Strawbridge and Clothier of Philadelphia.
     Programs included rest rooms, a library, annual pic-
     nics, entertainment activities, a lunch room, pen-

sions, a chorus, an athletic association, a savings
and loan association, a cottage for employee vacations, and medical care including a pioneering dental
care program. Programs were maintained even through
the Depression.

230 Lief, Alfred. The Firestone story: a history of the
     Firestone Tire and Rubber Company. New York, McGraw-
     Hill, 1951. 437 p.
         Chapters 5 and 6 describe welfare practices of
     the Firestone Tire and Rubber Company. Welfare de-
     veloped out of Firestone's desire to recapture the
     intimate contact he had with his employees when the
     plant was small. Programs included picnics, a res-
     taurant with low-cost meals, a baseball diamond,
     stock ownership, free life insurance, and Firestone
     Park. A club house was built with a library, class-
     rooms, athletic facilities, and medical and dental
     departments. The company built homes and sold them
     to employees at cost.

231 Lief, Alfred. Harvey Firestone, free man of enterprise.
     New York, McGraw-Hill, 1951. 324 p.
         A biography of the head of the Firestone Tire
     and Rubber Company. He set up an employee service
     department after a violent strike in order to promote
     better labor relations. Welfare benefits included a
     restaurant, housing sold to workers at cost, free
     life insurance, a stock purchase plan, a club house,
     Firestone Park, and free legal aid from lawyer
     Wendell Wilkie.

232 Lief, Alfred. "It floats": the story of Procter and
     Gamble. New York, Rinehart and Company, 1958. 338 p.
         Traces the development of welfare practices at the
     Procter and Gamble Company. Motivated by humanitar-
     ian concerns, the company instituted a profit-shar-
     ing/stock ownership program, a pension fund, and
     sickness, disability and life insurance. Employees
     were given seats on the company board of directors
     and a program of guaranteed employment was devised.

233 Lindsey, Almont. The Pullman Strike: the story of a
     unique experiment and of a great labor upheaval.

Chicago, University of Chicago Press, 1942. 385 p.
A history of the Pullman Strike and events leading
up to it. Chapters 2-4 describe the model town of
Pullman, Illinois, constructed to attract skilled
workers and discourage turnover. Describes methods
and problems of construction. The company provided
for all needs of workers and allowed them no control
over the management of the town. The lack of democracy under this paternalistic system was one reason
for the strike.

234 Lippencott, Charles A. "Promoting employee teamwork and
       welfare without paternalism: how the Studebaker
       Corporation handles the problem of industrial rela-
       tions." Industrial management, 71, March 1926, 146-
       150.
         Describes employee benefits at the Studebaker
       Corporation, where management believes, "An employer's
       best asset is a loyal and contented employee." The
       company sees welfare as an effort to restore personal
       relationships to industry but recognizes that em-
       ployees resent paternalism. "The sacrifice of inde-
       pendent manhood is too high a price to pay for any
       material benefits however great." Studebaker over-
       came the problem of paternalism by paying dividends
       for continuous service. This is not considered wel-
       fare because it is a benefit employees must earn
       through loyal service. Vacation, pension, stock pur-
       chase, and insurance plans operate on the same prin-
       ciple. The company also provides an educational
       program, medical care, and recreational facilities.

235 Metropolitan Life Insurance Company. (Pamphlets on wel-
       fare work) New York, 1912-.
         A collection of pamphlets on the welfare programs
       of the Metropolitan Life Insurance Company. Company
       programs include good working conditions, paid vaca-
       tions for all employees, sick pay, lunch service,
       comprehensive medical care including a tuberculosis
       sanatorium, vocational education, recreational and
       athletic facilities, and a savings fund. Titles of
       the pamphlets are: "The Visiting Nurse Service"
       (1912); "The Welfare Work of the Metropolitan Life
       Insurance Company" (1912-1918); "Memoirs of the San-
       atorium" (1916); "Welfare Work for Employees" (1915);

"Metropolitan Staff Savings Fund" (1915); "Rules
Governing Home Office Clerical Employees" (1915);
"Educational Activities for Employees of the Metro-
politan Life Insurance Company" (1915). (These pam-
phlets are available in the U.S. Department of Labor
Library).

236 Moore, Charles W. Timing a century: history of the
Waltham Watch Company. Cambridge, Harvard University
Press, 1945. 362 p.
Pages 109-111 and Chapter 11 discuss industrial
welfare at the Waltham Watch Company. The company's
"lavish expenditure" on industrial democracy and welfare, from 1910-1921, was characterized by high wages,
a company-subsidized cafeteria, pensions, recreational
facilities, a nursery, and medical services.
Productivity declined by 50% during those years.
A tightening of the reins, including wage and benefit
cuts, led to a strike in 1924. The strike failed and
no benefits were restored until employees unionized
after the Depression.

237 National Cash Register Company. Information and
rules for our factory and office employees. Dayton,
OH, National Cash Register Company, 1929. 67 p.
The employee handbook of the National Cash Register
Company, which tells employees, "This book will encourage you to put heart in your work." Dictates
standards of moral conduct both in and away from the
factory. Describes welfare benefits, which include a
dining hall and lunches, legal advice, baths on company time, umbrella and overshoe loans during storms,
parks, camps, club houses, paid vacations for all employees, a library, classes, and medical care.

238 National Cash Register Company. (Pamphlets on welfare
and educational work for employees.) Dayton, OH.
A brief history of the National Cash Register Company, including welfare programs. Describes the company library, lunch rooms, and educational programs.
The company encourages enrollment in its "owl classes"
by making educational attainment a criterion for
promotion. The medical department provided emergency
care, physical examinations, and minor dental care.

(These pamphlets are available at the U.S. Department
of Labor Library).

239 National Industrial Conference Board. Industrial rela-
     tions activities at Cheney Brothers. New York, 1929.
     87 p.
        Chapters 2 and 3 describe welfare programs of the
     Cheney Brothers Company. Medical benefits included
     dental, optical, and nursing care and hospital ar-
     rangements. Work councils gave employees a voice in
     management. Other programs included insurance, edu-
     cation, housing, cafeterias, pensions, savings plans,
     and recreation.

240 Nelson, Daniel. Managers and workers: origins of the
     new factory system in the United States, 1880-1920.
     Madison, University of Wisconsin Press, 1975.   234 p.
        Chapter 6 traces the history of various welfare
     programs in pioneer welfare companies. Motives for
     introducing welfare were to personalize labor rela-
     tions, improve company loyalty and morale, and pre-
     vent labor unrest. Discusses the advent of system-
     atic welfare and welfare secretaries. Emphasizes pro-
     grams of the Pullman Palace Car Company, the National
     Cash Register Company, William Filene's Sons, and
     Joseph Bancroft and Sons. Table 8 on page 116 lists
     companies with extensive welfare programs from 1905-
     1915.

241 Nelson, Daniel. "The new factory system and the unions:
     the National Cash Register Company dispute of 1901."
     Labor history, 15:2, Spring 1974, 163-178.
        Examines the effect of welfare work at the Nation-
     al Cash Register Company. National Cash Register
     Company, considered a model factory, motivated work-
     ers with a wide range of welfare programs. A lockout
     and series of strikes in 1901 were blamed on over-
     done and overbearing welfare programs but were really
     instigated by opposition to a particular heavy-handed
     foreman. After the strikes, a Labor Department was
     formed to limit the authority of foremen. The subse-
     quent success of welfare and the Labor Department un-
     dermined unions' strength and even eventually led to
     their demise.

242 Nelson, N.O. "My business life - I." World's work, 19,
    December 1909, 12387-12393. "My business life - II."
    19, January 1910, 12504-12511.
       An autobiographical description of the creation
    and growth of the N.O. Nelson Company, including the
    development of welfare programs to compensate for
    "the unfair division between capital and labor." The
    company introduced "fresh air missions," weekly boat
    excursions for employees. A profit-sharing plan was
    introduced for altruistic reasons. The company was
    not concerned with whether it reduced turnover or in-
    creased productivity. Emergency loans, kindergartens,
    and scholarships were also provided. To improve
    living and working conditions, the company built a
    new factory and a village for employees outside the
    city.

243 Nevins, Allan and Frank E. Hill. Ford: expansion and
    challenge, 1915-1933. New York, Charles Scribner's
    Sons, 1957. v. 2.
       A history of the Ford Motor Company. Chapter 13
    describes the company's welfare programs through
    which "paternalism was pushed to an unprecedented
    point." Programs included safety and comfort in the
    plant, medical care, and low priced stores. Immi-
    grant workers were required to attend company-spon-
    sored English classes and a trade school was opened
    for poor boys. Profit-sharing bonuses were paid out
    on the basis of employees' moral standing. Chapter
    20 discusses health care provisions including sani-
    tary working conditions and a medical staff and
    facilities.

244 New Jersey. Bureau of Statistics of Labor and Industry.
    "Industrial betterment institutions in New Jersey
    manufacturing establishments." Twenty-seventh
    annual report, 1904. Trenton (?). 153 p.
       Describes welfare programs of the Celluloid Com-
    pany, the Ferris Brothers Company, the Ingersoll-
    Sergeant Drill Company, the Sherwin-Williams Company,
    and the Weston Electrical Instrument Company. Cellu-
    loid Company programs included club houses, a library,
    an entertainment hall, and sickness and death bene-
    fits. Ferris Brothers provided a dining room and
    meals, umbrellas and rubber overshoes during storms,
    a recreation hall, and financial aid. Ingersoll-

Sergeant established a jointly funded sickness, disability, and death fund. Sherwin-Williams provided
shower-baths, lunch rooms, jointly funded sickness
and death benefits, a club room, and Thanksgiving
turkeys. Weston benefits included club rooms, a dining hall with low-cost meals, a library, a kitchen
and a dispensary.

245 New York Edison Company. Educational and other employee
     relations. New York, 1913. 57 p.
          Describes vocational education and other welfare
     work of the New York Edison Company. Outlines bene-
     fits and eligibility requirements of the Mutual
     Benefit Association. Discusses medical care, savings
     and loan provisions, and social, recreational, and
     athletic activities.

246 Norton, Augustus P. "Welfare work for civilian employees
     of the United States." Monthly labor review, 7:2,
     August 1918, 218-231.
          A survey of welfare work on civilian federal em-
     ployees during World War I. Describes restaurants in
     government buildings and enumerates federal recrea-
     tion facilities and programs. Discusses health bene-
     fits including emergency rooms, medical staff and
     visiting nurses. Costs of government welfare are
     estimated and evaluated in light of the programs'
     success in reducing turnover. Recommendations for
     improved welfare in Washington, D.C., are listed.

247 Ozanne, Robert. A Century of labor-management relations
     at McCormick and International Harvester. Madison,
     University of Wisconsin Press, 1967. 300 p.
          Traces the evolution of industrial welfare at the
     McCormick-International Harvester Company. A major
     purpose of welfare programs was to bolster the com-
     pany's public image in order to discourage the govern-
     ment from invoking anti-trust laws against it. Bene-
     fits included vocational education through the McCor-
     mick Institute, health, sanitation and recreation
     programs, a loan fund, profit-sharing, and sickness
     and accident benefits. A company union, established
     to keep independent unions out, gave workers a voice
     but no real power in determining labor policy. The
     company hired Gertrude Beeks as "social agent" to

administer welfare programs. She surveyed welfare
programs of numerous U.S. companies and used the results of the surveys to improve welfare programs at
McCormick-International Harvester Company.

248 Patterson, John H. "Altruism and sympathy as factors in
     works administration." Engineering magazine, 20:4,
     January 1901, 577-608.
         Suggests manufacturers and their workers should
     "unite in enthusiastic development of one another's
     interests." Advocates welfare as a means of winning
     workers' sympathy and assistance. Surveys a wide
     range of programs using examples from specific com-
     panies. General welfare considerations include
     "thoughtfulness for comfort in work," "opportunities
     for mental training and mental growth," provisions
     for old age and disability, and development of pleas-
     ant, attractive, and comfortable living conditions.

249 Phillips, R.E. "The betterment of working life." World's
     work, 1, December 1900, 157-169.
         Describes turn-of-the-century welfare measures of
     specific companies in Cleveland, Pittsburgh, and Day-
     ton, Ohio. Briefly outlines several programs includ-
     ing employee lunch rooms, libraries, medical and
     health benefits, community improvement projects,
     education, and recreational activities.

250 Report on condition of woman and child wage-earners in
     the United States. 61st Congress, 2nd Session, Sen-
     ate Document 645. (5635-5703) Washington, G.P.O.,
     1911-1912. 19 vols.
         These volumes represent a detailed report on con-
     ditions of employment for women and children in the
     early 20th Century. Scattered throughout the study
     are references to industrial welfare programs in var-
     ious industries. A number of volumes deal with the
     textile industry and Chapters 5 and 8 of Volume one
     detail working conditions and living conditions in a
     mill community. Each volume is indexed separately.

251 Ripley, Charles M. Life in a large manufacturing plant.
     Schenectady, NY, General Electric Company, Publications

Bureau, 1919. (Reprinted from General Electric
review for 1917 and 1918) 170 p.
   Sketches wide range of benefits available to General Electric Company employees. Some benefits are
managed by the Mutual Benefit Association, run and
funded by employees but partially subsidized by the
company. Association benefits are accident, illness,
and life insurance and social and recreational programs. Other benefits include pensions, medical
care, low cost restaurants, educational programs,
newspapers and a library.

252 Roland, Henry. "Six examples of successful shop manage-
       ment." Engineering magazine, 12:1, October 1896,
       69-85.
          Examines the labor policies of Whitin Shops of
       Whitinsville, Massachusetts, which never had a strike
       or serious labor problem. Management followed a
       policy of "full consideration of the effect of any
       business move on the earnings and peace of mind of
       the workmen." The company rented housing to workers
       at low rates and supported schools, churches, and a
       "Memorial Building" with assembly rooms, a library,
       and a music room. Suggests the labor harmony was due
       to the beautiful and healthful environment and the
       company's recognition of its duty to care for workers.

253 Shefferman, Nathan W. Employment methods. New York,
       Ronald Press, 1920. 573 p.
          An overview of personnel policies including chap-
       ters on industrial welfare. Chapter 14 discusses ed-
       ucational programs, including general education and
       English classes for immigrants. Chapters 26 and 27
       survey a wide range of welfare programs. Chapter 28
       examines functions, costs, and various services of
       company medical programs and Chapter 30 surveys the
       industrial housing problem. Discusses the relation
       of adequate housing to turnover and productivity and
       lists advantages and problems of providing worker
       housing.

254 Shuey, Edwin L. Factory people and their employers.
       New York, Lentilhon and Company, 1900. 224 p.
          "A Handbook of Practical Methods of Improving

Factory Conditions and the Relations of Employer and
Employe." Believes welfare is part of an employer's
responsibility to the employees who have made him
successful. Briefly describes notable programs of
specific companies. Benefits discussed include profit-sharing, recreation, community improvement, medical care, lunch rooms, libraries, housing, and mutual benefit associations.

255 Tead, Ordway and Henry C. Metcalf. Personnel adminis-
     tration: its principles and practice. New York,
     McGraw-Hill, 1920. 543 p.
     Pages 141-152 describe a number of job related
     benefits to improve the health and comfort of work-
     ers, including rest rooms, lunch rooms, sanitation,
     and health care. Chapter 23 discusses advantages
     and disadvantages of profit-sharing and stock pur-
     chase plans. Chapter 24 discusses general princi-
     ples of providing worker insurance, pensions, and
     unemployment compensation. Chapters 27-29 survey
     employee representation. Discusses reasons for rep-
     resentation, types of plan, provisions of good
     plans, details of administration, and limitations.

256 Tolman, William Howe. How a manufacturing concern pro-
     motes industrial hygiene. Washington, International
     Congress of Hygiene and Demography, 1912. 30 p.
     Describes welfare programs of the National Cash
     Register Company. The company transformed the dingy
     "Slidertown" section of Dayton, Ohio into "South
     Park," an attractive residential area. It land-
     scaped the factory area and planted gardens and gave
     prizes to employees and neighborhood boys who
     planted gardens. Other welfare included medical
     care, a gymnasium and recreational facilities, and
     health and industrial education. Air, light, water,
     food, and exercise were the key ingredients of the
     company's pleasant working conditions.

257 Tolman, William Howe. Industrial betterment. New York,
     Social Service Press, 1900. 82 p. (Monographs on
     American Social Economics #16. League for Social
     Service)
     A description of industrial welfare, based on the

philosophy that "when there is sympathy on the part
of the employer, and its realization on the part of
the employee, their interests become identical."
Describes a wide range of programs, using examples
of specific companies. Describes model homes, gardens, towns, and other facilities. Education was
offered to improve the quality of workers and their
children. Other welfare benefits include improved
working conditions, medical care and facilities,
company restaurants and lunch rooms, vacations, recreational facilities and activities, and savings
plans.

258   Tracy, Lena Harvey. How my heart sang: the story of
         pioneer industrial welfare work. New York, Richard
         R. Smith, 1950. 192 p.
         Chapters 6-12 describe pioneering welfare pro-
      grams of the National Cash Register Company, intro-
      duced in response to a series of strikes and product
      sabotage. Welfare work began when the company
      bought a cottage that was to become a saloon and
      built a kindergarten there instead. The author was
      hired as welfare director to supervise both employee
      betterment and community improvement projects. Im-
      proved working conditions, a lunch room, educational
      programs, and boys' and girls' clubs were features
      of the welfare efforts.

259   United Shoe Company. (Miscellaneous pamphlets on wel-
         fare work) 1911-1916.
         A collection of pamphlets describing welfare pro-
      grams of the United Shoe Machinery Factory in Bever-
      ly, Massachusetts. The company's motive for pro-
      viding welfare was "enlightened selfishness," since
      welfare benefited both the company and the workers
      by making the workers happier and more productive.
      Welfare programs included sanitary and pleasant
      working conditions, medical care and an emergency
      hospital, athletic and recreational programs and
      facilities, a club house, and housing sold to em-
      ployees at cost. A jointly funded mutual relief
      association provided sick, accident and death bene-
      fits. Pamphlet titles are: "Efficiency through
      hygiene," "Good sport, good health, good work," "The
      story of three partners," and "An industrial city."

(These pamphlets are available in the U.S. Department of Labor Library.)

260 U.S. Department of Labor. Working Conditions Service.
     Treatment of industrial problems by constructive
     methods. Washington, 1919. 15 p.
          Outlines the functions of the Working Conditions
     Service of the Department of Labor, which assists
     employers in improving working conditions. The
     Division of Industrial Hygiene and Medicine assists
     in identifying and eliminating health hazards in the
     work place and in developing comprehensive medical
     care programs. The Division of Labor Administration
     assists in developing a variety of personnel pro-
     grams including such welfare efforts as restaurants,
     and lunch rooms, housing, recreation, insurance,
     pensions, legal aid, and savings and loan programs.

261 "Wages and other conditions in government and in private
     employment." Monthly labor review, 29:2, August
     1929, 133-140.
          Summary of a report to Congress comparing wages
     and benefits of federal employees with wages and
     benefits of comparable private sector workers. In-
     cludes comparison of such welfare benefits as pen-
     sions, group insurance, sick leave, paid vacations,
     and medical service. Private industry provides
     more extensive and varied welfare benefits than the
     federal government.

262 Walker, Anne K. "Looking beyond the door of welfare
     service in the department store." The Modern hospi-
     tal, 7:2, August 1916, 119-122.
          Outlines extensive welfare efforts of B. Altman
     and Company, a major New York department store. The
     programs are designed to promote mental and physical
     health so employees are more useful on the job.
     Programs include a medical department and emergency
     hospital, a lunch program, recreation rooms, a li-
     brary, a school, and vocational classes.

263 "Welfare work in a bookbinding establishment." The
     Modern hospital, 7:2, August 1916, 122-123.

Traces the development of welfare programs in
the J.F. Tapley Company in New York City. Programs
include medical facilities, a visiting nurse, a
vacation fund, and a library.

264 Willcox, William R. Developments of the year in welfare
     work. New York, National Civic Federation, December
     11, 1913. 10 p.
         A report on the past year's welfare efforts by
     the National Civic Federation. Focuses on a survey
     of welfare in New York department stores from which
     a guidebook for developing welfare in the retail
     industry was compiled. Discusses improvements in
     department store welfare and examines inadequacies
     that still existed. National Civic Federation wel-
     fare recommendations to stores were often ignored
     because owners did not understand the importance
     of welfare. Other welfare efforts of the National
     Civic Federation included educational programs, wel-
     fare advice to employers, and cooperation in the
     development of New York City welfare programs. Pub-
     lications dealing with the welfare activities of
     various companies are listed.

265 Wuest, Robert. "Industrial betterment activities of the
     National Metal Trades Association." The Annals of
     the American Academy of Political and Social Science,
     44, November 1912, 74-85.
         An examination of the industrial welfare programs
     of the National Metal Trades Association, an em-
     ployer association of metal products manufacturers.
     Programs include industrial education and scholar-
     ships for apprentices, cooperative profit-sharing,
     safety and hygiene projects, accident compensation
     and a magazine for workers.

266 Young Men's Christian Association. International Com-
     mittee, Industrial Department. Among industrial
     workers...(ways and means) a handbook for associa-
     tions in industrial fields. New York, 1916. 118 p.

         A handbook on how to establish YMCAs for indus-
     trial workers. Suggests ways to elicit support and
     financial contributions from employers and workers.
     Discusses variety of welfare programs that may be
     instituted through YMCAs.

INDUSTRIAL WELFARE PROGRAMS IN FOUR INDUSTRIES

Mining, railroads, steel, and textiles are considered separately in the bibliography because of the major role they played in the welfare movement. Mining was particularly known for employee representation and company towns. Company towns and related benefits were the primary welfare benefits in the textile industry. Company stores gained particular notoriety in the textile and mining industries. Welfare in the steel and railroad industries focused on pensions and jointly funded employee relief plans, which provided sickness, accident, and death benefits. Employee representation was also a common feature in these two industries. One particularly useful periodical for the textile industry is the Cotton History Review (1960-61) which became the Textile History Review (1962-64).

MINING

267 "Anaconda Copper has a model town at Conda, Idaho."
     Engineering and mining journal, 130:5, September 8,
     1930, 240.
          Describes Conda, Idaho, a phosphate mining town
     of the Anaconda Copper Mining Company. The town
     features attractive, four-room cottages with modern
     conveniences, beautiful gardens, and a company store.
     Tennis courts, a baseball diamond, and a recreation
     hall provide leisure time activity.

268 "Bituminous mine workers and their homes." In Report of
     the U.S. Coal Commission. 68th Congress, 2nd Ses-
     sion, Senate Document 195, Part III. (8402, v. 3)

Washington, G.P.O., 1925. 1399-1646.
A survey of living conditions in the bituminous
coal industry. Discusses generally poor conditions
of company-owned housing. Describes unsanitary,
ramshackle conditions, the lack of trees and gardens, inadequate water, sewerage, and light, and
inadequate disease prevention and medical service.
Considers the adequacy of educational and religious
facilities and services. Discusses high rents in
company housing and high prices in company stores.

269 Bituminous Operators' Special Committee. The Company
     town. (Pamphlet submitted to the U.S. Coal Commis-
     sion, September 8, 1923) In U.S. Coal Commission
     Records, entry 8, box 3, Federal Records Center,
     Suitland, MD.

270 Camp and plant, v. 1-5, 1901-1904.
     The weekly magazine of the sociological depart-
     ment of the Colorado Fuel and Iron Company; includes
     a variety of articles on company welfare programs.

271 Chafee, Zechariah, Jr. "Company towns in the soft coal
     fields." Independent, 111:3851, September 15,
     1923, 102-104.
     Outlines U.S. Coal Commission report on company
     towns in the bituminous coal industry. Describes
     facilities and services commonly provided and advo-
     cates transferring control of the towns to the work-
     ers.

272 Chanler, W.C. "Civil liberties in the soft coal fields:
     the point of view of the operators." Independent,
     111:3853, October 13, 1923, 162-163.
     A defense of company-owned mining towns. Argues
     that company towns are an unwelcome operating ex-
     pense, forced on companies because no other housing
     was available for workers. Contends that company
     dominance of lives and workers' loss of liberty are
     not as severe as writers have suggested. Claims
     loss of some freedom is compensated for by a gain in
     other civil rights, such as protection from violence
     and the right to work without union interference.

273 Collier, Peter and David Horowitz. <u>The Rockefellers:
     an American dynasty</u>. New York, Holt, Rinehart and
     Winston, 1976. 746 p.
          Chapter 8 describes the employee representation
     plan introduced at the Colorado Fuel and Iron Com-
     pany in the wake of a bitter, violent strike and
     public outcry against the company. Under the plan,
     employee representatives and management would decide
     issues concerning working and living conditions,
     safety, sanitation, housing, and education. De-
     scribes John D. Rockefeller Jr.'s selling of the plan
     to the workers.

274 "The Colorado Coal Miners' Strike." U.S. Commission on
     Industrial Relations. <u>Report and Testimony</u>, v. 7
     and 8, 6345-7425. 64th Congress, 1st Session, Docu-
     ment No. 415. (Senate Document v. 25, 26, No. 6935-
     6936)
          Testimony before the Commission on Industrial
     Relations on the Colorado Coal Miners' Strike of
     1913 and 1914. Includes descriptions of unhealthy
     and dangerous working and living conditions. De-
     scribes the violence of the strike and drives for
     union recognition. Discusses the development of the
     Coal Miners' Welfare Association, a joint venture
     designed to promote the welfare of miners. The
     president of the Colorado Fuel and Iron Company
     denies that miners were forced to shop at the com-
     pany store and describes the company hospital,
     housing, and other conditions.

275 (Colorado Coal Miners' Strike) "Further proceedings
     relating to Colorado strike, large foundations,
     and industrial control." U.S. Commission on Indus-
     trial Relations. <u>Report and Testimony</u>, v. 8, 9, 7761-
     8480. 64th Congress, 1st Session, Document 415.
     (Senate Document v. 26, 27, No. 6936-6937)
          Testimony before the U.S. Commission on Indus-
     trial Relations on the Colorado coal miners' strike
     of 1913 and 1914. Includes testimony by John D.
     Rockefeller Jr., a major stockholder in the Colo-
     rado Fuel and Iron Company. Rockefeller testified
     that he favors associations of employees as long as
     they do not disregard rights of employers and claims
     he was not responsible for the company's policy of

union opposition. Advocates the establishment of
an employee representation plan to allow the company
and workers to confer over labor issues.

276   (Colorado Fuel and Iron Company) Annual report of the
      Sociological Department of the Colorado Fuel and
      Iron Company, 1903-1906, 1907-1909.
            Annual reports on programs and facilities pro-
      vided to employees of the Colorado Fuel and Iron
      Company and their families. Special emphasis is
      placed on schools, education, and playgrounds for
      children. Other programs include clubs, libraries,
      bands, an art exhibit, churches, lectures, enter-
      tainment, and sanitation. Reports include several
      photographs.

277   (Colorado Fuel and Iron Company) Report of the Medical
      Department of the Colorado Fuel and Iron Company for
      1906-1907, 1908-1909.
            Annual reports of medical care provided to em-
      ployees of the Colorado Fuel and Iron Company.
      Lists types and frequency of workers' diseases and
      injuries and discusses methods of treatment. De-
      scribes nursing school and hospital facilities and
      equipment. Projects future medical and sanitary
      needs and problems.

278   Colorado Fuel and Iron Company Industrial Bulletin.
      v. 1-14, 1915-1929.
            The company publication of the Colorado Fuel and
      Iron Company. Includes descriptions and examples
      of various welfare programs.

279   "Colorado Fuel and Iron Industrial Representation
      Plan." Monthly review of U.S. Bureau of Labor Sta-
      tistics (Monthly labor review), 1:6, December 1915,
      12-22.
            Describes agreement between employees and the
      Colorado Fuel and Iron Company. Agreement outlines
      rules for establishing and administering a company-
      sponsored union and sets up employee/employer com-
      mittees to consider working conditions and welfare
      issues. Committees make recommendations to company
      but company makes decisions on all matters. Text

of plan is reprinted.

280 Emmet, Boris. Labor relations in the Fairmont, West
     Virginia bituminous coal field. U.S. Department of
     Labor, Bureau of Labor Statistics, Bulletin 361.
     Washington, G.P.O., 1924. 86 p.
        Pages 71-86 outline the employee representation
     and non-union collective bargaining plan of the
     large coal company in Fairmont, West Virginia. The
     plan features employee committees, an employee com-
     missioner who works for the interests of employees,
     and an employer commissioner who represents the com-
     pany in labor matters. Includes text of the agree-
     ment and rules of administration. Other welfare
     programs of the company include group insurance,
     playgrounds, recreation centers, housing, and
     company stores.

281 "The employe services of the Consolidation Coal Company."
     Law and labor, 12:11, November 1930, 245-246.
        Describes welfare programs of the Consolidation
     Coal Company, including a medical staff, recreation-
     al facilities, company stores, company-funded health,
     accident and life insurance, housing, and an employee
     representation plan to give workers an avenue for ap-
     pealing complaints.

282 Fowler, George L. "Social and industrial conditions in
     the Pocahontas coal fields." Engineering magazine,
     27:3, June 1904, 383-396.
        A survey of living conditions in the coal mining
     area of Pocahontas, West Virginia. Explains the
     procedure of using scrip in company stores. Denies
     that companies compel workers to shop at company
     stores and claims goods at most stores are not over-
     priced. Surveys various types of housing and dis-
     cusses the unsanitary conditions of many of them.

283 Gates, William B. Michigan copper and Boston dollars:
     an economic history of the Michigan copper mining
     industry. Cambridge, Harvard University Press, 1951.
     301 p.
        Chapter 4 outlines welfare in the Michigan copper

mines. Prior to the Civil War, company housing,
churches, and schools were unclean and poorly built.
Inflexible company rules governed every detail of
life. After the war, Calumet and Hecla, the largest
company, developed "enlightened paternalism" and
gained a reputation for treating employees well.
Housing, schools, and churches were sturdy and
comfortable. A number of benefits, including sickness, disability, and death benefits, hospitals,
health insurance, libraries, and several community
service and improvement programs were introduced.

284 Ginger, Ray. "Company sponsored welfare plans in the
       anthracite industry before 1900." Bulletin of the
       Business Historical Society, 27:2, June 1953, 112–
       120.
            This article deals principally with the medical
       and insurance benefits provided by the major coal
       companies. Additionally it offers hypothetical an-
       swers to three questions: 1) why did companies in-
       stall certain programs? 2) did these plans mitigate
       labor unrest? and 3) how well or poorly were the
       plans managed?

285 Jensen, Vernon H. Heritage of conflict: labor rela-
       tions in the nonferrous metals industry up to 1930.
       Ithaca, Cornell University Press, 1950. 495 p.
            Pages 253 and 272-274 describe welfare programs
       of the Homestake Mining Company in South Dakota and
       the Calumet and Hecla Company in Michigan copper
       mines. The Homestake program, established after the
       local union was ousted, included a hospital depart-
       ment, recreation building, free library and kinder-
       garten. Calumet and Hecla offered such an extensive
       range of benefits that it controlled every aspect
       of workers' lives. Domination by both companies
       at least partially negated the benefits of welfare
       measures.

286 Korson, George. Coal dust on the fiddle: songs and
       stories of the bituminous industry. Halboro, PA,
       Folklore Associates, 1964. 460 p.
            Chapters 2 and 3 describe living conditions in
       company-owned mining camps. Towns and houses were

ramshackle and dirty. Company schools were poor
and no provisions were made for old and disabled
workers. Inadequate medical care featured over-
worked doctors who often practiced more folklore
than medicine. High prices at the company store
kept miners in constant debt and at the mercy of
their employers.

287 Labor difficulties in the coal fields of Colorado. 64th
     Congress, 1st Session, House of Representatives,
     Document No. 859. Washington, G.P.O., 1916. 1-16.
     (7099)
          Pages 5-9 of this report of the Colorado Coal
     Commission outline plan for cooperation between em-
     ployees and employers in the Colorado Fuel and Iron
     Company. Plan includes establishing and administer-
     ing a company-sponsored union, with joint committees
     to consider welfare issues and working conditions.
     Committees make recommendations to company but do
     not have authority to initiate programs.

288 Lewis, Lawrence. "Uplifting 17,000 employees." World's
     work, 9:5, March 1905, 5939-5950.
          Enumerates welfare efforts of the Colorado Fuel
     and Iron Company. Designed to draw workers out of
     filth and violence. The company replaced unsanitary
     living quarters with model housing, provided English
     classes to overcome language barriers, built a
     reading room and library, funded schools and a medi-
     cal staff, taught sanitation and hygiene, and started
     a day nursery and camp magazine.

289 McGill, Nettie P. The Welfare of children in bituminous
     coal mining communities in West Virginia. U.S. De-
     partment of Labor, Bureau of Labor Statistics, Bul-
     letin 117. Washington, G.P.O., 1923. 77 p.
          A survey of employer welfare programs affecting
     children in 11 West Virginia mining villages. Based
     on visits to every home with children under age 18,
     survey examined such welfare benefits as company
     housing, schools, health and medical care, recrea-
     tion, and safety conditions for children who worked
     in the mines.

290 Magnusson, Leifur. "Company housing in the anthracite
     region of Pennsylvania." Monthly labor review,
     10:5, May 1920, 186-195.
          Survey of housing of 24 Pennsylvania coal com-
     panies. Describes towns and housing conditions, in-
     cluding the age, types, and sizes of houses. Lists
     rents and discusses upkeep and costs of maintenance.
     Describes two model housing projects and includes
     floor plans.

291 Magnusson, Leifur. "Company housing in the bituminous
     coal fields." Monthly labor review, 10:4, April
     1920, 215-222.
          Survey of housing in coal mining towns. Found
     most homes were owned by companies and did not have
     the conveniences of average city housing. Estimates
     age, size, and type of houses and lists average
     rents in various regions.

292 Magnusson, Leifur. "A modern copper mining town."
     Monthly labor review, 7:3, September 1918, 278-284.
          Describes copper mining town of Tyrone, New Mex-
     ico. The Phelps-Dodge Corporation provides housing,
     a hospital, recreational facilities, utilities, fire
     and police protection, and a library. American
     workers are entitled to better housing than Mexican
     workers. Costs of housing to the company and rental
     rates to workers are listed.

293 Mather, William G. Some observations on the principle
     of benefit funds and their place in the Lake Superior
     iron mining industry. 1898. 13 p.
          Describes pensions, housing, medical care, and
     education provided to employees of Lake Superior
     iron mining companies. Since labor is the main
     cost of producing iron ore, keeping workers happy
     and content will increase the efficiency of produc-
     tion.

294 Morris, Homer Lawrence. The Plight of the bituminous
     coal miner. Philadelphia, University of Pennsylvania
     Press, 1934. 253 p.
          Analyzes the decline of the bituminous coal in-

dustry and describes the effects of high unemployment of coal miners. Chapter 6 describes living in
company-controlled communities. Since companies
provide housing and most other facilities, they determine the standard of living of their employees.
Describes poor housing, high prices in company
stores, and exploitative leases. Companies control
what is taught and preached by financing schools
and churches. Even without high unemployment, miners
are trapped in the industry because they are largely
illiterate, untrained for any other job, and entire-
ly dependent on the company for all means of exist-
ence.

295 Obenauer, Marie L. "Living conditions in the anthracite
region and composition of the mining population."
In Report of the U.S. Coal Commission, Senate Document 195, Part II, 68th Congress, 2nd Session, (8402,
v. 1) Washington, G.P.O., 1925. 527-572.
A survey of living conditions in the anthracite
region of Pennsylvania, based on the 1920 census and
visits to mining families. Compares conditions in
company owned houses and towns to conditions in independently owned mining towns. Finds that company
towns have less developed water, sewer, and lighting
systems but have a lower cost of living and lower
rents.

296 "Report of the Colorado Coal Commission." Monthly labor
review, 2:4, April 1916, 47-49.
Briefly summarizes 1916 report of Colorado Coal
Commission. Mentions a variety of welfare measures,
including housing, recreational facilities, and
schools. Also discusses the joint employer/employee
cooperation plan of the Colorado Fuel and Iron Company.

297 Report of the United States Coal Commission, 68th Congress, 2nd Session, Senate Document 195, Parts I-V.
(8402, v. 1-3) Washington, G.P.O., 1925.
Complete 5-part report of United States Coal Commission investigation of the coal mining industry.
A report in Part I on civil rights in the coal
fields describes housing and other services provided

when new mines opened. Emphasizes company dominance
of mining towns, which deprived workers of freedom.
A section of Part II describes living conditions in
the anthracite mining region. Only 10% of miners
lived in company-owned housing. Independent housing
was of generally higher quality with better facilities but rents in company housing were lower. In
Part III, a similar study examines bituminous coal
towns, most of which were company-owned. Outlines
quality and incidence of several welfare measures,
including housing, sanitation, churches, medical
services, and recreation. Description and photographs of best and worst towns are presented.

298   Report on the Colorado strike investigation. 63rd
          Congress, 3rd Session, House Document 1630. Wash-
          ington, G.P.O., 1915. (6889) 53 p.
              Results of investigation by the House Committee
          on Mines and Mining of the 1913 Colorado Coal Mine
          Strike. Pages 38-40 describe living conditions in
          the mining camps. Employees were required to live in
          substandard company housing and trade in the company
          store. Report criticizes the mining camps for lack of
          welfare programs as only one camp had any recreation
          or amusement facilities.

299   Rochester, Anna. Labor and coal. New York, Interna-
          tional Publishers, 1931. 255 p.
              Chapter 5 attacks company mining towns, claiming
          they are not welfare programs but rather a weapon
          for controlling the workers. Some companies require
          employees to live in crowded, unsanitary housing.
          Workers are often either forced to shop in over-
          priced company stores or are lured in by easy credit.
          Other sections of book attack industry for lack of
          other welfare programs.

300   Rockefeller, John D., Jr. The Colorado Industrial Plan.
          1916. 94 p.
              A collection of essays and speeches by John D.
          Rockefeller Jr. on the employee representation plan
          of the Colorado Fuel and Iron Company. The Colorado
          plan is based on the idea that the interests of em-
          ployers and employees should be mutual, not antago-

nistic. Labor and capital should be partners since
both can prosper if they work in harmony. The text
of the plan is provided.

301 Rockefeller, John D., Jr. The Personal relation in in-
     dustry. New York, Boni and Liveright, 1923. 149 p.
        A collection of addresses by John D. Rockefeller
     Jr. focusing mainly on the employee representation
     plan of the Colorado Fuel and Iron Company. Based on
     Rockefeller's philosophy that "the purpose of indus-
     try is quite as much the advancement of social well-
     being as the production of wealth," the plan im-
     proves employee benefits and gives workers a voice
     in labor policy. The plan guarantees a minimum wage,
     provides an 8-hour day for some workers, stabilizes
     rents on company housing, and provides for the build-
     ing of bath houses and club houses. The Appendix
     presents the text of the plan.

302 "Rockefeller interests in Colorado." U.S. Commission on
     Industrial Relations. Report and Testimony, v. 9,
     8481-8948. 64th Congress, 1st Session, Document
     415. (Senate Document v. 27, No. 6937)
        A hearing before the U.S. Commission on Indus-
     trial Relations to determine the extent of John D.
     Rockefeller Jr.'s responsibility for poor living and
     working conditions and violence in the mining camps
     of the Colorado Fuel and Iron Company. Rockefeller,
     a major stockholder in the company, claimed he had
     little knowledge of workers' conditions. Includes
     testimony on the condition of worker housing, the
     company store, sanitation in the camps, the avail-
     ability of recreation, and general working and
     living conditions. Includes testimony of MacKenzie
     King, eventual prime minister of Canada, who helped
     Rockefeller improve labor conditions and introduce
     an employee representation plan.

303 "Rockefeller organizes and recognizes a 'union'." Amer-
     ican federationist, 22:11, November 1915, 975-977.
        Samuel Gompers mocks John D. Rockefeller Jr's
     attempts to understand the lives of his employees at
     the Colorado Fuel and Iron Company. Attacks Rocke-
     feller's proposal for a company union as a pretext
     to keep the United Mine Workers out. Contends com-

pany unions will give employees no opportunity to
push for meaningful demands. Rockefeller should
give workers higher wages to spend as they wish
rather than using the money to unilaterally introduce welfare programs.

304 Selekman, Ben M. and Mary Van Kleeck. Employees' repre-
       sentation in coal mines: a study of Colorado Fuel
       and Iron Company. New York, Russell Sage Founda-
       tion, 1924. 454 p.
          A study of employee representation at the Colo-
       rado Fuel and Iron Company, introduced following
       a long and bitter strike. Describes the election of
       representatives, functions and powers of joint com-
       mittees and representatives, and costs of adminis-
       tration. Examines the success of committees in im-
       proving housing, medical service, education, and rec-
       reation. Considers differences between employee
       representation and trade unions. The company
       claimed the plan was not intended to discriminate
       against union members but union organizers were of-
       ten banned from the camps. The United Mine Workers
       opposed the representation plan, claiming only a
       powerful union could protect employee interests.
       Appendix A presents the text of the plan.

305 Spencer, William. "Copperton - a model home town for
       Utah copper employees." Engineering and mining
       journal, 125:9, March 3, 1928, 369-372.
          Describes the building of Copperton, Utah, owned
       by the Utah Copper Company. In building the town,
       the company attempted to avoid the crowded, smokey
       congestion caused by poor planning in its nearby
       town of Bingham. The company provided comfortable
       houses, a hospital, a park, a playground, tennis
       courts, and a baseball park.

306 (Union Pacific Coal Company) History of the Union Pacific
       coal mines, 1868-1940. Omaha, Colonial Press, 1940.
       265 p.
          A history of several Union Pacific coal mining
       towns. Includes town-by-town descriptions of wel-
       fare benefits provided by the company. Housing
       was the primary benefit but the company also often

provided schools, churches, recreational and entertainment facilities and activities, company stores,
and various community improvement measures.

307 White, Joseph H. **Houses for mining towns**. U.S. Department of the Interior, Bureau of Mines, Bulletin 87.
Washington, G.P.O., 1914. 64 p.

308 Wilson, Isabella C. "Welfare work in a mining town."
Journal of home economics, 11:1, January 1919, 21-
23.
Outlines efforts of the Logan Mining Company to
make Earling, West Virginia a healthier, more pleasant
place to live. Residents were taught gardening,
cooking, canning and a number of sanitary habits
such as collecting garbage and fencing hogs. A
playground for the children was also provided.

309 Zinke, George W. "Minnequa Plant of Colorado Fuel and
Iron Corporation and two locals of United Steelworkers of America." In **Causes of industrial peace under collective bargaining**. Case Study #9. Washington, National Planning Association, 1950. 93 p.
Chapter 3 outlines the employee representation
plan of the Minnequa Plant of the Colorado Fuel and
Iron Company. The "Rockefeller Plan," formed in
response to a violent strike in 1913, was considered
a model company union. Employee representatives
made recommendations on labor policy but the company
was under no obligation to accept them.

RAILROADS

310 Atterbury, W.W. **Employe representation of the Pennsylvania Railroad**. (Address before the Chicago General
Office Association) 1934. 17 p.
A speech on employee representation by the president of the Pennsylvania Railroad. Traces the development from a tradition of individual bargaining
to a recognition of the right to bargain collective-
ly. Objects to the government's attempt, through
the Railway Labor Act, to scrap the successful em-

ployee representation plan and substitute collective
bargaining with trade unions. Denies that the plan
is a company union and says it is simply a means of
adjusting differences.

311 Brown, James Douglas. Railway labor survey. New York,
     (Social Science Research Council) 1933. 153 p.
         A survey of industrial relations on the rail-
     roads. Discusses company unions as a means of sta-
     bilizing labor unrest. Provides a brief history of
     company unions and their replacement by brotherhood
     unions. Many aspects of company unions, including
     company financing, were outlawed by the Railway
     Emergency Act. A brief overview of railroad pen-
     sions is also provided. Employees were rarely
     guaranteed payments. Most employees did not qualify
     for pensions because they lost seniority during
     strikes and layoffs and did not meet continuous
     service requirements. Railroad pension expendi-
     tures are estimated.

312 "Conditions of labor on Pennsylvania Railroad." U.S. Com-
     mission on Industrial Relations. Report and Testi-
     mony, v. 11, 10067-10449. 64th Congress, 1st Ses-
     sion, Document 415. (6939) 1915.
         Testimony before the U.S. Commission on Indus-
     trial Relations on labor conditions on the Pennsyl-
     vania Railroad. Includes descriptions by railroad
     and union officials of the employees' voluntary re-
     lief department, which paid sickness and death bene-
     fits if they left the company even though the fund
     was primarily employee funded. The union also
     claimed employees were forced to join the relief
     association.

313 Core, H.E. An employee's view of how the plan of em-
     ployee representation on the Pennsylvania Railroad
     actually works. 1927? 7 P.
         An address by the general chairman of the Brother-
     hood of Locomotive Firemen and Enginemen describing
     the cooperative plan of the Pennsylvania Railroad.
     The plan was introduced to provide a means for
     mutual discussion and agreement on working conditions
     and to eliminate delay in the grievance procedure.
     A joint court of review interpreted work rules. The

plan helped reduce labor disputes.

314 "Employee representation on railroads." Monthly labor
     review, 20:5, May 1925, 31-32.
          Partial text of speech by the vice-president of
     the Pennsylvania Railroad. Outlines company's rep-
     resentation plan, established on the philosophy
     that cooperation of employees is essential to prog-
     ress and prosperity. All issues of wages and work-
     ing conditions are decided by a 2/3 vote of a joint
     worker/management committee. Tie votes are taken
     to arbitration. Employees are allowed to join in-
     dependent unions but the company deals only with
     employees, not outside representatives.

315 Higgins, Neal. "Two early pension plans: the B&O and
     Pennsylvania Railroad programs." In Essays in eco-
     nomic and business history, edited by James H. Soltow,
     East Lansing, Michigan State University, Graduate
     School of Business Administration, Division of Re-
     search, 1979. (Michigan State University Business
     Studies) 97-107 p.
          Discussion of the two major railroad pension
     plans from their inception in 1884 and 1900 respec-
     tively through July 1937. About half the article is
     devoted to tables including annual statistics on
     number of pensioners, payments, and pension expenses.

316 Hunt, E.B. "Pennsylvania railroad voluntary relief de-
     partment." Proceedings of the Conference on Social
     Insurance. U.S. Department of Labor, Bureau of
     Labor Statistics, Bulletin 212. Washington, G.P.O.,
     1917, 491-496 p.
          Description of the jointly funded voluntary re-
     lief fund of the Pennsylvania railroad, which pays
     sickness, accident and death benefits and includes
     a pension provision. Membership is used both to
     protect workers and to give them incentive to stay
     with the company, thus reducing turnover.

317 Jacobs, H.W. "The square deal to the railroad em-
     ployee." Engineering magazine, 33:3, June 1907,

328-352.

Surveys welfare programs on the railroads, established to foster a better "esprit de corps" between management and employees. "To combat the evils of the saloon," companies built other places for workers to spend time while they were on the road, including reading rooms, recreation halls, company cottages, and parks. Pensions and medical benefits were provided to encourage loyal service. Eligibility requirements for pensions and methods of determining benefits are discussed.

318 Johnson, Emory R. "Railway departments for the relief and insurance of employees." Annals of the American Academy of Political and Social Science, 6, November 1895, 424-468.

Describes jointly funded employee relief plans in the railroad industry, which provided accident, illness, and death benefits, pensions, medical care, and savings funds. Traces the history of railway relief departments and describes details of relief plans. Employee membership was often compulsory. Companies introduced the plans to help the workers, to develop employee loyalty in order to prevent strikes and encourage high quality service, and because they believed the funds would relieve them of legal liability in case of accident.

319 Johnson, Emory R. "Railway relief departments." Bulletin of the Department of Labor, 2:8, January 1897, 37-57.

Outlines relief plans of six major railroads. Funded by employees but subsidized and managed by companies, plans included sickness, accident, and death benefits, and sometimes hospital and medical care. Five plans also provided pensions and the Baltimore and Ohio Railroad included savings and loan provisions. Purpose of plans was to encourage better service and lower turnover among workers.

320 Latta, Samuel W. Rest houses for railroad men: how the railroad men regard such conveniences. New York, Welfare Department of the National Civic Federation, 1906. 29 p.

A description of rest houses built by railroad

companies to provide lodgings for traveling railroad men. Describes facilities of model houses including reading, game, and recreation rooms, a library, and sleeping, cooking and bathing facilities.
Rest houses were a means of keeping railroad men out
of saloons. Railroad men discuss benefits and inadequacies of the facilities.

321 McKillips, Budd L. "Company unions on the railroads."
     The Nation, 142:3679, January 8, 1936, 48-50.
         Traces the history of company unions. Describes
     strikebreaking tactics, yellow-dog contracts, and
     the role of company unions in keeping independent
     unions out. Companies absolutely controlled company
     unions: picked officers, approved constitutions,
     and drafted all "agreements." The Railway Labor Act
     outlawed company unions and independent unions grad-
     ually took over in spite of stiff opposition from
     the companies.

322 Menkel, William. "'Welfare work' on American rail-
     roads." Review of reviews, 38, October 1908, 449-
     463.
         Overview of welfare programs of railroads. Out-
     lines pioneering welfare programs of the railroad
     departments of YMCAs and traces the adoption of
     similar programs by railroad companies. Describes
     typical examples of club houses, reading rooms,
     rest houses, educational opportunities, pensions,
     relief funds, hospital and medical care, savings
     funds, and housing. Concludes that welfare work in
     the railroad industry has brought companies and men
     closer together, has increased worker efficiency,
     and has helped eliminate labor unrest.

323 Pennsylvania Railroad Company. Employe representation.
     The Pennsylvania Railroad Plan. Philadelphia,
     1925. 95 p.
         Describes the Pennsylvania Railroad Employee Rep-
     resentation Plan, created to fulfill the company's
     promise that "It is not necessary for Pennsylvania
     Railroad employees to resort to a strike in order
     to get a square deal." Employees and management are
     equally represented. Joint decisions are final but
     they must be passed by a 2/3 vote. The company

guarantees the independence of representatives. The
text of the plan is provided.

324 Pennsylvania Railroad Company. Employe representation
     in the Pennsylvania Railroad system. Philadelphia,
     1922. 63 p.
          Outlines purposes and origins of the Pennsylvania
     Railroad Employee Representation Plan. Describes
     joint committees, election of representatives, and
     grievance procedure under the plan. Includes text
     of the plan.

325 "Pennsylvania Railroad pension departments: systems
     east and west of Pittsburgh and Erie, Pennsylvania,
     status to and including the year 1907." Annals of
     the American Academy of Political and Social Science,
     33:2, March 1909, 258-264.
          Describes pension plan of the Pennsylvania Rail-
     road. Lists age limits, years of service required,
     terms of benefit payments, and costs to the company.

326 Randolph, A. Philip. "Porters fight paternalism."
     American federationist, 37:6, June 1930, 666-673.
          Analyzes discontent of Pullman Company porters,
     which stemmed from dissatisfaction with the employee
     representation plan. Porters resented the plan be-
     cause it failed to adjust grievances. It was im-
     posed on them without their consents, and election
     and wage conferences were manipulated by management.
     Examines details of company domination and other in-
     justices in employment conditions.

327 "Results of cooperation of workers and management on
     railroads." Monthly labor review, 25:1, July 1927,
     30-33.
          Evaluates the "Baltimore and Ohio Plan" of union-
     management cooperation, introduced to stabilize em-
     ployment, increase efficiency, and instill mutual
     trust between workers and management. Employee com-
     mittees, with union approval, made suggestions to
     management and, in return, benefits derived from
     suggestions were shared with workers. Results of
     the plan included reduced turnover, increased and

higher quality output, and improved morale. The
plan originated with the Baltimore and Ohio Railroad and spread to Canadian National Railways,
Chicago and Northwestern Railway Company and Chicago, Milwaukee, and St. Paul Railway Company.

328 Riebenack, M. "Pennsylvania Railroad pension depart-
      ments." Annals of the American Academy of Political
      and Social Science, 33:2, March 1909, 34-40.
          Outlines pension program in the railroad indus-
      try. Traces development of programs and lists eli-
      bility requirements, benefit payment schedules, and
      total company expenditures.

329 Schmidt, Richard E. "Illinois Central Railroad opens
      new hospital." The Modern hospital, 7:2, August
      1916, 98-104.
          A description of the Illinois Central Railroad's
      new hospital and medical facilities in Chicago.

330 Taylor, Elva M. "Employee representation on American
      railroads." American federationist, 33:9 and 10,
      September and October 1926, 1103-1108 and 1201-1217.
          Traces the history of employee representation
      plans in the railroad industry, introduced in an
      atmosphere of volatile relations between companies
      and the many trade unions that represented railroad
      employees. Union leaders attacked the plans, which
      focused on grievance settlement, were controlled by
      the companies and gave no real power or represen-
      tation to workers. Unions rebelled against company
      attempts to bar union members from employee repre-
      sentation councils.

331 "Union-management cooperation on the railroads." Monthly
      labor review, 32:5, May 1931, 44-46.
          Outlines union-management cooperation plans of
      three U.S. railroads: Baltimore and Ohio; Chicago
      and North Western; and Chicago, Milwaukee, St. Paul
      and Pacific. The plans are designed to provide job
      security to mechanical department employees while,
      at the same time, improving efficiency and quality
      of work. Management discusses all proposed tool
      and equipment changes with union representatives.

332   Willoughby, William F. Workingman's insurance. New
      York, Thomas Y. Crowell, 1898. 386 p.
          Chapter 9 surveys insurance programs of railroad
      companies, where insurance was especially necessary
      because of the hazardous work. Describes programs
      of specific companies and lists costs, benefit
      levels, eligibility requirements, and details of
      administration. Insurance was jointly funded by
      the company and employees. Author contends the
      companies should take full responsibility for pay-
      ing accident benefits.

333   Wood, Louis Aubrey. Union-management cooperation on the
      railroads. New Haven, Yale University Press, 1931.
      326 p.
          A survey of employee representation on railroads,
      introduced to promote more peaceful relations with
      workers and railroad unions. Traces the background
      and development of representation plans and describes
      their functions and structure on several railroads.
      Joint committees were formed to decide labor issues
      but unions retained the rights to bargain collec-
      tively and to strike. Results of the plans were
      improved work performance and morale and less labor
      unrest. Attitudes of management and employees toward
      the plans are discussed.

STEEL

334   Bethlehem Steel Company. Employee representation.
      South Bethlehem, PA, 1919. 84 p.
          Sketches the development of the employee rep-
      resentation plan of the Bethlehem Steel Company.
      Describes the first election and provides brief biog-
      raphies of representatives at various plants. Does
      not give details of plan.

335   Bethlehem Steel Corporation and subsidiary companies
      relief plan. 1st-6th Annual Reports, 1926-1931.
      24 pages each.
          Annual financial and statistical reports on ac-
      cident, illness, and death benefits paid by the

Bethlehem Steel Corporation. Describes the jointly
funded relief fund and lists both employer and employee contributions to the fund. Summarizes number of benefits paid out and average amounts of payments.

336 Blackford, Mansel G. "Scientific management and welfare
     work in early twentieth century American business:
     the Buckeye Steel Castings Company." Ohio history,
     90:3, Summer 1981, 238-258.
         Describes personnel policies of the Buckeye Steel
     Castings Company where scientific management and
     welfare were combined to maximize efficiency while
     minimizing labor unrest. The company believed it
     had a duty to promote "a wholesome community condi-
     tion" and provide healthy and pleasant working con-
     ditions. Welfare included a medical staff and fa-
     cilities, a company kitchen, a baseball field, pic-
     nics, life insurance, housing, educational and reli-
     gious classes, and social and athletic programs.
     Reasons for providing these programs were genuine
     humanitarianism, to lower turnover and production
     costs, to promote loyalty, to attract high quality
     workers, and to "Americanize foreign employees."

337 Bolling, Raynal C. "Results of the voluntary relief
     plan for the United States Steel Corporation."
     Annals of the American Academy of Political and
     Social Science, 38, September 1911, 35-44.
         Text of speech by assistant solicitor general of
     the United States Steel Corporation which describes
     company's accident relief and safety plans. Under
     the relief plan, injured workers are compensated
     even if injury was their own fault. Workers do not
     contribute to relief fund, which pays a variable
     percentage of lost wages, because the company con-
     siders the uncompensated portion of lost wages to
     be the employee's contribution.

338 Bolling, Raynal C. "United States Steel Corporation and
     labor conditions." Annals of the American Academy
     of Political and Social Science, 42, July 1912, 38-
     47.
         Outlines the $5 million a year welfare program of
     the United States Steel Corporation. Programs in-

clude stock purchase plans, accident benefits, medical
care, pensions, sanitation, swimming pools, playgrounds, gardens, lunch rooms, and a variety of other
programs at individual factories. The company avoids
paternalism and claims to operate an open shop, nei-
ther favoring, nor discriminating against union members.

339 Brody, David. Steelworkers in America: the non-union
     era. Cambridge, Harvard University Press, 1960.
     303 p.
        A scholarly study of the development of the steel
     industry, including a discussion of the role of wel-
     fare. Companies tied skilled workers to their jobs
     by providing housing or home loans, a stock subscrip-
     tion plan, bonuses for "faithful service," pensions,
     and accident and death benefits. Discusses the in-
     adequacy of benefits and describes life in company
     towns. Slavic laborers did not receive the benefits
     given to English-speaking skilled workers. Examines
     the "new era of cooperation," when several benefits
     were introduced for all workers in an effort to coun-
     teract public outrage over conditions in the steel mills.

340 Calder, John. "Five years of employee representation
     under 'The Bethlehem Plan'." Iron age, 3:24, June 14,
     1923, 1689-1696.
        Traces the history and describes the operation of
     the employee representation plan of the Bethlehem
     Steel Corporation. The plan was developed to encour-
     age industrial peace during World War I. Under the
     plan, employee representatives operated with complete
     independence from the company and were given full ac-
     cess to company information. The plan fostered a
     spirit of mutuality and cooperation that stabilized
     labor relations.

341 "Carnegie on employees as partners." New outlook, 74,
     May 16, 1903, 147-148.
        Summarizes speech by Andrew Carnegie in which he
     attributes his success to securing the effective
     cooperation of his workers. He made department heads
     partners through stock ownership. A savings plan

was instituted for wage earners because they could
not afford the risk of stock ownership.

342 Clark, Lindley D. "Recent action relating to employers'
     liability and workmen's compensation." Bulletin of
     the Bureau of Labor, Washington, D.C.: Department
     of Commerce and Labor, 1910, 675-714 p.
        Pages 698-700 describe accident relief benefits
     of the United States Steel Corporation and the In-
     ternational Harvester Company. Both funds cover on-
     the-job injuries and are entirely company funded.
     Negligence does not disqualify workers from receiv-
     ing benefits.

343 Close, Charles L. Welfare work in the steel industry.
     New York, 1920. 45 p.
        An overview of welfare programs of the U.S. Steel
     Corporation and its subsidiaries. Restaurants were
     provided to keep up workers' energy levels. English
     classes were part of the education and Americaniza-
     tion program for foreign employees. Pensions were
     jointly funded by the companies and the Carnegie
     Pension Fund. Other welfare benefits included medi-
     cal care, accident relief, gardens, housing, play-
     grounds, athletic facilities and activities, and a
     stock subscription plan.

344 Collective bargaining in the steel industry: why steel
     favors employee representation plans and is opposed
     to professional trade unions. 1934. 14 p.
        Defends the steel industry's opposition to trade
     unions, claiming that unions try to impose them-
     selves on unwilling workers. Says employee repre-
     sentation plans are better because they are cooper-
     ative efforts of all employees. Compares the har-
     mony and cooperation of employee representation
     to the antagonism of trade unions where decisions are
     often made by non-employee leaders. For employee
     representation to succeed, employees must be given
     the right to independent meetings and elections.

345 Darlington, Thomas. "Gardens in connection with work-
     men's houses in iron, steel and allied industries."

Monthly bulletin of the American Iron and Steel
Institute, 1:3, March 1913, 67-99.
        A pictoral and poetic essay on workers' gardens
in the iron and steel industries. Philosophizes on
the value of the beauty and peace of gardens and il-
lustrates with several pages of photographs. Gardens also reduce the cost of living by saving food
expenses.

346 Darlington, Thomas. "Present scope of welfare work in
        the iron and steel industry." The Modern hospital,
        7:2, August 1916, 91-94.
            An enumeration of welfare programs in the iron
        and steel industries with special emphasis on health-
        related areas such as hygiene, sanitation, pollution
        control and medical facilities.

347 Darlington, Thomas and Sidney McCurdy. Present scope of
        welfare work in the iron and steel industry. New
        York, American Iron and Steel Institute, 1914. 16 p.
            An overview of welfare work by iron and steel
        companies. The goal of the industry's welfare was to
        develop a strong and healthy work force. Programs
        included sanitary and healthy working conditions,
        sanitation work in company villages, medical care,
        a rest farm for wives in poor health, home economic
        classes for wives and daughters, playgrounds and
        schools for children, cafeterias, housing, and gar-
        dens.

348 Erskine, J.B. "United States Steel and Carnegie Pension
        Fund." Proceedings of the Conference on Social In-
        surance. U.S. Department of Labor Bureau of Labor
        Statistics, Bulletin 212. Washington, G.P.O., 1917.
        742-746.
            Outlines pension fund jointly established by the
        United States Steel Corporation and Andrew Carnegie.
        Enumerates qualification requirements and details of
        administration.

349 "Expenses of employee services carried on by the United
        States Steel Corporation." Industrial relations
        (Bloomfield's labor digest) 18:37, September 13,

1924, 2083.
A chart listing welfare expenses of the United
States Steel Corporation from 1912 to 1923. Lists
wide variety of facilities and services and number
of each provided.

350 Garrety, John A. "The United States Steel Corporation
        versus labor: the early years." Labor history,
        1:1, Winter 1960, 3-38
        Traces the history of labor relations of the
United States Steel Corporation. Due to its wide
variety of operation, the Corporation had to deal
with a wide variety of workers and labor problems.
U.S. Steel wanted to keep unions out of plants where
they had not already organized. Traces the evolu-
tion from tough labor policy to a conciliatory approach which included welfare programs. A subsidized stock purchase plan was introduced to stimu-
late loyalty and efficiency. The Corporation built
housing, schools, playgrounds, and sports facilities
and installed a pension system. An accident relief
fund based benefit payments on the seriousness of
the injury, the size of the workers' family, and
length of service. This system of welfare was considered a failure when workers called a massive
strike in 1919. "Paternalism failed because it was
unilaterally conceived and inherently degrading to
the beneficiaries."

351 Goodrich, Arthur. "The United States Steel Corporation
        profit-sharing plan." World's work, 5:4, February
        1903, 3055-3058.
        Outlines profit-sharing plan of the United States
Steel Corporation. Traces the history of the plan
and suggests reasons for potential failure. The
plan, developed to improve workers' loyalty, gives
workers an opportunity to buy company stocks and
pays interest even before the stocks are paid off.

352 Greer, P. "United States Steel Corporation's industrial
        welfare and its ideals." Pennsylvania manufactur-
        ers' journal, 7:2, April 1926, 3-8.

353 "Group insurance plan of the United States Steel Corpor-
       ation." Monthly labor review, 41:2, August 1935,
       337-338.
            Describes the jointly funded group insurance plan
       of the United States Steel Corporation. Eligibility
       is not restricted by age, occupation, sex, or physi-
       cal conditions. Benefit levels and employee payments
       are based on salary.

354 Gulick, Charles A. Labor policy of the United States
       Steel Corporation. New York, Columbia University,
       1924. (Studies in History, Economics and Public Law,
       66:1, #258) 200 p.
            Chapters 5 and 6 survey welfare benefits of the
       United States Steel Corporation. A pension fund
       began as a gift from Andrew Carnegie. English
       classes were offered to immigrant workers and schools
       were built. Extensive medical benefits included vis-
       iting nurses, low cost hospitals and dental clinics
       and an accident relief fund. Other programs were
       stock purchasing plans, sanitation programs, movies
       and other recreation, athletic facilities, libraries,
       housing, pensions, and community development projects.
       Survey included specific list of annual welfare expen-
       ditures. U.S. Steel welfare programs were criticized
       as being part of a comprehensive union avoidance
       campaign.

355 Kaylor, R.J. "Youngstown Sheet and Tube's company hospi-
       tal." The Modern hospital, 7:2, August 1916, 109-110.
            Describes the emergency hospital at Youngstown
       Sheet and Tube Company, available to employees and
       their families. The hospital is intended for emer-
       gency care and treatment of minor illnesses and in-
       juries. Serious or long-term cases are transferred
       to city hospitals. The company's medical efforts
       also include visiting nurses and free vaccinations
       to workers and their families.

356 Labor conditions in the iron and steel industry. 62nd
       Congress, 1st Session, Senate Document 110, 4 vols.
       (Senate Document 18-21:6096-6099) 1911.
            Chapters 12-14 examine physical conditions of
       work in the iron and steel industry and the effect

of working conditions on productivity. Chapter 15
describes the use of scrip in company stores and
discusses jointly funded accident funds and medical
benefits. Chapter 16 surveys company housing and
stores, including descriptions of housing conditions
in sample towns. Chapter 17 describes pension
funds, profit-sharing, stock ownership and plant
and community sanitation. Outlines the pension systems of the U.S. Steel Corporation and the Wiscon-
sin Steel Company and profit-sharing plans of U.S.
Steel and the Youngstown Sheet and Tube Company.
Appendix N contains the text of U.S. Steel's stock
subscription plan.

357 Magnusson, Leifur. "A modern industrial suburb." Month-
        ly labor review, 6:4, April 1918, 1-25.
        Describes the company town of Morgan Park, Minne-
        sota owned by the Morgan Park Company, a subsidiary
        of the United States Steel Corporation. Describes
        housing, public utilities and facilities, and layout
        of the town. The company donated land and financed
        a schoolhouse, playground, churches, club house, and
        recreational grounds. Comfortable, modern housing
        is provided at low rent. The company takes respon-
        sibility for maintenance, garbage collection, sewer-
        age, and other services. Prizes are awarded for
        neat gardens and houses. The company attempts to
        run the town cooperatively with employees rather
        than imposing regulations and prohibitions.

358 Mulligan, William H. "The corporation community: life
        in Sparrows Point, Maryland." In Papers presented
        at the 26th annual meeting of the Business History
        Conference, 6-8 March 1980, edited by Paul Uselding.
        (Business and Economic History, Second Series, v. 9,
        136-138 p.) Urbana, University of Illinois, College
        of Commerce and Business Administration, 1980.

        Account of a steel town near Baltimore, Maryland.
        Author describes the paternalism of this company
        town as "neither benevolent nor sinister" but as a
        rational response to a series of interrelated prob-
        lems.

359 Report on conditions of employment in the iron and
     steel industry in the United States. v. 3: Work-
     ing conditions and the relations of employers and
     employees. 62nd Congress 1st Session. Senate
     Document 110. (6098) Washington, G.P.O., 1913.
     594 p.
          Chapters 16 and 17 outline welfare programs in
     the iron and steel industry. Chapter 16 describes
     company housing and stores. Compares housing of
     skilled and unskilled workers and compares condi-
     tions in different parts of the country. Examines
     company control of workers' lives through housing
     regulations. Chapter 17 describes pension funds,
     profit-sharing plans and plant and community sani-
     tation. Discusses pension systems of the United
     States Steel Corporation and the Wisconsin Steel
     Company and profit-sharing plans of the Youngstown
     Sheet and Tube Company and the United States Steel
     Corporation.

360 Selekman, Ben M. Employees' representation in steel
     works: a study of the industrial representation
     plan of the Minnequa Steel Works of the Colorado
     Fuel and Iron Company. New York, Russell Sage
     Foundation, 1924. 293 p.
          Examines employee representation at the Minnequa
     Steel Works. Describes the introduction of the plan
     and its essential features. A joint committee of
     employees and employers was formed to discuss mat-
     ters of mutual interest. The committee improved
     medical care and cut prices in the company store
     and was used to discuss grievances. Workers' major
     criticism of the plan was that it allowed them no
     voice in determining wages. The greatest gain of
     the committee was the 8-hour day.

361 Skaggs, Julian C. "Paternalism at Lukens, 1825-1886."
     In Papers presented at the 26th annual meeting of
     the Business History Conference, 6-8 March 1980,
     edited by Paul Uselding. (Business and economic
     history, Second Series, v. 9, 128-135 p.) Urbana,
     University of Illinois, College of Commerce and
     Business Administration, 1980.
          Describes the paternalistic welfare program of
     Lukens Rolling Mill. The company believed it had
     a duty to provide steady work to employees and

often found odd jobs for workers during slack periods. The employee-employer relationship was based
on "mutual loyalty, respect, and tolerance." The
company provided low cost housing to workers and
eventually developed a mutual benefit association
and cooperative store. The paternalistic system
came to an end when workers went on strike in 1886.

362 "Special retirement adjustments in the steel industry."
       Monthly labor review, 29:2, August 1929, 99-101.
       Describes policy of the Bethlehem Steel Corpora-
tion and associated companies to provide for employees who are no longer efficient or whose jobs
no longer exist. If employees don't meet normal
pension eligibility requirements, they are sometimes placed on reduced pension. Arrangements de-
pend on purpose of discharge and age and physical
condition of the employee.

363 Stein, Rose M. "Steel robots that come alive." The
       Nation, 142:3683, February 5, 1936, 160-161.
       Describes increasing militance of company unions
in steel industry. Employee representation plans
were structured to prevent effective collective action. Employees of several companies met and for-
mulated demands for increased wages and benefits.
When the companies flatly refused the demands, some
company unions disbanded to form independent unions.

364 Wilson, Edward. "The organization of an open shop under
       the Midvale Plan." Annals of the American Academy
       of Political and Social Science, 85, September 1919,
       214-219.
       Describes a plan for a company-sponsored union
at the Midvale Steel and Ordnance Company. Under
the plan, the union is given autonomy equal to
that of an independent union but it holds meetings
on company time and property. Apparently the major
purpose of the union is not to negotiate with the
company but simply to give employees a chance to
voice their suggestions and desires. The company
retains unilateral decision making authority. The
union also establishes and administers a grievance
process.

TEXTILES

365 American Cotton Manufacturers' Association. Mill Stores
         Committee. The Cotton mill worker and his needs.
         Charlotte, NC, 1934. 38 p.
             An investigation of company stores in the textile
         industry. Approves of the use of scrip instead of
         money because it is convenient for the worker and
         discourages extravagance. Claims workers benefit
         from company stores because they are convenient,
         they will extend credit, prices are competitive,
         profits are small, and quality is high.

366 Bagnall, William R. The Textile industries of the United
         States. v. I, 1639-1810. Cambridge, MA, The River-
         side Press, 1893. 613 p.
             Pages 301-305 describe welfare programs of the
         Peace Dale Manufacturing Company. The company built
         single family houses and sold them to workers on an
         installment plan. Profit-sharing helped ensure a
         peaceful labor climate. The company helped finance
         a church, library, school, and music hall.

367 Ballard, S. Thurston. "Welfare work and profit-sharing."
         American industries, 8:2, September 1, 1908, 18-19.
             Describes the profit-sharing plan of Ballard
         Mills in Louisville, Kentucky, introduced to get
         "more earnest and efficient work" from employees by
         making them feel like partners in the business.
         The company also provided a cafeteria and free
         lunches, shower baths, and a baseball diamond. A
         billiard table was provided instead of a library in
         the belief that "If you want to give them something,
         let it be something they want." A jointly funded
         mutual benefit association provides sick benefits.

368 Berglund, Abraham et al. Labor in the industrial South.
         Charlottesville, University of Virginia, Institute
         for Research in the Social Sciences, 1930. 176 p.
             Chapter 8 compares welfare work in southern cot-
         ton mills to older New England mills which no long-
         er need welfare because municipalities have taken
         over social programs. Southern welfare benefits

include community houses with recreation facilities,
schools, medical facilities and services, relief
funds, and housing. The types of programs needed
vary according to a mill's distance from an established town.

369   Bernstein, Irving. The Lean years: a history of the
      American worker, 1920-1933. Baltimore, Penguin
      Books, 1960. 577 p.
         Pages 1-43 examine the labor movement in the
      cotton mills of the Southern Piedmont. Includes
      discussion of housing and a variety of other facili-
      ties and services provided by the mills. Since
      mills owned everything in the villages, they were
      able to control all aspects of workers' lives. The
      mill owner "has the power to discharge the worker
      at the mill, to refuse him credit at his store, to
      have him expelled from church, to bar his children
      from school, and to withhold the service of a doc-
      tor or hospital."

370   Blanshard, Paul. Labor in southern cotton mills. New
      York, New Republic, Inc., 1927. 88 p.
         Surveys living conditions in southern cotton
      mill villages. Considers low rents and other bene-
      fits as compensation for low wages but finds the
      total cost of living is actually higher in the South
      than in the North. Finds southern mills do not
      spend more on welfare than northern mills. De-
      scribes mill villages and considers the psychologi-
      cal effects of living in houses that are all alike.
      Considers company ownership of housing a benefit
      to workers because their freedom of movement is not
      restricted by home ownership. Defends paternalism
      as necessary to transform illiterate mountain and
      farming people into a modern industrial community.
      Presents statistics on benefits provided in the vil-
      lages and discusses apathy of workers toward the
      benefits.

371   Blicksilver, Jack. Cotton manufacturing in the South-
      east, an historical analysis. Atlanta, Georgia
      College of Business Administration, Bureau of Busi-
      ness and Economic Research, School of Business
      Administration, (Studies in Business and Economics,

Bulletin 5) 1959. 176 p.
Pages 33-36, 68-81, and 127-128 discuss welfare
in southern cotton mills. Considers and rejects
claim that welfare benefits and subsidized housing
compensate for low wages. Discusses trend toward
improvement in company housing. Suggests paternal
domination may have been necessary to teach workers
to live in a community setting but workers resented
it because they felt welfare money should have been
used to increase wages.

372 Calvert, Bruce T. The Story of a silk mill. New York,
     Belding Brothers and Company, 1914. 28 p.
     A narrative description of the development and
     operations of Belding Brothers and Company silk
     mill. Includes discussion of welfare programs. The
     Belding Brothers believed it was their responsibil-
     ity to care for the welfare of the girls who worked
     in the mill because "If we want fine people we must
     have fine mothers." Stresses the need for cleanli-
     ness in the mill to make conditions as pleasant as
     possible. Describes the model factory town with
     clean, modern facilities, schools, churches, sports
     and recreational facilities, a park, low-cost hous-
     ing, and a company doctor.

373 "Company housing in the cotton textile industry in Mas-
     sachusetts." Monthly labor review, 19:2, August
     1924, 437-38.
     Results of a questionnaire on workers' housing
     sent to all Massachusetts textile companies in
     1924. Lists percentage of companies that owned
     workers' housing and the percentage of employees
     that lived in company housing. Describes types
     of houses, rents, and various facilities provided.

374 Cook, John Harrison. A Study of mill schools in North
     Carolina. New York, Columbia University Press,
     1925. 55 p.
     Surveys 119 mill schools in North Carolina
     cotton mill towns. Classifies each school ac-
     cording to degree of financial support and control
     by the mills. Twenty-six schools were company-
     funded but mill owners did not try to control what
     was taught.

375 Davis, Jean. "The economics of welfare work in the cot-
        ton mills of the southern states." In The Indus-
        trial South. Emory University, Georgia, Banner
        Press, 1929. 49-57 p.
           Questions whether welfare work should be consid-
        ered charity or a cost of doing business. Con-
        cludes that this depends on whether welfare leads
        to cost savings through greater efficiency. Exam-
        ines whether welfare in industry is sufficient to
        make up for low wages.

376 deVyver, Frank Traver. "Paternalism - North and South."
        American federationist, 37:11, November 1930,
        1353-1358.
           Examines paternalism in the textile industry.
        Suggests southern mills must provide more welfare
        benefits than northern mills because southern mills
        are in less developed areas. northern mill work-
        ers receive benefits from the cities they live in
        but Southern workers must depend on the mills for
        these services. Suggests southern mills should not
        be condemned for providing needed welfare programs.

377 deVyver, Frank Traver. "Southern textile mills revis-
        ited." Southern economic journal, 4:4, April 1938,
        466-473.
           A longitudinal investigation of 66 southern cot-
        ton mill villages, undertaken to determine whether
        welfare was substantial enough to offset low wages.
        Considers the effects of the Depression and social
        and labor legislation on welfare programs. Found
        that the Depression had little effect on housing
        rents, church aid, and subsidized sports but led to
        discontinuance of free water and electricity and
        cutbacks in education and health programs. Con-
        cludes that some of the best mills with the most
        extensive welfare programs were among the least
        successful at keeping unions out.

378 Draper, E.S. "Attractive development work in southern
        mill villages." Textile world, 77:7, February 15,
        1930, 26-27.
           Describes improvements in southern mill villages
        in 1929, including new housing developments and im-
        provements in existing villages.

379 Edge, Arthur B., Jr. "Fuller E. Callaway: founder of
        Callaway Mills," <u>Cotton history review</u>, 1:2, April
        1960, 35-46.
        An address delivered in 1954 before the Newcomen
     Society in North America, extolling the business
     acumen of Fuller E. Callaway. His career began by
     selling spools of thread at the age of eight and
     ended as owner of a complex of nine textile mills.
     His welfare activities included comfortable homes
     for his employees, schools, hospitals, recreational
     facilities, and medical and dental clinics, and the
     establishment of the Textile Benefit Association.
     He felt that people were one's best investment and
     that they paid the biggest dividends.

380 Edmonds, R.W. <u>Cotton mill labor conditions in the South
        and New England</u>. Baltimore, Manufacturers' Record
        Publishing Company, 1925. 61 p.
        A series of letters on conditions in cotton
     mills, reprinted from <u>Barron's</u> weekly financial
     paper in New York and from the <u>Manufacturer's jour-
     nal</u>. Includes a letter on educational and recrea-
     tional facilities and housing conditions. Includes
     examples of model welfare programs.

381 Ellis, Leonora Beck. "A model factory town." <u>Forum</u>,
        32:1, September 1901, 60-65.
        A detailed description of Pelzer, South Caro-
     lina, a cotton mill town known for extensive wel-
     fare programs and its lack of labor problems. Pro-
     grams include recreation and entertainment, free
     education, libraries, churches, care for the dis-
     abled, free medical care, free sewerage, banks, and
     profit-sharing. A brief summary of welfare programs
     in other cotton mill towns is also provided.

382 Ely, Richard T. "An American industrial experiment."
        <u>Harper's monthly magazine</u>, 195:625, June 1902, 39-
        45.
        Analyzes the cotton mill town of Pelzer, South
     Carolina, a product of "pure autocracy in industrial
     affairs" plus "paternalistic benevolence." The Pel-
     zer Corporation owns and dominates the town but
     governs with sufficient benevolence that residents
     are not entirely stifled. Welfare programs include

housing, compulsory education for children, a library, recreational facilities, and a savings bank.

383 Few, William P. "Constructive philanthropy of a southern
     cotton mill." South Atlantic quarterly, 8:1, Jan-
     uary 1909, 82-90.
          Describes welfare programs of the Victor Manufac-
     turing Company, a cotton mill in Greers, South Caro-
     lina. Based on the belief that welfare makes work-
     ers happier and more productive, the company built
     and funded a church, schools, a library and a vari-
     ety of recreational facilities. Classes and lec-
     tures broadened workers' knowledge on a wide range
     of topics.

384 Gilman, Glenn. Human relations in the industrial South-
     east; a study of the textile industry. Chapel Hill,
     University of North Carolina Press, 1956. 327 p.
          Overview of southern textile industry. Pages
     149-159 and 225-226 in particular focus on welfare
     programs which were based on the philosophy of
     treating employees as "poor white workers" rather
     than "poor white trash." Mill villages developed
     out of necessity since other housing was often un-
     available at mill sites. Paternalism was often re-
     sented and segregating mill children into separate
     schools encouraged class bias.

385 Hatch, Harold A. "The partnership plan of the Garner
     Print Works and Bleachery." Bleachery life, 1:2,
     1-2.
          The text of a speech on the employee participa-
     tion plan of the Garner Print Works and Bleachery
     in Wappingers Falls, New York. Employees control
     housing, recreation, and education programs and re-
     ceive 48 percent of net profits. Their contribution
     to the partnership is faithful service to the com-
     pany. Profit-sharing was introduced to spread
     wealth rather than concentrating it in the hands of
     a few and leaving the rest in poverty.

386 Heiss, M.W. "The southern mill village: a viewpoint."
     Journal of social forces, 2:3, March 1924, 345-350.
          A historical overview of the development of

southern mill villages. Paternalism was necessary
when mills were first built because people were
poor and uneducated and did not know how to live in
a community environment. Companies established
schools and welfare departments to build better
workers. Medical care, churches, housing and other
benefits were provided. Since workers have become
established and prosperous citizens, the author predicts a trend away from paternalism toward industrial democracy.

387 Herring, Harriet L. "Cycles of cotton mill criticism."
     South Atlantic quarterly, 28:2, 1929, 113-125.
          An examination of criticisms and defenses of con-
     ditions in New England and southern textile mills.
     Describes the flood of literature published in de-
     fense and praise of mill welfare. Welfare work was
     one defense used to counter criticisms of poor work-
     ing conditions. Paternalism was defended on the
     grounds that it was a justifiable means of improving
     working conditions.

388 Herring, Harriet L. Passing of the mill village: revo-
     lution in a southern institution. Chapel Hill, Uni-
     versity of North Carolina Press, 1949. 137 p.
          Pages 3-7 discuss the tradition of company owner-
     ship of mill villages. Companies had to provide
     housing for workers because mills were often built
     far from established towns. Examines changing pub-
     lic opinion of mill villages throughout the welfare
     era. Chapter 8 discusses the failure of unionism
     in the southern mills due to the fact that workers
     were dependent on companies for housing and could
     be evicted for union activity. Additionally, unions
     sometimes opposed the sale of mill houses to the
     workers because they thought home ownership would
     make the workers less militant.

389 Herring, Harriet L. "Towards preliminary social analy-
     sis: I. The southern mill system faces a new
     issue." Social forces, 8, 1930, 350-359.
          An examination of conditions that led to a series
     of violent strikes in southern cotton mill villages.
     Traces the history of paternalism as a system of
     industrial management and examines criticisms of

the system. Discusses paternalism as a tool for
both controlling and helping the worker. Considers
the possibility of replacing paternalism with collective bargaining and suggests problems of organization, including worker inertia and public opposition to unions.

390 Herring, Harriet L. Welfare work in mill villages; the
        story of extra-mill activities in North Carolina.
        Chapel Hill, University of North Carolina Press,
        1929. 406 p.
            Traces the development of welfare work in 322
        North Carolina cotton mill villages. Examines full
        range of benefits, many of which developed out of
        necessity in villages isolated from established
        towns. Discusses variations in the type and scope
        of welfare offered. Chapters on general history
        and philosophy of welfare work present a scholarly
        overview of industrial welfare. Although this work
        deals primarily with the textile industry, its depth
        of analysis of programs and welfare issues make it
        a broadly comprehensive study of industrial welfare
        in general.

391 "Industrial democracy." American federationist, 37:4,
        April 1930, 402-403.
            William Green criticizes the Dan River Mill em-
        ployee representation plan as "the kind of industrial
        democracy whose backbone management could break at
        will." Denounces the Bemberg Glantzstoff Company for
        firing union members in violation of its agreement
        not to discriminate against them. Calls employee
        representation an extension of management and a
        repudiation of democracy.

392 Josephson, Hannah. The Golden threads: New England's
        mill girls and magnates. New York, Duell, Sloan
        & Pearce, 1949. 325 p.
            Describes "showplace" cotton mills of Lowell,
        Massachusetts. Companies provided room and board
        for girls who came to work in the mills. One com-
        pany built a school, library, and church. Factories
        were pleasant and well-ventilated. Conditions de-
        clined in the 1840s due to falling profits which led
        to speed-ups and cuts in benefits. Unrest and a

drive to unionize resulted.

393 Knowlton, Evelyn H. Pepperell's progress; history of a
       cotton textile company, 1844-1945. Cambridge,
       Harvard University Press, 1948. 511 p.
         Scattered throughout this work are short descrip-
       tions of Pepperell's industrial welfare activities,
       which are easily identified through the index.

394 Kohn, August. The Cotton mills of South Carolina.
       Charleston, SC, Press of Walker, Evans and Cogswell
       Company, 1903. 40 p.
         A series of articles in The News and courier of
       Charleston, South Carolina, examining conditions in
       cotton mills and cotton mill villages. Includes
       discussion of companies providing education and re-
       ligious training and health care. Believes condi-
       tions in mill villages are good and says companies
       genuinely try to care for needs of workers.

395 Lahne, Herbert J. The Cotton mill worker. New York,
       Farrar and Rinehart, 1944. 303 p.
         Chapters 3-5 describe the "all-embracing pater-
       nal system" in cotton mill villages. Describes and
       compares New England and southern villages. Their
       locations were determined by where water power could
       be found. Describes a broad range of conditions
       from model villages to ramshackle slums. Discusses
       the scrip payment system which tied employees to the
       mill by encouraging them to build a debt at the com-
       pany store. Companies often required employees to
       live in mill housing as a condition of employment.
       During strikes, workers were evicted and their credit
       at the store was cut. Companies supported churches
       and schools and thus controlled what was taught and
       preached.

396 Lander, Ernest McPherson, Jr. The Textile industry in
       antebellum South Carolina. Baton Rouge, Louisiana
       State University Press, 1969. 122 p.
         Pages 60-61 and Chapter 6 describe welfare in
       South Carolina cotton mills. Focuses on system of
       paternalism of the Graniteville Manufacturing Com-
       pany, including cottages and gardens, churches,

schools, and "rigid rules for the betterment of
their morals."

397 Lemert, Benjamin F. Cotton textile industry of the
       southern Appalachian Piedmont. Chapel Hill,
       University of North Carolina Press, 1933. 188 p.
         A study of the cotton-textile industry in the
       South. Pages 69-70 and 135-136 describe condi-
       tions in company-owned houses and villages. Finds
       living conditions of mill workers generally superior
       to conditions of non-mill families. Discusses the
       decline in the number of workers living in company
       housing as the region developed and provided in-
       creasing opportunity to live elsewhere.

398 Lozier, J.W. "Rural textile mill communities and the
       transition to industrialism in America, 1800-1840."
       In Working papers from the Regional Economic History
       Research Center. Greenville, Wilmington, Eleutherian
       Mills-Hagley Foundation, 1981. 78-96 p. v. 4,
       no. 4, 1981 edited by Glenn Porter and William H.
       Mulligan, Jr.)
         A discussion of numerous industrial welfare meas-
       ures found throughout rural mill villages including
       company housing, stores, schools, churches, etc.
       Authors attribute the phenomenon of industrial wel-
       fare during the pre-1850 years to inherent paternal-
       ism on the part of the mill owners.

399 MacDonald, Lois. "Some conditions and attitudes of
       Southern cotton mill villagers." In The Industrial
       South. Atlanta, GA, Emory University, 1929. 35-47
       p.
         Surveys attitudes of 187 families toward life in
       mill villages. Describes housing and living condi-
       tions and concludes that welfare has little effect
       on workers' lives.

400 MacDonald, Lois. Southern mill hills. New York, Alex L.
       Hillman, 1928. 151 p.
         Chapter 2 describes typical cotton mill villages.
       Companies provided schools, low cost housing, and
       many other welfare benefits. Examines the effects
       of paternalism including workers dependence on the

company and inferiority complexes. Everything in
the towns was controlled by the mills. The company
controlled churches and even dictated types of ser-
mons.

401 McLaurin, Melton A. Paternalism and protest, southern
     cotton textile workers and organized labor, 1875-
     1905. Westport, CT, Greenwood Publishing Corpora-
     tion, 1971. 265 p.
          Chapters 2 and 3 describe paternalism in southern
     cotton mill villages. The mills completely dominat-
     ed workers' lives since they financed housing,
     schools, churches, stores, and other services. Mo-
     tives for welfare included concern for the moral
     welfare of workers, a need to attract workers, and
     anti-unionism. Mill owners were ultimately success-
     ful in defeating unions because of workers' total
     social and economic dependence on paternalistic wel-
     fare programs.

402 Mitchell, Broadus. William Gregg: factory master of the
     old South. New York, Octagon Books, 1966. 331 p.
          A biography of William Gregg, a leader in the
     textile industry and industrial welfare in South
     Carolina. Analyzes his development of cotton mills
     into a profitable industry. Mills provided employ-
     ment for poor whites and brought them out of "deg-
     radation and poverty" by feeding, clothing, and
     housing them. Describes sturdy, comfortable, and
     clean housing, churches, and schools. Chapter 4
     defends paternalism as necessary to bring the people
     out of their poverty. Chapter 5 describes Gregg's
     goal of eliminating illiteracy among his workers.
     He enforced compulsory education in mill school for
     all children under age 12. Supervision of workers'
     morals was included in his welfare programs.

403 National Civic Federation. Woman's Department. Commit-
     tee on Welfare Work for Industrial Employees. Exam-
     ples of welfare work in the cotton industry. New
     York, 1910. 16 p.
          Traces the development of welfare work in the
     textile industry. Describes a wide range of bene-
     fits, using examples from several companies. Bene-
     fits include schools, housing, recreational and

athletic facilities, and medical care. Costs to
companies are estimated.

404 Nelson, Daniel and Stuart Campbell. "Taylorism versus
         welfare work in American industry: H.L. Gantt and
         the Bancrofts." Business history review, 46:1,
         Spring 1972, 1-16.
             Discusses welfare at Joseph Bancroft and Sons
         Company, the first firm to introduce both Taylorism
         and welfare measures. Welfare included housing,
         schools, low cost meals, in-plant laundry service,
         an emergency room, a library, and sewing and cooking
         classes. Employees resisted the introduction of
         Taylorism because its tactics clashed with the spir-
         it of welfare. Taylorism was discarded in favor of
         welfare.

405 Nelson, Henry Loomis. "The Cheneys' village at South
         Manchester, Connecticut." Harper's Weekly, 34:1728,
         February 1, 1890, 87-88.
             Describes the model village of South Manchester,
         Connecticut, owned by Cheney Brothers silk mill.
         Describes the village as a large park with attrac-
         tive, comfortable housing and many beauties of na-
         ture. Compares the town to "bad villages," where
         workers live in squalor and depravity. The company
         did not intrude on the private lives of workers.

406 Newman, Dale. "Work and community life in a southern tex-
         tile town." Labor history, 19:2, Spring 1978, 204-
         225.
             Describes company domination of the cotton mill
         town of LeClay, North Carolina. The Roseville Cot-
         ton Mills owned workers' housing, stores, theater,
         churches, and schools and provided all community
         services. Poor education and economic insecurity
         made workers totally dependent on the company and
         deterred them from taking collective action.

407 Nichols, Jeannette Paddock. "Does the mill village fos-
         ter any social types?" Journal of social forces,
         2:3, March 1924, 350-357.
             Examines idea that southern cotton mill workers

are a socially unique group, secure and isolated
under paternalism. Traces history of mills and
mill villages, including the Cotton Mill Campaign,
when mills were built to provide jobs for poor
whites. Describes workers' housing and discusses
attempts of company welfare workers to teach hygiene, homemaking, and community development. Education was poor because children went to work as
soon as they were old enough.

408 Parker, Thomas F. "The South Carolina cotton mill - a
        manufacturer's view." The South Atlantic quarterly,
        8:4, October 1909, 328-337.
        A defense of South Carolina cotton mills, popu-
     larly criticized for low wages, poor working con-
     ditions, and paternalism. Argues that the develop-
     ment of the cotton textile industry brought the peo-
     ple of South Carolina out of "the depths of poverty
     and ignorance." By employing thousands of workers,
     mills lifted the whole state out of depression.
     Factories are modern and provide good working condi-
     tions. Defends paternalism by claiming that critics
     don't know the true conditions in mill villages.

409 Parker, Thomas F. The South Carolina cotton mill vil-
        lage and the South Carolina cotton mill. Green-
        ville, SC, 1911. 22 p. (Reprinted from South Atlan-
        tic quarterly, October 1909-1910)
        A manufacturer's view of welfare in the textile
     industry. Says welfare is the company's attempt to
     meet local needs. Claims paternalism is necessary
     under the circumstances because people were living
     in such poverty before the mills came in. The com-
     panies provide schools, housing, and churches at
     substantial expense to themselves.

410 Pope, Liston. Millhands and preachers. New Haven, Yale
        University Press, 1942. 369 p.
        An analysis of the interaction between churches
     and cotton mills in Gaston County, North Carolina.
     Chapters 3 and 8 outline mill support of churches.
     Mill owners often financed church construction and
     supplemented ministers' salaries. Through financial
     leverage, mill owners not only controlled the num-
     ber and denominations of churches but also often

controlled religious teachings. The division of
welfare duties between churches and mills is discussed in Chapter 8.

411 Potwin, Marjorie A. Cotton mill people of the Piedmont;
      a study in social change. New York, Columbia
      University Press, 1927. 166 p.
         A sociological study of southern cotton mill
      workers, who represented a "new" social order, a
      population shifting from farms to industry. Stresses
      the independence of workers and the importance of
      personal liberty even though the workers were depend-
      ent on the mills in many respects. Mills provided
      housing, schools, churches, and a wide range of
      other benefits. In Saxon Mills, South Carolina,
      the company provided medical care, a store, elec-
      tricity, indoor plumbing, a community center, a
      playground and athletic facilities. Due to racial
      problems in public schools, workers turned to the
      company for a separate mill school.

412 Report on conditions of woman and child wage earners in
        the United States. v. I: Cotton textile industry.
      61st Congress, 2d Session, Senate Document 645.
      (5685) Washington, G.P.O., 1910. 1044 p.
         Chapters 5 and 8 compare cotton mill welfarism of
      the South and New England. Chapter 5 compares work-
      ing conditions such as lighting, ventilation, and
      sanitation and concludes that southern mills are
      generally better, largely because New England mills
      are older. Chapter 8 examines mill village provi-
      sions such as housing, schools, churches, and other
      welfare programs. Company-owned housing was deemed gen-
      erally superior to other worker housing. Most mill-spon-
      sored schools, and other welfare programs were in the
      South since cities and states provided those benefits in
      New England.

413 Rhyne, Jennings J. Some Southern cotton mill workers
        and their villages. Chapel Hill, University of
      North Carolina Press, 1930. 214 p.
         A survey of southern cotton mill villages, based
      on interviews with 500 North Carolina families.
      Describes various types of mill villages and exam-
      ines how the typical mill worker spends his day.
      Discusses the growth of mill villages including the

development of housing, the company store, and
various welfare activities. Compares housing conditions, education, and community activities in
rural villages, towns, suburban villages, and company-controlled towns.

414 Robinson, Harriet Jane. Loom and spindle. New York,
       Boston, T.Y. Crowell and Company, 1898. 216 p.
       Describes life among the mill girls of Lowell,
       Massachusetts. The companies kept watch over the
       girls' morals by requiring them to attend church,
       by supervising their living habits with boarding
       house mothers, and by requiring them to sign an
       oath of morality. The companies provided comfort-
       able lodgings, food, and pleasant working condi-
       tions. The Lowell offering, a literary magazine,
       contained stories and articles written by the mill
       girls.

415 Schwenning, Gustav T. "A pragmatic view of employee
       welfare work." Reprinted in Contemporary industrial
       processes, 10:2, Chapel Hill, University of North
       Carolina, Extension Bulletin, 1930. 8 p.
       Examines criticisms of employer paternalism,
       focusing on the southern textile industry. Briefly
       traces the history of welfare in textiles. Pater-
       nalism was necessary in the industry because it was
       used to help rebuild the South after the Civil War.
       It was also necessary because cotton mills were
       built far from towns thus companies had to furnish
       housing and other facilities.

416 Selekman, Ben M. Sharing management with the workers:
       a study of the partnership plan of the Dutchess
       Bleachery. New York, Russell Sage Foundation, 1924.
       142 p.
       Examines the employee partnership Plan of Dutchess
       Bleachery, Inc. An employee representative served
       on the company's Board of Directors and an employee
       Board of Operatives administered company housing,
       education, and recreation. A Board of Managers,
       comprised of six employees and six managers, super-
       vised business operations. Profit-sharing and an
       unemployment fund were features of the program.
       Study discusses effects of employee participation

on the success of the business. The Partnership
Plan resulted in improved worker housing, improved
morale, lower turnover, and greater efficiency.
Obstacles to full success of the plan included low
pay, uninspiring work, and workers' suspicion of
management motives.

417   Shaffer, E.T.H. "Southern mill people." The Yale re-
          view, 19, 1929, 325-340.
          Analysis of awakening labor consciousness in
      southern cotton mill towns. Traces historical de-
      velopment of mill villages from docile and paternal-
      isticly governed to discontented and impersonally
      run. Includes brief enumeration of welfare benefits
      in the Piedmont area of the Carolinas.

418   Simpson, William Hayes. Life in mill communities. Clinton,
          SC, P.C. Press, 1943. 105 p.
          Survey of employer welfare in 82 South Carolina
      cotton mill towns. Compares variety and quality of
      programs, including company-subsidized housing,
      churches, schools and recreational facilities.
      Mills commonly provided some sort of medical service
      although few had hospitals and some companies
      offered hospital insurance. Eighteen mills ran
      company stores where employees could buy on credit.
      Mills often extended interest-free loans to workers
      who lacked collateral for bank loans.

419   Simpson, William Hayes. Some aspects of America's tex-
          tile industry. Columbia, University of South Caro-
          lina, Division of General Studies, 1966. 127 p.
          Chapter 2 describes cotton mill villages in New
      England and the South. Housing was built out of
      necessity rather than paternalism because most mills
      were not located near established towns. Mills also
      provided benefits such as hospitals, sewerage,
      water, libraries and churches. Pages 19-21 enumer-
      ate recreational programs sponsored by a number of
      mills. Most housing was eventually sold to workers
      and other buyers but many mills continued to provide
      the other benefits.

420 Smith, Robert Sidney. <u>Mill on the Dan</u>. Durham, Duke
        University Press, 1950. 570 p.
           A history of Dan River cotton mills which had
        "a consistent record of corporate investment in the
        moral and physical well-being of the workers and
        their families." Pages 105-112 and Chapter 5 de-
        scribe a wide variety of welfare programs provided
        or supported by the company. The mill village of
        Schoolfield was built because the mill was not near
        an established town and because of "the desire of
        management to supervise every aspect of community
        life that related to the workers' efficiency."
        Health care included a hospital, nursery, and home
        nursing service. The company provided housing and
        supported recreational facilities, a company store,
        and churches. It subsidized the YMCA which provided
        movies, bathing facilities, evening classes, and
        athletic facilities. An employee representation
        plan was adopted to stop unions. A Cabinet, Sen-
        ate, and House of Representatives, comprised of
        labor and management representatives, dealt with
        labor issues. The representatives adopted group
        life insurance and medical care provisions for work-
        ers.

421 Stewart, Peter. "A brief history of the Peace Dale Manu-
        facturing Company." <u>Textile history review</u>, 4:1,
        January 1963, 12-23.
           Pages 19-21 describe labor relations at the
        Peace Dale Manufacturing Company. A profit-sharing
        plan paid employees a percentage of their annual
        wages and helped strengthen labor relations. "En-
        lightened paternalism" led to the construction of
        several public buildings. A weavers' strike in 1906
        partially destroyed the spirit of mutual understand-
        ing.

422 Stewart, Peter. "Paternalism in a New England mill vil-
        lage." <u>Textile history review</u>, 4:2, April 1963,
        59-65.
           Description of industrial welfare activities of
        the Peace Dale Manufacturing Company where harmony
        between the owners and workers existed for close to
        100 years. Distinction is made between economic and
        benevolent paternalism although generally both types
        of paternalism existed simultaneously. Welfare

measures included a town hall, library, recreational
facilities, churches, schools, stores, savings and
loan plans, health clinics, pensions, and well-built
and beautiful homes.

423 Stewart, Peter. "A profit-sharing system for the Peace
     Dale Mill in Rhode Island." Textile history review,
     4:3, July 1963, 126-133.
         Describes profit-sharing plan of the woolen mills
     of the Peace Dale Manufacturing Company. The pro-
     gram was installed to instill a spirit of coopera-
     tion among workers and because the owner believed
     the amount paid to labor should equal labor's con-
     tribution to the value of manufactured goods. The
     success of the program is questionable because out-
     put and quality improved only slightly and profit-
     sharing was discontinued after a few years.

424 Sturdivant, Joanna Farrell. "Employee representation
     plan of the Durham Hosiery Mills." Social forces,
     4:3, March 1926, 625-628. (Reprinted in Herring's
     Welfare work in mill villages.)
         Describes the employee representation plan of
     Durham Hosiery Mills, introduced to offer employees
     something better than unions. Plan included Cabi-
     net of executives, Senate of department heads and
     foremen, and House of Representatives of elected
     employees. Bills that passed both Houses were con-
     sidered by the Cabinet. Two-thirds of both houses
     could override a Cabinet veto on matters not af-
     fecting finances, working hours, or company policy.
     Plan led to such welfare benefits as improved hous-
     ing, recreational facilities, and nurses. Employ-
     ees abandoned the plan during layoffs and wage cuts
     of the Depression.

425 Taylor, James H. "Manufacturers in South Carolina."
     Cotton history review, 1:3, July 1960, 131-137.
         Describes model cotton mill town of Graniteville,
     South Carolina. After boarding houses failed to
     attract workers, individual cottages were built to
     provide for whole families.

426 Thompson, Holland. <u>From the cotton field to the cotton</u>
     <u>mill; a study of industrial transition in North</u>
     <u>Carolina</u>. New York, Macmillan, 1906. 284 p.
          Chapter 9 describes social life in cotton mill
     villages. Companies subsidized churches and schools
     which provided social activities as well as religion
     and education for the communities. Other sources of
     diversion were rarely available to mill workers.
     Chapter 11 describes provision for day-to-day work-
     ers' needs. Companies provided medical care, fuel,
     supplies, and paid funeral expenses.

427 Titus, Edward Kirk. "An instructive factory village."
     <u>World's work</u>, 9, January 1905, 5752-5754.
          Describes the model cotton mill village of Lud-
     low, Massachusetts. The company provides and main-
     tains comfortable housing, a library, recreation
     and athletic facilities, education and a school; and
     a boarding house, including meals, for unmarried wom-
     en.

428 Usselman, Steven W. "Scientific management without Tay-
     lor: management innovations at Bancroft." In <u>Work-</u>
     <u>ing papers from the Regional Economic History Re-</u>
     <u>search Center</u>. Greenville, Wilmington, DE, Eleu-
     therian Mills-Hagley Foundation, 1981. 47-77 p.
     (v. 4, no. 4, 1981, edited by Glenn Porter and Wil-
     liam H. Mulligan, Jr.)
          Examines Joseph Bancroft and Sons Company, a cot-
     ton textile finishing firm of Wilmington, Delaware.
     Studies the interaction between scientific manage-
     ment and industrial welfare, both of which were in
     extensive use in the firm. By adopting a pragmatic
     approach the company established a centralized con-
     trol of labor and production and integrated the fi-
     nancial and operational departments with notable suc-
     cess.

429 VanKleeck, Mary. "Sharing management with workers."
     <u>Journal of social forces</u>, 3:3, March 1925, 506-
     510.
          Examines the Partnership Plan of Dutchess Bleach-
     ery, Inc, instituted in an atmosphere of labor
     unrest. The plan gave workers a voice in operating

the business, opened the company's financial re-
cords, and provided for profit-sharing. An employee
board took charge of repairing company houses and
supervising educational and recreational facilities.
An unemployment benefit fund was installed. The
Partnership Plan did not threaten the function of
the union and worker morale and efficiency were improved.

430 Ware, Caroline F. The Early New England cotton manufac-
     ture. Boston, Houghton Mifflin Company, 1931. 349
     p.
         Pages 200-203 and 256-260 describe boarding
     houses provided by northern cotton mills to attract
     a labor supply of "respectable girls." Most board-
     ing houses had matrons who looked after the girls'
     morals. Describes generally crowded but comfortable
     living conditions in typical boarding houses.

COMPANY TOWNS AND WORKERS' HOUSING

Examinations and general surveys of company towns and company-
owned worker housing in all industries except mining, textiles,
steel, and railroads, which are treated in separate sections of
this bibliography. Works describe conditions, costs, and services provided. Model towns, especially Pullman, Illinois, are
described.

431 Allen, James B. "The company town: a passing phase of
        Utah's industrial development." Utah historical
        quarterly, 34:2, Spring 1966, 138-160.
            A history of company towns in Utah. All property
        was owned by the company and the company acted as em-
        ployer, landlord, merchant, government, and police.
        Describes typical company towns and examines the ade-
        quacy of housing, schools, and sports and recreation-
        al facilities. Most towns were segregated into
        American and immigrant sections and were character-
        ized by "drab uniformity." Company towns were used
        as a tool against unions because workers were forced
        out of their houses during strikes.

432 Allen, James B. The Company town in the American West.
        Norman, University of Oklahoma Press, 1966. 205 p.
            An overview of company towns in the West. Exam-
        ines reasons for development, their relationship to
        the development of certain industries, and living
        conditions compared to non-company towns. Focuses
        especially on company towns in the lumber, copper,
        and coal industries. Describes community layout,
        beautification projects, housing, rents, religion,
        and education and estimates company costs. Con-
        cludes that no single stereotype describes all com-
        pany towns. Some were dirty and ramshackle while
        others were sanitary and well maintained. Some com-

132

panies exploited workers while others had their best
interests at heart.

433   Allen, Leslie H. Industrial housing problems. Boston,
      Aberthaw Construction Company, 1917. 31 p.
      Claims poor housing conditions and the unavail-
      ability of housing are causing high labor turnover.
      Also suggests workers in crowded, unsanitary housing
      are less productive. Believes employers have a re-
      sponsibility to provide workers with adequate housing.
      Discusses building problems and essential features of
      good housing. Warns against overcrowding and cautions
      employers to strictly supervise housing and education
      of workers.

434   Allen, Leslie H. "The problem of industrial housing."
      Industrial management, 54:3, December 1917, 396-404.
      Proposes that employers must build houses and con-
      sider them an operating expense in order to attract
      and maintain workers. Describes overcrowding and
      poor sanitation in workers' housing, problems which
      affect workers' health and lower productivity. Lists
      essential features of adequate housing and estimates
      the proportion of costs workers can be expected to
      bear.

435   Allen, Leslie H. The Workman's home: its influence upon
      production in the factory and labor turnover. Boston,
      Aberthaw Construction Company, 1918. 23 p.
      A survey of housing conditions of employees of
      840 companies. Concludes that poor housing is the
      main reason for employee turnover. Presents comments
      of various employers on the housing problem and dis-
      cusses financial barriers to building worker housing.

436   Buder, Stanley. Pullman: an experiment in industrial
      order and community planning. New York, Oxford
      University Press, 1967. 263 p.
      Describes George Pullman's efforts to create a
      showplace company town. He believed adequate housing
      was necessary for social well-being and would solve
      labor problems. He emphasized aesthetics because he
      believed beauty improved the individual. Describes

planning and developing the town's physical and
social character. Due to the isolation of the town,
Pullman was also forced to construct a school, stores,
churches, and other municipal facilities. Discusses
public and employee opinions of the town, relations
between the company and the community, and the degree
of company dominance over the workers. Examines the
company's loss of control over the town due to the
strike.

437 Cleland, Robert Glass. _A History of Phelps Dodge, 1934-
     1950_. New York, Alfred A. Knopf, 1952. 307 p.
         Pages 72-73, 109-110, and Chapter 10 describe the
     obligation felt by Phelps Dodge and Company to care
     for the "religious, moral, and physical well-being of
     its employees." The company's welfare programs in
     Pennsylvania lumber camps and Arizona copper mining
     camps included comfortable homes, medical care, rea-
     sonably priced stores, churches, schools, libraries,
     and recreation centers. By 1917, the company was
     providing pensions and jointly funded insurance. The
     company was strongly opposed to unions and its welfare
     programs were aimed at keeping them out.

438 Creel, George. "The feudal towns of Texas." _Harper's
     weekly_, 60:3031, January 23, 1915, 76-78.
         Describes the company lumber towns of Jasper and
     Kirbyville, Texas.

439 Eaton, Charles H. "Pullman and paternalism." _American
     journal of politics_, 5, 1894, 571-579.
         Argues that paternalism does not exist in Pullman,
     Illinois. Although the Pullman Palace Car Company
     provides many of the town's facilities, it does not
     control their use. The company does not control
     stores, the theater is not operated as a business,
     and workers are not required to attend company-funded
     churches. Workers are not forced to live in company
     housing but choose to do so because it is superior
     to other housing in the area. Workers are not intim-
     idated in any way.

440 Ely, Richard T. "Pullman; a social study." Harper's
       monthly magazine, 70, 1885, 452-466.
          Analyzes paternalistic attempt by the Pullman
       Palace Car Company to build an ideal town in Pull-
       man, Illinois. The town is clean and attractive,
       provides comfortable, low-cost housing and features
       a variety of facilities such as a theater, shops,
       and a library. But the success of the town is tem-
       pered by workers' loss of liberty. The Pullman Com-
       pany and a few smaller companies own and control
       every aspect of the town. Workers are not free to
       criticize the town or companies and may be evicted
       at any time.

441 Going, Charles Buxton. "Village communities of the fac-
       tory." Engineering magazine, 21:1, April 1901,
       59-74.
          Suggests employers should care for the well-being
       of their workers. Cautions that welfare programs
       should be carefully devised to avoid paternalism.
       Claims the model town experiment in Pullman, Illi-
       nois, failed because of over interest and "chafing
       restrictions" by management. Emphasizes the need
       to establish "a feeling of mutual regard and sym-
       pathy" between the employer and his workers. Sur-
       veys model company towns of several companies and
       suggests that their success resulted from cooperation
       between management and employees.

442 Hanger, G.W.W. Housing of working people in the United
       States by employers. U.S. Department of Labor, Bu-
       reau of Labor Statistics, Bulletin 54. Washington,
       G.P.O., September 1904. 1191-1243.
          Surveys housing provided for workers by 16 com-
       panies. Describes housing of each company, estimates
       costs to employers and rents charged workers, and
       discusses other welfare benefits provided. Provides
       particularly detailed description of welfare at the
       Colorado Fuel and Iron Company. Includes many photo-
       graphs and floor plans.

443 Magnusson, Leifur. "Employers' housing in the United
       States." Monthly review of the U.S. Bureau of Labor
       Statistics (Monthly labor review) 5:5, November 1917,
       35-60.

A survey of 213 companies that provided housing
for workers. Discusses construction and maintenance
problems in company towns. Describes types of houses,
number of rooms, rents, costs to companies and
modern conveniences provided. Companies provided
housing to attract and maintain better workers, to
foster a loyal, contented, and efficient work force,
to control workers, and to make sure workers had
adequate living conditions. Suggests the need for
less uniformity of houses and the planting of trees
and gardens to break the monotony. Presents housing
statistics by industry.

444 Magnusson, Leifur. "Housing and the land problem."
     Monthly labor review, 6:5, May 1918, 268-277.
          Discusses problems of companies that must move out
     of cities to obtain land. Examines problems of com-
     pany towns built in these new areas. Considers the
     potential for expansion, adequacy of town planning,
     and the rising cost of land. The disadvantage of
     company housing is that it places no responsibility
     on tenants. Describes various plans of financing
     and control of housing.

445 Magnusson, Leifur. Housing by employers in the United
     States. U.S. Department of Labor, Bureau of Labor
     Statistics, Bulletin 263. Washington, G.P.O., 1920.
     283 p.
          A survey of above average housing provided by 213
     employers. Surveys types and conditions of houses,
     provision of utilities, community services provided,
     maintenance, and costs to employers. Describes char-
     acteristics of typical company towns and houses.
     Housing was generally supplied because many companies
     were located outside established towns, and to at-
     tract and maintain good workers.

446 Magnusson, Leifur. "Methods of sale of company houses."
     Monthly labor review, 8:4, April 1919, 227-232.
          Examines the practice of companies selling housing
     to their workers. The practice was most common in
     the coal and iron and steel industries. Discusses
     mortgage provisions, average payments, and provisions
     to minimize risks for workers and companies. Com-
     panies sold houses to reduce turnover by encouraging

workers to stay in the area.

447 Magnusson, Leifur. "Sanitary aspects of company hous-
         ing." Monthly labor review, 8:1, January 1919, 289-
         291.
            A survey of sanitary aspects of housing of over
         200 companies. Discusses maintenance and upkeep
         of housing and surrounding areas, the enforcement of
         sanitary regulations, and provisions for sewerage and
         water systems.

448 Meakin, Bridgett. Model factories and villages; ideal
         conditions of labour and housing. London, T. Fisher
         Unwin, 1905. 480 p.
            Pages 382-416 and 443-474 describe model company
         towns in the United States. Discusses problems of
         constructing and maintaining housing for workers and
         suggests ways of circumventing problems through care-
         ful urban planning.

449 Mortimer, George. "George F. Johnson and his 'Square
         Deal Towns'." American magazine, 41, January 1921,
         36-37+.
            Describes the history and development of the Endi-
         cott-Johnson shoe manufacturing company. The company
         built two model towns, called "Square Deal Towns,"
         with comfortable housing, modern conveniences, gar-
         dens, swimming pools, and a racetrack. Conditions
         were so good unions didn't even bother trying to
         organize in the model towns.

450 Sennett, Richard. Authority. New York, Alfred A. Knopf,
         1980. 206 p.
            Pages 62-83 present a philosophical analysis of
         workers' rebellion against George Pullman's paternal-
         ism. Examines reasons for a strike in what was con-
         sidered a model company town. Describes the town and
         rigid rules of morality imposed on employees who
         lived there. Pullman refused to sell homes to em-
         ployees and controlled all aspects of their lives.
         Rebellion against paternalism was a major cause of
         the strike.

451 Snavely, J.R. "The industrial community development at
        Hershey, Pennsylvania." American landscape archi-
        tect, 3:5, November 1930, 24-36.
           A largely pictoral description of Hershey, Penn-
        sylvania, the "Chocolate Town." The Hershey Company
        funds a variety of community projects including
        schools, a park, community beautification, public
        utilities, churches, and athletic and social facili-
        ties.

452 Thackwell, Rhys G. "An industrial village of home
        owners." American city, 36:5, May 1927, 669-671.
           Describes the company town of Kohler, Wisconsin.
        The houses were built, maintained, and sold at cost
        by the Kohler Company. Town features recreational
        facilities, a laundry, and an employee lunch room
        in the factory. In spite of company ownership, Kohler
        was intended to be an independent community run with-
        out employer paternalism.

453 Vance, Rupert B. How the other half is housed. (South-
        ern Policy Papers No. 4) Chapel Hill, University of
        North Carolina Press, 1936. 16 p.
           A pictoral survey of southern farm housing. While
        only one page depicts company housing, the photo-
        graphs of other houses show the poor living condi-
        tions in the area before mills moved in and company
        housing became available. Adequate housing is de-
        picted to provide a comparison to substandard condi-
        tions.

454 "Welfare work in company towns." Monthly labor review,
        25:2, August 1927, 90-96.
           Discussion of welfare work in company towns, often
        necessary due to isolation from other communities.
        Considers balance between the necessity of employers
        providing essential services and employer domination
        of workers' lives. Outlines various facilities and
        services provided, including medical and health serv-
        ices, education, clubs, and community centers and
        describes model programs.

455 Wood, Edith Elmer. <u>The Housing of the unskilled wage</u>
     <u>earner</u>. New York, Macmillan, 1919. 321 p.
          A survey of workers in the United States. Notes
     that many workers' salaries are not sufficient to
     provide adequate housing. Pages 114-129 describe
     model housing provided by employers, including de-
     scriptions of New England mill towns; Pullman, Illi-
     nois; LeClaire, Illinois; Goodyear Heights, and
     several other company towns. Finds that standards
     in employer-owned towns are not always satisfactory
     and criticizes the paternalistic structure of the
     towns.

SPECIFIC PROGRAMS

Surveys of several companies' programs and descriptions of programs of individual companies. Discusses characteristics of programs, their value to employees and employers, and reasons for introducing them.

1. Cafeterias and lunch rooms -- Describes cafeterias, restaurants, lunch rooms, and free or low cost meals provided by the employers.
2. Company stores -- Includes both pros and cons of the company store and the scrip system.
3. Economic security -- Includes any program dealing with employees' financial well-being. Stock ownership and profit-sharing are excluded from this category because such plans were sometimes more of an economic risk than security for workers. (See Sections VII.5 and VII.7 for these programs.) The effect of the Depression on these programs will primarily be found in this section.
   a. Mutual benefit associations -- Mutual benefit associations were usually funded jointly by the employer and workers. They provided sickness, accident, and death benefits and sometimes medical care and pensions.
   b. Pensions -- Contains plans of specific companies, general surveys, and government hearings.
   c. Unemployment insurance -- Includes various forms of dismissal compensation, especially prevalent during the Depression.
   d. Miscellaneous -- Includes savings plans, employment stabilization of guaranteed employment, group insurance, cooperative buying, and investment opportunities for workers.
4. Health -- Descriptions of medical care, company doctors, visiting nurses, dentists, psychiatric care, hospitals, and sanitariums provided for workers by employers. Some works are studies of health condi-

140

tions in various industries. The responsibility of
the employer to care for the health of employees is
sometimes considered.

5. Profit-sharing -- Includes philosophical discussions,
descriptions of general characteristics, and company
plans for profit-sharing. Discusses employee protections from loss, effects of the Depression, organized
labor's reactions, and successes and failures.

6. Recreation -- Includes descriptions of employer-pro-
vided activities and facilities for athletics, parties, picnics, musical groups, club houses, and cultural events.

7. Stock ownership -- Descriptions and characteristics
of plans, including discussions of risks to employees
and protections from loss. Effects of the stock
market crash on stock programs are found in this
section.

8. Vacations -- Discusses paid vacations for both office
employees and production workers and vacation homes
and resorts provided by employers.

9. Miscellaneous -- Includes such topics as loan plans,
cooperative farming, employee counseling, rest
periods, and factory beautification.

CAFETERIAS AND LUNCH ROOMS

456 The Employee betterment book: a practical treatise on
     industrial lunch rooms and other industrial welfare
     projects. Chicago, Albert Pick and Company, 1920.
     71 p.
        Describes model industrial welfare programs. Dis-
     cusses costs and problems of benefits such as lunch
     rooms, club rooms, rest rooms, and athletic and rec-
     reational facilities. Pages 20-29 describe the
     model cafeteria of the Westinghouse Electric and Manu-
     facturing Company, the largest cafeteria in the world.
     The cafeteria was installed to increase worker effi-
     ciency by providing nutritious meals. The cafete-
     ria's operations are discussed in detail.

457 "Lunch rooms in industrial establishments." Monthly
     labor review, 24:3, March 1927, 13-22.
        Bureau of Labor Statistics survey of lunch room

services provided by 303 out of 430 firms. Examines
costs to employers and prices charged for meals, discusses various types of facilities, and estimates the
number of employees who use them. Lunch rooms were
usually provided if no other eating places were near-
by and when employers wanted workers to have a nour-
ishing meal so they would be healthier and more efficient.

458 National Industrial Conference Board. Industrial lunch
rooms. New York, 1928. 65 p.
An examination of company lunch rooms. Discusses
how to determine whether a lunch room is needed and
what type of services and facilities are appropriate.
Lunch rooms range from a room where bag lunches are
eaten to full restaurant facilities. Discusses typical lunch room layouts, equipment used, managing
food service, and costs to employees. Most lunch
rooms are installed because plants are too far away
from home or restaurants.

459 Rossy, C.S. "Factory employees' restaurant." Industrial
management, 55:3, March 1918, 236-237.
Describes the employees' restaurant of the Norwalk
Tire and Rubber Company, established in the belief
that well fed workers are more productive. The
restaurant serves buffet style, "help yourself" meals
to avoid the costs of paying food servers.

460 Whitney, Anice L. "Health and welfare activities in the
Government Printing Office." Monthly labor review,
16:5, May 1923, 1-13.
Article focuses on cooperative employer/employee
welfare efforts of the Government Printing Office
(GPO) which employed over 4000 workers. Organization
and partial funding of projects and activities came
from an employee group called the GPO Cafeteria and
Recreation Association. The bulk of the funding came
directly from GPO. Cafeteria and recreation facilities highlighted the welfare effort. As part of an
absentee control program, GPO provided medical services, including a medical staff, ambulance service,
and emergency care.

461 Whitney, Anice L. "Lunch rooms for employees." <u>Monthly</u>
        <u>labor review</u>, 5:12, December 1917, 207-215.
            A survey of 224 companies that provided lunch
        rooms for employees. Suggests the provision of warm,
        wholesome meals is one of the most important types
        of industrial betterment. Describes kinds of services
        and estimates the number of employees using the
        facilities. Estimates costs to companies of various
        types of facilities and discusses average prices
        charged for meals.

COMPANY STORES

462 "Company cooperative stores in the United States." <u>Month-</u>
        <u>ly labor review</u>, 13:6, December 1921, 185-186.
            A synopsis of a Metropolitan Life Insurance survey
        of company cooperative stores. The purpose of the
        stores was to make merchandise available to workers
        at reduced prices. Lists six types of buying plans
        and discusses the implications of company versus em-
        ployee management.

463 "Company stores and the scrip system." <u>Monthly labor</u>
        <u>review</u>, 41:7, July 1935, 45-53.
            A survey of 961 company stores. Found the quality
        of goods was the same as at independent stores but
        food prices were higher. The extension of credit
        by company stores forced employees to shop there.
        Describes types of stores, the extent of employee
        patronage, the amount of credit extended, payment of
        wages in scrip, and compulsion to trade at the com-
        pany stores. Presents price comparison statistics.

464 Creamer, Daniel. "Legislation on company stores in the
        United States." <u>American federationist</u>, 43:4,
        April 1936, 365-375.
            Discusses the inadequacies of legislation govern-
        ing company stores. The distinguishing feature of
        all company stores was their ability to make deduc-
        tions from workers' paychecks. Workers who failed
        to patronize company stores risked dismissal. Scrip
        and credit were used to tie workers to the company.
        Legislation included prohibitions against coerced
        patronage, regulation of the redeemability and ne-

gotiability of scrip, and blanket prohibitions against
company stores. The laws are criticized as inadequate
and too easily circumvented.

465   Johnson, Ole S. The Industrial store: its history, oper-
        ations and economic significance. Atlanta, University
        of Georgia, Division of Research, School of Business
        Administration, 1952. 171 p.
          A study of company stores. Major functions in-
        cluded providing goods for workers, acting as a cred-
        it agency, providing a source of revenue for the
        company, attracting and maintaining a labor force,
        and promoting better labor relations. Traces the
        history of company stores, including their develop-
        ment in the coal, railroad, textile, mining, and lum-
        ber industries. Describes store operations of sever-
        al companies and compares prices at company and in-
        dependent stores. Examines the controversy over pay-
        ing workers in scrip so they can only shop at the
        company store and discusses company control over
        workers through credit at the stores.

466   "Legislation relating to payment of wages in scrip, pro-
        tection of employees as traders, and company stores."
        Monthly labor review, 43:1, July 1936, 74-76.
          Surveys laws which protected workers from exploi-
        tation at company stores. Laws included restrictions
        on the use of scrip as a substitute for wages, pro-
        hibitions against coerced patronage, regulation of
        the prices of goods sold, and general restrictions
        against company ownership of stores.

467   National Association of Corporation Schools. Bulletin,
        8, April 1921, 157-164.
          (Cooperative stores)

468   Report of the Industrial Commission on Labor Legislation.
        v. 5 of the Commissioners' Reports. Washington,
        G.P.O., 1900. 308 p.
          Of particular interest are pages 55-64 which deal
        with methods of wage payment, company stores, relief
        societies, and company physicians.

ECONOMIC SECURITY

MUTUAL BENEFIT ASSOCIATIONS

469   Bacon, Helen.   How to conduct a mutual aid association.
        Detroit?   1917?   14 p.
           A survey of 83 successful mutual benefit associa-
        tions in the Detroit area.   Discusses membership,
        dues, benefit levels, medical provisions, and varia-
        tions among plans.

470   Brundage, Dean Kennedy.   "A survey of the work of em-
        ployees' mutual benefit associations."   Public
        health reports, 46:36, September 4, 1931, 2102-
        2119.
           Investigates the extent to which mutual benefit
        associations have gone beyond payment of benefits to
        develop health care programs.   Surveys 602 companies
        and reports the size and age of mutual benefit asso-
        ciations, benefit levels, and company contributions.
        Suggests ways to improve the programs.

471   Chandler, W.L.   "Benefit funds: a summary and analysis
        of benefit funds in 461 industrial establishments."
        System, 25:3, March 1914.

472   Chandler, W.L.   "Conclusions from a survey of over 500
        employees' benefit associations."   In Proceedings of
        the Employment Managers' Conference, Philadelphia,
        PA, April 2 and 3, 1917.   U.S. Department of Labor,
        Bureau of Labor Statistics, Bulletin 227.   Washing-
        ton, G.P.O., 1917.   158-167 p.   (Same article is
        also in Annals of the American Academy of Political
        and Social Science, 71, May 1917, 156-166.)
           Explains the value of jointly funded employee
        benefit associations, which provide sick benefits
        and medical service for workers.   By promoting the
        health of workers, benefit associations make workers
        more efficient and reduce absenteeism.   Suggests
        health and accident insurance has more immediate
        benefit for workers than life insurance.   Describes
        the development of the Mutual Benefit Association
        of the Dodge Manufacturing Company, which paid divi-

dends back to employees when the treasury was large.
Emphasizes the need to "sell" the plan to workers to
develop their interest and enthusiasm. Discusses the
advantages of voluntary membership and considers op-
timal benefit levels.

473 Chandler, W.L. "The employees benefit association."
     Industrial management, 55:1-4, 6, January-June 1918,
     34-39, 109-115, 219-224, 293-297, 465-470.
        A 5-part examination of 61 problems in organizing,
     developing, and operating industrial mutual benefit
     associations. Based on a study of 579 companies.
     Includes consideration of benefits to both workers
     and companies, problems of financing, costs to em-
     ployees and companies, the role of workmen's compen-
     sation and other laws, membership requirements, de-
     tails of administration, terms of benefit payments,
     and types of benefits that may be provided.

474 Industrial relations, Bloomfield's Labor Digest. Em-
     ployees' mutual benefit associations: their organ-
     ization, methods, and administration. Boston, Bloom-
     field and Bloomfield, 1922. 19 p.
        An overview of mutual benefit associations. Anal-
     yzes and compares associations that are entirely em-
     ployee administered, jointly administered, and en-
     tirely company administered. Discusses eligibility
     requirements, dues, and details of benefits.

475 Jackson, John. "Mutual aid associations of Strawbridge
     and Clothier." Proceedings of the Employment Man-
     agers' Conference. U.S. Department of Labor, Bureau
     of Labor Statistics, Bulletin 227. Washington,
     G.P.O., 1917. 1968-1972 p.
        Summarizes work of the Strawbridge and Clothier
     mutual benefit association. A relief fund, financed
     jointly by the company and workers, pays sick and
     death benefits. The company pays interest on a work-
     er savings fund and jointly supports a pension plan.
     The Mutual Aid Association also includes a chorus, an
     orchestra, and an athletic association.

476 National Association of Corporation Schools. Bulletin,
     7, October 1920, 445-449.
        (Benefit associations)

477 National Industrial Conference Board. Experience with
     mutual benefit associations in the United States.
     Research Report #65. New York, 1923. 155 p.
        A survey of sickness, accident, death, and unem-
     ployment benefits provided through mutual benefit
     associations. Some associations were entirely run
     by employees but others were jointly funded and ad-
     ministered with employers. Some included medical
     service. Describes eligibility requirements, dues
     and benefits, and details of administration. Es-
     timates costs to employers and employees under var-
     ious plans. The Appendix lists companies with mutual
     benefit associations.

478 National Industrial Conference Board. A Manual for mu-
     tual benefit associations. Research Report #66
     (Supplement to Report #65) New York, 1924. 48 p.
        A handbook on how to form mutual benefit associa-
     tions. Discusses company financing, participation
     in administration, voluntary or compulsory member-
     ship, eligibility requirements, dues, and benefit
     levels. Appendix A provides model by-laws and Appen-
     dix B lists companies with mutual benefit associa-
     tions.

479 National Industrial Conference Board. The Present status
     of mutual benefit associations. New York, 1931.
     104 p.
        Describes the organization and administration of
     mutual benefit associations, which developed to pro-
     tect employees from loss of earning power. Examines
     types and amounts of benefits, including sickness,
     disability, and death benefits and medical care.
     Discusses joint employee/employer financing of the
     programs.

480 "Present status of industrial mutual benefit associa-
     tions." Monthly labor review, 33:1, July 1931, 75-
     76.
        A survey of 398 companies with mutual benefit

associations. The purposes of the associations are
to provide low-cost accident, sickness, and death
benefits to workers, to decrease absences and turnover and to improve morale. Survey notes a trend
toward compulsory membership.

481 Price, C.W. "Employees' benefit association of the In-
        ternational Harvester Company." Annals of the Ameri-
        can Academy of Political and Social Science, 33:2,
        March 1909, 246-257.
            Describes International Harvester's Employee Bene-
        fit Association. The association is funded by com-
        pany and employee contributions and pays sickness,
        disability, and death benefits. Article explains
        funding and administration and lists amount of bene-
        fits paid for specific injuries and illnesses. Eval-
        uates pros and cons of features of various benefit
        programs.

482 Princeton University. Industrial Relations Section. Mem-
        orandum: mutual benefit associations. Princeton,
        NJ, 1929. 18 p.
            A survey of 100 mutual benefit associations. De-
        scribes eligibility requirements, dues, company con-
        tributions, and benefit rates. Considers the poten-
        tial for paternalism in administration and gives
        suggestions for management of associations. Dis-
        cusses sickness, accident, and death benefits and
        hospital care provided through the plans.

483 Ranney, George A. "Employees' Benefit Association of the
        International Harvester companies." Proceedings of
        the Conference on Social Insurance. U.S. Department
        of Labor, Bureau of Labor Statistics, Bulletin 212.
        Washington, G.P.O., 1917. 482-490 p.
            Report on the details and functioning of Inter-
        national Harvester's mutual benefit system, which
        was designed to protect employees from loss of earn-
        ing power. The jointly funded system paid sickness,
        injury and death benefits to member workers.

484 Schmidt, Emerson P. Industrial relations in urban trans-
        portation. Minneapolis, University of Minnesota
        Press, 1937. 264 p.

Pages 95-101 discuss industrial welfare in the street railway industry. Examines the prevalence of joint funds which provided sick and death benefits. Describes mutual benefit funds of numerous public railway companies. The dominant employer motive for contributing to the funds was "greater profit through improved industrial relations." Organized labor claimed they were "a trick to ward off the union and lull the employees into a false sense of security." Discusses the extension of welfare policies to include pensions and group insurance.

485 Swope, Gerard. "Management cooperation with workers for economic welfare." Annals of the American Academy of Political and Social Science, 154, March 1931, 131-137.

Explains welfare programs of the General Electric Company. Most programs are funded jointly by the company and workers in the belief that "things should not be done for nor to people but by and with people." Programs include group life insurance, a company savings bond plan, pensions, and an unemployment and loan fund.

486 "Work of employees' mutual benefit associations." Monthly labor review, 33:5, November 1931. 75-78.

A survey of 315 companies with mutual benefit associations. Lists range and methods of computation of benefits. Includes company recommendations on changes in programs and opinions as to the effectiveness of associations in improving employees' health.

PENSIONS

487 "Annuity plan of a large manufacturing company." Monthly labor review, 30:2, February 1930, 45-46.

Explains pension plan of the Westinghouse Electric and Manufacturing Company. Employees are given an opportunity to buy annuity units in addition to those provided by the company. Price of units varies with the employees' age. Employees who leave the company receive credit for purchased annuity units.

488   Brandeis, Louis D. <u>Business, a profession</u>. Boston,
      Small, Maynard and Company, 1914. 327 p.
           Pages 65-81 advocate the use of pension plans in
      industry. Pensions are needed so older unproductive
      workers can be humanely retired. Criticizes U.S.
      pension plans for being discretionary and therefore
      a form of strike insurance since older workers avoid
      labor trouble for fear of losing their pensions. Ad-
      vocates right to partial accrued pension for employees
      who leave the company before retirement age and sug-
      gests that plans guarantee payment upon retirement.

489   "Commercial telegraph companies." U.S. Commission on Indus-
      trial Relations. <u>Report and Testimony</u>, v. 10, 9291-
      9541. 64th Congress, 1st Session, Document 415,
      (Senate Document 415, 6938) 1915.
           Testimony before the U.S. Commission on Industrial
      Relations concerning the labor policies of the Western
      Union Telegraph Company. Included is information on
      pensions and sick benefits which were provided as "a
      contribution toward the progress of society," and to
      attract a higher class of workers.

490   Conant, Luther, Jr. <u>A Critical analysis of industrial
      pension systems</u>. New York, Macmillan, 1922. 262 p.
           Overview of industrial pension plans. Suggests
      plans should not be started without careful consider-
      ation of whether their financial obligations can be
      met. Outlines reasons for pensions and examines at-
      titudes of scholars, businessmen, and labor leaders
      toward them. Describes various types of plans and
      presents arguments for and against each. Appendix
      1 outlines plans of several companies.

491   Fitch, John A. "For value received; a discussion of in-
      dustrial pensions." <u>Survey</u>, 40, May 25, 1918, 221-224.
           Surveys pension plans of several companies, with
      special emphasis on the plan of Sears, Roebuck and
      Company. Criticizes most plans because they are used
      as weapons to keep employees from stirring up trouble
      and to force them to stay with the company twenty
      or more years. Even then, the employer may refuse to
      pay pensions earned. The Sears plan is the exception
      since it guarantees benefits and requires only ten
      years service before benefits may be drawn.

492 "Industrial pension plans in the Depression, United
     States and Canada." Monthly labor review, 36:5, May
     1933, 1062-1064.
         Discusses conflicting trends of unprecedented
     growth of new pension plans during the Depression
     and the rapid curtailment of plans in force before
     the Depression. This shift is seen as a move to
     decrease the burden on employers by shifting from
     entirely company-funded plans to plans which require
     employee contribution.

493 Latimer, Murray W. Industrial pension systems in the
     United States and Canada. New York, Industrial Rela-
     tions Counselors, 1932. 561 p.
         An overview and financial analysis of pension sys-
     tems. Traces the history of the pension movement and
     describes traits of programs in various industries.
     Surveys eligibility requirements and methods of de-
     termining benefit levels. Compares advantages and
     disadvantages of contributory and noncontributory
     plans. Discusses the rapid growth in the number of
     pensioners and amount of payments as more and more
     employees become eligible for benefits. Reasons for
     providing pensions include: to provide for workers
     who no longer perform effectively, to discourage
     turnover, and to improve a company's public image.

494 National Civic Federation. Old age annuities: a prac-
     tical guide for an economically sound solution of
     the pension problem. New York, 1925. 11 p.
         An examination of industrial pensions. Shortcom-
     ings of pension plans were that they were only pro-
     vided by a small percentage of companies, employees
     who changed companies received no benefits, and
     benefits were not guaranteed to employees who earned
     them. Suggests that workers be required to contrib-
     ute to the plans. Employees who leave a company be-
     fore reaching retirement age would be entitled to
     accrued benefits. Warns employers to set enough
     money aside to pay for future liabilities.

495 National Civic Federation. Old age annuities: recommenda-
     tions to industrial establishments for the study and
     formulation of funded pension plans. New York, 1926.
     10 p.

Practical guidelines for companies trying to improve their pension programs. The major problem is
overcoming insolvency of the old programs and developing financial guidelines to make sure such debts
don't build up in the future. Discusses technicali-
ties of employee and employer contributed portions of
pension funds. Considers problems of providing for
employees who are already near retirement age when
the pension program is introduced.

496 National Civic Federation. Industrial Welfare Department.
     Old age pension conference. New York, 1927. 43 p.
     A collection of addresses on pension plans. Sug-
gests pensions should be secure, suited to employees'
needs, and not exclusively dependent on continuous
service. The value of pensions to employers is their
encouragement of loyal and continuous service. Con-
tributory plans are suggested to encourage employee
savings. Employees who leave pension plans of the
Western Clock Company, All America Cables, Inc., the
Equitable Trust Company, and the Otis Elevator Company are described.

497 National Industrial Conference Board. Industrial pen-
     sions in the United States. New York, 1925. 157 p.
     Part I is a general survey of pension plans. Out-
lines types of plans, eligibility requirements, and
payment levels. Purposes of pensions are to reduce
turnover, to reward long service, and to provide a
means of retiring workers who are no longer useful
to the company. Unions opposed pension plans because
they make workers obliged to employers and weaken
union power.
     Part II outlines practical considerations to guide
employers in organizing and administering pension
systems.

498 "Pension plans in American industry." Industrial rela-
     tions, 8:7, October 15, 1921.

499 "Private companies in the United States having old-age
     pension systems." Monthly review of the Bureau of
     Labor Statistics (Monthly labor review) 2:6, June
     1916, 110-112.

> List of companies with pension plans. Classified
> by industry.

500 "Problems of old-age pensions in industry." Monthly
       labor review, 24:3, March 1927, 48-54.
       Survey by the Pennsylvania Old Age Pension Commis-
sion of pension provisions of over 1600 companies.
Three hundred seventy had formal pension plans
and another 224 provided benefits to specially deserv-
ing workers. Examines reasons companies pay the rising
costs of pension plans. Reasons include needing a
humane way to retire employees who have become unpro-
ductive, providing incentive for low turnover, and
using the threat of losing benefits to keep older
ployees from causing labor trouble.

501 Roland, Henry. "Six examples of successful shop manage-
       ment." Engineering magazine, 13:1, April 1897, 10-
       19.
       Describes the pension and life insurance plan of
Alfred Dodge and Sons. Pensions were provided as a
compassionate means of weeding older employees from the
work force. Benefits were based on length of service
so employees with long service might draw pensions
that exceeded working wages. Pensions were jointly
funded with employees contributing one percent of
their wages and were supplemented by an endowment
fund which rewarded workers for productivity. Life
insurance was company funded and benefits were based
on length of service.

502 "Safeguarding the employees' interest under industrial
       pension plans." Monthly labor review, 29:3, Septem-
       ber 1929, 95-96.
       Criticizes industrial pension plans because they
force workers to remain with one company and they
give workers a false sense of security since benefits can be withheld at the company's discretion.
Describes how the Western Clock Company overcame
these problems. Its jointly funded plan may be con-
tinued even if an employee leaves the company. The
company stops contributing when the worker leaves but
he is still entitled to what was already accumulated
and may continue his share of contributions to the
fund.

503 Squier, Lee Welling. Old age dependency in the United
        States: a complete survey of the pension movement.
        New York, Macmillan, 1912. 361 p.
           A comprehensive survey of all forms of pension
        systems, including pensions provided to workers by
        employers. Finds that only a small proportion of
        industrial establishments have pension plans. Brief-
        ly describes plans of several companies as well as
        plans for government employees. Pensions are given
        because "to keep worn-out, incapacitated men on the
        payroll is an economic waste," but it is inhumane to
        discharge them without financial consideration.

504 Westinghouse Electric and Manufacturing Company. Service
        pensions, regulations. East Pittsburgh, PA, 1915.
        14 p.
           Text of regulations governing the employer-funded
        pension plan of the Westinghouse Electric and Manu-
        facturing Company. The company may repeal the plan
        at any time but may not discontinue payments to indi-
        viduals already on pension. The company may refuse
        to award pensions to any individual employee and em-
        ployees who leave the company completely forfeit el-
        igibility.

505 Wood, L.D. "Industrial pension plans." American feder-
        ationist, 33:7, July 1926, 858-861.
           Analysis of pension plans based on survey of 300
        firms. Outlines age and service requirements and costs
        to employers. Finds that since most pensions may be
        withheld at the discretion of the company, they do
        not provide adequate security and protection to work-
        ers. Claims many companies with new plans are not
        making provisions for the large expenditures that
        will be required as the number of pensioners in-
        creases. Suggests employers should set aside suf-
        ficient funding to guarantee future payments.

UNEMPLOYMENT BENEFITS

506 "Dismissal-compensation plans." Monthly labor review,
        36:3, March 1933, 496-497.
           Synopsis of Princeton University study of dismis-
        sal-compensation plans based on visits to 80 large

companies. Found that dismissal-compensation plans
had spread rapidly due to the Depression and over
half of the companies visited had instituted such
plans in the past two years.

507 "The dismissal wage." <u>Monthly labor review</u>, 30:4, April
      1930, 1-5.
         Examines trend toward payment of dismissal wages
      to employees laid off due to lack of work. Such
      payments give workers time to look for new jobs.
      Lists companies which pay dismissal wages and dis-
      cusses variations in the programs.

508 Draper, Ernest G. and Henry S. Dennison. "Progressive
      employers favor unemployment reserve funds." <u>Amer-
      ican labor legislation review</u>, 21:1, 1931?
         Advocates the introduction of unemployment reserve
      funds in industry. Claims they will make business
      more efficient by encouraging companies to spread
      production over the year to avoid unemployment pay-
      ments. Describes the successful operation of the unem-
      ployment fund of the Dennison Manufacturing Company.

509 Fowler, Charles Burnell. "Private unemployment benefit
      schemes in the United States." Article III. <u>Ameri-
      can federationist</u>, 41:3, March 1934, 253-260.
         Pages 257-260 examine company plans to provide
      unemployment relief for employees. Plans were used to
      suppress trade unions by providing benefits so
      workers wouldn't need unions to demand them. De-
      scribes benefits, payments and emergency provisions
      of the General Electric plan. Criticizes the finan-
      cial instability and narrow coverage of the plan.
      Lists other criticisms of company unemployment plans.

510 Gilson, Mary B. "Existing plans for unemployment in-
      surance in the United States." <u>American federation-
      ist</u>, 35:9, September 1928, 1114-1122.
         Discusses efforts by employers to minimize un-
      employment by stabilizing production and distribution
      and describes plans to provide unemployment benefits
      when layoffs are inevitable. Some companies pro-
      vided financial benefits while others transferred

workers to temporary jobs during the slack season.
Describes eligibility requirements and levels and
duration of benefits.

511 Hawkins, Everett D. "Dismissal compensation in American
        industry." Monthly labor review, 39:5, November 1934,
        1067-1077.
            A survey of dismissal compensation in 212 com-
        panies known to make such payments. Outlines dif-
        fering eligibility requirements and benefit levels.
        Benefits were most often paid by large corporations.
        The growth of dismissal compensation plans acceler-
        ated during the Depression when many companies were
        forced to lay off employees.

512 National Association of Corporation Schools. Bulletin,
        6, October 1919, 449-454.
            (Dismissal wage practices)

513 "Operation of unemployment-benefit plans in the United
        States during 1931 and 1932; Part I. Company and
        joint agreement plans." Monthly labor review, 35:6,
        December 1932, 1225-1251.
            Bureau of Labor Statistics survey of unemployment
        plans of specific companies and industries and an
        evaluation of how the plans are surviving the De-
        pression. Programs given the most attention include
        plans of the Dennison Manufacturing Company, Columbia
        Conserve Company, Dutchess Bleachery, Leeds and
        Northrup, Procter and Gamble, General Electric and
        the garment industry.

514 "Retirement and unemployment plans of Hill Brothers Com-
        pany." Monthly labor review, 37:5, November 1933,
        1096-1097.
            Describes three reserve funds of the Hill Brothers
        shoe manufacturing company. One fund is employee
        funded and covers seasonal slack or shutdown periods.
        The second reserve, jointly funded, pays long-term
        unemployment benefits. The third fund is employer
        funded and pays retirement benefits at the discretion
        of management.

515 "Revision of unemployment-pension plan of the General
         Electric Company." Monthly labor review, 39:6,
         December 1934, 1363-1365.
             Outlines General Electric's unemployment plan,
         which was revised to require all permanent employees
         to participate. Employee contributions are matched
         by the company. In addition to unemployment benefits,
         the plan also provides loans for emergencies and spe-
         cial needs.

516 Schwenning, G.T. "Dismissal compensation: a list of
         references." Monthly labor review, 34:2, February
         1932, 478-492.
             Many of these citations deal with dismissal com-
         pensation plans of specific companies.

517 "Stabilization and unemployment pension plan of the
         General Electric Company." Law and labor, 12:8,
         August 1930, 180-183.
             Text of a plan to stabilize employment and provide
         pensions and unemployment benefits to employees of
         the General Electric Company. A joint company/em-
         ployee fund provides pensions, loans, and compensa-
         tion during temporary layoffs. In addition, the
         company pledges to stabilize employment by building
         inventory and cutting hours in slack times and using
         overtime instead of hiring during peak production.

518 Stewart, Bryce M. Unemployment benefits in the United
         States: the plans and their setting. New York,
         Industrial Relations Counselors, 1930. 727 p.
             Section 3 describes company plans to provide un-
         employment benefits for workers. Presents detailed
         descriptions of plans of several companies, including
         descriptions of funding procedures, eligibility re-
         quirements, duration and amount of benefits, details
         of administration, and experience with each plan.
         Provides extensive statistical data on the plans.

519 "Unemployment-benefit plans in the United States."
         Monthly labor review, 33:6, December 1931, 31-46.
             Synopsis of study of 79 unemployment benefit or
         guaranteed employment plans. Briefly outlines plans
         of specific companies and describes various types of

plans including company plans, joint contribution
funds, and guaranteed employment plans. Lists terms
and requirements of benefit payments. For full text
of study, see Bureau of Labor Statistics Bulletin 544.

520 Unemployment-benefit plans in the United States and unem-
        ployment insurance in foreign countries. U.S. Depart-
        ment of Labor, Bureau of Labor Statistics, Bulletin
        544. Washington, G.P.O., 1931. 385 p.
        A survey of all known unemployment benefit pro-
        grams which either guaranteed employment or provided
        financial benefits to laid off workers. Includes
        detailed reports of company plans. Estimates the
        number of employees covered, costs to companies, and
        amounts of benefits paid. Lists companies with dis-
        continued plans and gives reasons for discontinuance.

521 "Unemployment insurance plan of the National Electrical
        Manufacturers' Association." Monthly labor review,
        35:1, July 1932, 22-26.
        Text of "Nema" plan, an unemployment benefit plan
        adopted by 300 companies that are members of the
        National Electrical Manufacturers' Association. Out-
        lines eligibility requirements, amount of employee
        and company contributions, terms of benefit payments,
        and details of administration. Fund may also be
        used for employee loans.

522 Whitney, Anice L. "Operation of unemployment-benefit
        plans in the United States up to 1934: Part I."
        Monthly labor review, 38:6, June 1934, 1288-1318.
        Overview of company unemployment benefit plans in
        1934. Several plans were established during the
        Depression but many more were discontinued during
        that period. Companies with plans are listed and
        various types of programs are discussed. Plans of
        specific companies and of the garment and lace in-
        dustry are briefly outlined.

MISCELLANEOUS

523 "Annuity and benefit plans for employees of the Standard
        Oil Company." Monthly labor review, 7:1, July 1918,

168-169.
Discusses pensions and sickness, accident, and
death benefits of the Standard Oil Company of New
Jersey. Presents text of a letter to employees ex-
plaining the programs.

524 Bloomfield Daniel (ed.) Problems of labor. New York,
     H.W. Wilson Company, 1920. 436 p.
     A collection of reprinted periodical articles on
     labor issues. Pages 313-331 reprint the following
     articles on industrial insurance:

        1) Schereschewsky, J.W. "Industrial Insurance."
            Public health reports, 29:3, June 5, 1914.
                Discusses industrial sickness insurance
                as "a logical means by which society may
                equitably distribute the costs resulting
                from physical inefficiency." Argues the
                need for greater emphasis on the preven-
                tion of illness and suggests insurance
                should be combined with a health care
                program.

        2) Lapp, John A. "Health Insurance." Proceed-
            ings: National Conference of Social Work,
            June 1919.
                Advocates national industrial insurance
                as a means of distributing the economic
                shock of accident and illness. Suggests
                compulsory membership to keep premium
                costs low.

        3) Kimball, H.W. "Group Insurance." Indus-
            trial management, 57, February 1919, 154-
            156.
                An overview of group industrial insur-
                ance. Outlines terms of policies, el-
                igibility requirements, and premiums.
                Discusses arguments for and against
                group insurance. Trade unions considered
                group insurance a tool to keep workers
                quiet and contented and believed its
                cost should be paid out as wages.

525 Chandler, W.L. "Financing aids for employees." Indus-
     trial management, 54:1, October 1917, 36-43.

Examines ways employers can share their financial
wisdom with workers without being paternalistic.
Discusses one company's establishment of a cooperative
store which bought in bulk resulting in lower prices
to workers. Suggests the necessity of companies providing comfortable housing at a reasonable price when
it is not otherwise available. Describes advantages
of employee benefit associations and thrift clubs
which help employees develop their own benefit programs.

526 "Continuance of group life insurance during layoffs."
       Monthly labor review, 33:3, September 1931, 57.
            Announcement by the General Electric Company that
       it will continue to provide life insurance to em-
       ployees laid off during the Depression.

527 "Encouragement of thrift by employers." Monthly labor
       review, 25:4, October 1927, 78-82.
            A survey of 196 companies with plans to encourage
       employee thrift. Plans include savings and loan
       funds, building funds, profit-sharing plans, stock
       ownership, vacations and Christmas savings funds,
       cooperative buying, discounts on company goods, legal
       aid, and advice on investments and expenditures.
       Outlines types of plans and the number of companies
       providing each. Includes examples of model programs.

528 Frederick, F.G. (ed.) The Swope plan: details, criti-
       cisms, analysis. New York, The Business Bourse, 1931.
       221 p.
            Investigates the employment stabilization plan of
       Gerard Swope, president of the General Electric Com-
       pany. The plan would establish trade associations of
       companies, under the supervision of the Federal Trade
       Commission or some other agency. Workers' compensa-
       tion, life and disability insurance, pensions and
       unemployment benefits are features of the plan. If
       an employee moves from one association company to
       another, these benefits are transferable. The plan
       was criticized as socialistic and monopolistic. Crit-
       icism, praise, and suggestions of businessmen, labor
       leaders, and other critics are presented.

529 "Group insurance." Monthly labor review, 35:1, July 1932,
     53-56.
          Examines trend toward group insurance, which grew
     in popularity even during the Depression. The pro-
     tection of the plans was so important to workers that
     they managed to pay their share even when their wages
     and hours were cut. Enumerates various types of
     group insurance available and outlines eligibility re-
     quirements and benefit limits.

530 "Guaranteed-employment plan in meatpacking." Monthly
     labor review, 40:6, June 1935, 1462-1463.
          Outlines guaranteed wage and employment program of
     the George A. Hormel meatpacking company, instituted
     because a shortage of hogs threatened large layoffs.
     The company paid fixed weekly salaries by loaning
     hours to employees when there was not enough work to
     go around. Employees would repay the hours when
     business was heavy. If business did not pick up by
     1939, workers would not have to pay back the hours.

531 Henderson, Charles Richmond. Industrial insurance in the
     United States. 2nd ed. Chicago, University of Chi-
     cago Press, 1908. 454 p.
          Chapter 7 describes industrial insurance programs
     of several companies. Claims public opinion is rap-
     idly forcing companies to take financial responsibil-
     ity for waste of life caused by industrial accidents
     and illness. Describes insurance, pensions, and joint-
     ly funded relief funds. Chapter 8 surveys insurance
     plans of railroads. Says railroad companies have
     made "the most important contribution to the promo-
     tion of industrial insurance." Appendices F, G, H, K,
     and L provide texts of benefit association agreements
     of the United Traction and Electric Company, Swift
     and Company, the International Harvester Company,
     Scottsdale Iron and Steel Works, and the Studebaker
     Brothers Manufacturing Company.

532 National Civic Federation. Ninth annual meeting. New
     York, 1909. 347 p.
          Proceedings of the 1908 National Civic Federation
     Conference. Part II presents addresses on industrial
     insurance for workers. Compares costs and benefits
     of industrial insurance versus private insurance.

Describes programs of several companies.

533 National Industrial Conference Board. <u>Employee thrift
     and investment plans</u>. New York, 1929. 114 p.
     A survey of savings and investment plans of 319
     companies. Outlines various savings incentive pro-
     grams and investment plans such as investment in the
     company, investment trusts, and employer-supplemented
     funds. Examines benefits of such plans to both em-
     ployers and workers.

534 "Personnel plans of representative banks." <u>Monthly labor
     review</u>, 41:1, July 1935, 56-61.
     Analyzes personnel plans of 30 banks. Welfare pro-
     grams focus on economic security on the theory that
     employees in debt cannot be trusted to handle large
     sums of money. Economic programs include savings
     plans, stock ownership, group insurance, pensions,
     and sick pay. Medical care, paid vacations and lunch
     rooms are other common benefits. Many banks pay for
     vocational college courses and English classes.

535 "Personnel work and cooperation within industrial plants."
     <u>Proceedings of the Academy of Political Science</u>, 9,
     1922, 539-572.
     A collection of addresses on personnel programs in
     industry. Discusses problems implementing successful
     programs and suggests employee cooperation and con-
     fidence is essential to success. Describes economic
     security plans of several companies. The Dennison
     Manufacturing Company stabilized employment by spread-
     ing manufacturing over the year. The American
     Rolling Mills Company instituted a joint employee/em-
     ployer advisory committee to oversee group insurance
     and stock ownership programs. Dutchess Bleachery
     and the Rockland Finishing Company provided unemploy-
     ment benefits and the American Telephone and Tele-
     graph Company introduced stock ownership.

536 Pound, Arthur. <u>The Turning wheel: the story of General
     Motors through twenty years, 1908-1933</u>. Garden City,
     NY, Doubleday, Doran and Company, 1934. 517 p.
     Chapter 28 describes employee/employer cooperative
     programs of the General Motors Corporation. A bonus

plan awarded stock to employees who made special contributions to the company. Under the savings and investment plan, GM contributed from 25¢ to $1 into the
investment fund for every dollar an employee put into
the Savings Fund. Employees received interest on
savings and, upon maturity of the Investment Fund,
employees received their portions of its accrued benefits. Other programs included General Motors Institute for vocational training and cooperative housing
construction and gardening programs.

537 Public Service Corporation of New Jersey. Welfare Com-
         mittee. Annual reports, 1st-5th. 1911-1915.
         Each edition summarizes the year's welfare work
      of the Public Service Corporation of New Jersey.
      Benefits include pensions and disability, illness,
      and death payments. Eligibility requirements and
      costs of programs to the company are discussed.

538 "Pullman employees." U.S. Commission on Industrial Rela-
         tions. Report and Testimony, v. 10, 9545-9695. 64th
         Congress, 1st Session, Document 415. (Senate Docu-
         ment, 28:6938) 1915.
         Testimony before the U.S. Commission on Industrial
      Relations on labor conditions for Pullman employees.
      Includes descriptions of sick pay and death benefit
      programs. Describes benefit levels and eligibility
      requirements of the pension plans. Considers the ade-
      quacy of sleeping quarters and other facilities pro-
      vided for traveling porters and conductors.

539 Ripley, Charles M. Life in a large manufacturing plant.
         Schenectady, NY, General Electric Company, Publica-
         tions Bureau, 1919. (Reprinted from General Electric
         review for 1917 and 1918) 170 p.
         Sketches pension, insurance, and other benefits
      available to General Electric Company employees.
      Some benefits are managed by the Mutual Benefit Asso-
      ciation, run and funded by employees but partially
      subsidized by the company. Other benefits include
      social and recreational programs, medical care, low
      cost restaurants, educational programs, newspapers,
      and a library.

540 Weinstein, James. The Corporate ideal in the liberal
        state, 1900-1918. Boston, Beacon Press, 1968. 263 p.
        Chapters 1 and 2 include a sketch of welfare poli-
     cies of the National Civic Federation, an association
     comprised primarily of businessmen with some labor
     representatives. Describes the role of the Federation
     in encouraging such welfare programs as profit-sharing,
     pensions, sick and accident insurance, and stock pur-
     chase plans. Chapter 2 briefly outlines welfare poli-
     cies of the International Harvester Company and United
     States Steel Corporation, both NCF members and leaders
     in industrial welfare.

541 Westinghouse Electric and Manufacturing Company. Relief
        Department regulations. East Pittsburgh, PA, 1915.
        48 p.
        Describes the sickness, accident, and death fund of
     the Westinghouse Electric and Manufacturing Company.
     The plan is employee funded but the company pays in-
     terest and administrative costs. Eligibility require-
     ments, dues, and benefit levels are outlined.

542 Whitney, Anice L. "Establishment disability funds, pen-
        sion funds, and group insurance for employees."
        Monthly labor review, 6:2, February 1918, 192-204.
        Survey of pension, group insurance, and sickness,
     injury and death benefits in 431 companies. Lists
     number of companies providing each benefit. Discusses
     employee dues, employer contributions, variations in
     benefit levels, and eligibility requirements.

HEALTH

543 DeHart, Sanford. "The industrial dentist." Industrial
        management, 73:2, February 1927, 90-92.
        An overview of the increasingly popular benefit of
     industrial dentists. Surveys companies that offer
     free dental service and others that operate on a self-
     paying basis. Reports results of a study that shows
     employees in companies with dental service are health-
     ier overall than employees without such service. In-
     dustrial dentists teach employees the importance of
     dental hygiene and repair defective teeth that could
     have caused serious physical and mental disorders.

544 "Dental work in factories a success." Industrial rela-
      tions, 11:11, July 8, 1922.

545 "Discussion of personnel problems at International Mental
      Hygiene Congress." Monthly labor review, 30:6, June
      1930, 67-70.
          A description of R.H. Macy Company's experiment in
      mental hygiene. The company provided psychiatric
      treatment for employees with poor work records and
      modified working conditions to improve physical and
      mental health. The psychiatric program was also used
      as a means of selecting executives and preventing
      accidents in company cars.

546 "Does industrial medicine pay?" Monthly labor review,
      9:4, October 1919, 235-237.
          Synopsis of article by Dr. Harry E. Mock in the
      Journal of industrial hygiene. Dr. Mock advocates
      giving pre-employment physicals to prevent loss both
      to the company and employees. Companies avoid hiring
      unproductive employees and wasting training costs and
      employees are not given jobs beyond their physical
      capabilities. Prevents spread of contagious diseases
      to other employees.

547 Emmons, Arthur B. Health control in mercantile life:
      a problem of conserving human energy. New York,
      Harper and Brothers, 1926. 234 p.
          A study of health conditions in 25 east coast
      retail stores. Includes discussion of such welfare
      programs as medical care, sanitary and comfortable
      working conditions, lunch rooms, health education,
      and sickness and disability benefits. Concludes
      that fitness of workers is essential to effective
      operation of business since accident and illness cost
      time and money. Examines the effect of health-related
      welfare programs on reducing absenteeism and suggests
      ways merchants can preserve the health of their em-
      ployees.

548 Falk, I.S., Don M. Griswold, and Hazel I. Spicer. A Com-
      munity medical service organized under industrial
      auspices in Roanoke Rapids (North Carolina). Chica-
      go, University of Chicago Press, 1932. (Publica-

tions of the Committee on the Costs of Medical Care:
No. 20) 105 p.
   Describes a health care program provided in Roanoke
Rapids, North Carolina by Roanoke Mills Company, Rose-
mary Manufacturing Company, Patterson Mills Company,
Halifax Paper Company, and Virginia Electric and Power
Company. Surveys 526 families to determine if medi-
cal needs are adequately met by the program. Con-
cludes that general quality of health care is good
but points out some inadequacies.

549 Foley, Edna L. "The visiting nurse in industry." The
     Modern hospital, 7:2, August 1916, 125-127.
        Outlines duties and responsibilities of visiting
     nurses. As a link between management and workers,
     nurses need to be well-trained with experience in
     social work. By promoting a healthy and productive
     work force, the nurse benefits both the company and
     its workers.

550 Frankel, Lee K. "Systematic health service for employ-
     ees." The Modern hospital, 7:2, August 1916, 87-90.
        Describes health and medical benefits for employ-
     ees of the Metropolitan Life Insurance Company. Bene-
     fits include annual physical examinations, a dispen-
     sary, optical and dental services, and tuberculosis
     care.

551 Geier, Otto P. "Health of the working force." Industrial
     management, 54: 1, October 1917, 13-19.
        Advocates the need for medical care in industry
     to prevent illnesses which result in loss of wages
     to workers and loss of manpower to companies. Argues
     that providing medical care should be considered an
     investment since healthy workers are more willing and
     able to work. Considers health programs more impor-
     tant than other forms of welfare since they care for
     more basic needs. Stresses preventive medicine,
     including physical exams and sanitary control in the
     plant, as most effective in insuring a continuously
     productive work force.

552 Goldwater, S.S. "The conservation of the health of in-
     dustrial workers." The Modern hospital, 7:2, August

1916, 124-125.
An editorial advocating the employer's responsibility to care for the health of employees. Special emphasis is placed on controlling occupational health hazards. Several reasons for supporting industrial welfare are suggested, including making the workers healthier and more productive, conserving the nation's resources, and simple human compassion.

553 Hoskins, Jean. "Service work of the Eastern Manufacturing Company." Proceedings of the Employment Managers' Conference. U.S. Department of Labor, Bureau of Labor Statistics, Bulletin 227. Washington, G.P.O., 1917. 153-157 p.
Describes development of welfare practices in the Eastern Manufacturing Company, a pulp and paper mill in Bangor, Maine. Benefits include a dispensary and medical services, a library, recreational facilities, and a sanitation and hygiene program.

554 "Industrial health service in small plants." Monthly labor review, 30:3, March 1930, 65.
Sketches program of the Philadelphia Health Council and Tuberculosis Committee to provide health supervision to small firms. This cooperative program allows small companies to provide medical coverage for employees at lower rates than they would pay independently.

555 "Industrial medical service in a group of Chicago plants." Monthly labor review, 29:6, December 1929, 52-54.
Survey of the nature and scope of medical services in Chicago firms. Examines administration of programs and concludes that the extent of services depends on the size of the company. Recommends employing physicians part-time so they can develop outside medical interests and thus provide better care to workers.

556 Jones, Mark M. "Development of the health of Thomas A. Edison Interests." Industrial management, 55:6, June 1918, 491-493.

Describes the work of the Health Department of
Thomas A. Edison Interests, which deals with occupational disease, injury, illness, sanitation, and
health education, and includes two fully-equipped
hospitals. The purpose of the Health Department is
to "maintain personnel as efficient producing units
capable of such effort as their primary qualifica-
tions may warrant." The programs also include sickness and injury benefits in some cases.

557 Lambert, Alexander. "Provision for medical care under
       health insurance." The Modern hospital, 7:2, August
       1916, 95-97.
          Presents the value of health insurance in industry.
       Enumerates available health insurance benefits and
       discusses details of administering various plans.

558 "Medical and hospital service for industrial employees."
       Monthly labor review, 24:1, January 1927, 7-19.
          Survey of medical benefits provided by about 450
       companies. Lists number of companies providing
       various types of services and facilities and esti-
       mates costs of various programs. Discusses advance-
       ments in medical care and describes special services
       such as dental care, visiting nurses, and tuberculosis
       treatment.

559 "Medical care for 15,000 workers and their families."
       Monthly labor review, 31:6, December 1930, 89-91.
          Outlines extensive medical provisions of the
       Endicott-Johnson Corporation. The company provides
       free medical care, sick benefits, pensions, and wid-
       ows' allowances. Facilities include 3 medical cen-
       ters, traveling clinics, convalescent homes, and tuber-
       culosis cottages.

560 Metropolitan Life Insurance Company. Welfare work for
       policy holders (and other related pamphlets) New
       York, 1915-1919.
          A collection of pamphlets which outline efforts
       of the Metropolitan Life Insurance Company to help
       establish welfare programs in companies that sub-
       scribe to Metropolitan insurance policies. The pam-
       phlets examine the effects of a number of welfare

programs in improving mortality and disability rates.
The Industrial Health series of pamphlets includes
volumes on physical exams, dental care, working conditions, and first aid. Titles of other pamphlets
are: "Twenty-five Years of Life Conservation" (1935);
"Educating for a Longer Life" (1927 and 1928); and
"Men, Women and Morale" (1919). (These pamphlets are
available in the U.S. Department of Labor Library)

561 "Minimum standard for medical service in industry."
        Monthly labor review, 41:3, September 1935, 637-640.
        Outlines recommendations by the American College
     of Surgeons for the provision of adequate medical
     services in industry. Minimum standards include com-
     petent staff and adequate facilities. Companies that
     meet standards are placed on a list of approved fa-
     cilities. Recommendations resulted from a survey
     that found nearly all of 925 companies had inadequate
     programs.

562 National Industrial Conference Board. Cost of health
        service in industry. Research Report #37. New York,
        1921. 33 p.
        Presents statistics on the costs of industrial
     medical departments. A survey of 207 companies shows
     the average cost is $4.43 per employee per year,
     ranging from $1.84 in the tobacco industry to $24.40
     in mining. Lists average costs by industry and de-
     scribes variations in benefits provided.

563 National Industrial Conference Board. Health services in
        industry. Research Report #34. New York, 1921.
        61 p.
        An overview of company medical programs. Empha-
     sizes preventive medicine and accident avoidance.
     Describes the functions and role of the industrial
     physical. Presents statistics on industrial medical
     care in New England and surveys various types of
     equipment, facilities, and procedures. Discusses the
     value of physical exams and medical records.

564 National Industrial Conference Board. Medical supervi-
        sion and service in industry. New York, 1931.
        125 p.

Survey of medical benefits of 443 companies. The
purpose of medical programs was to protect the health
of employees so they would be happier and more productive. Functions of medical departments, costs to employers, staff and equipment, and the treatment and
prevention of illnesses and accidents are discussed.

565 Price, George M. "Cloak, suit, skirt, dress, and waist
     industries." The Modern hospital, 7:2, August 1916,
     111-114.
          Summarizes work of the New York Joint Board of
     Sanitation Control, which polices sanitary, health,
     and safety standards in the garment industry. The
     Board provides physical examinations to workers and
     promotes industrial health programs, especially for
     the care of tuberculosis. It also educates workers
     on safety and health regulations and practices.

566 Schwartz, Jerome L. "Early history of prepaid medical
     care plans." Bulletin of the history of medicine,
     39:5, September-October 1965, 450-475.
          A survey of pre-1929 medical plans, including
     plans of various companies and industries. Examines
     "contract practices," under which physicians cared
     for all employees of a company for a fixed rate. The
     American Medical Association condemned contract prac-
     tices, claiming they resulted in inferior medical
     care and lower medical standards. The development of
     company-sponsored group insurance is also outlined.

567 Scovill Manufacturing Company. Fifth annual report of
     the industrial hospital. Waterbury, CT, 1919. 28 p.
          Describes operations of a hospital for employees
     of the Scovill Manufacturing Company. The hospital
     was installed to provide for the physical and mental
     welfare of workers. The hospital staff and facili-
     ties are described.

568 "Sick leave with pay for factory workers." Monthly labor
     review, 24:4, April 1927, 33-34.
          A Bureau of Labor Statistics study of company sick
     leave policies. Only 15 companies had sick leave
     plans but several other companies occasionally paid
     benefits and decided each case individually. Most

companies paid no benefits although their employees
sometimes received benefits through mutual benefit
associations or group insurance. Study describes
plans of the few companies that had them.

569 Sitzer, L. Grace Powell. "Wrigley doesn't apologize for
       welfare work." Factory and industrial management,
       77:3, March 1929, 501-502.
         Sketches welfare efforts of the William Wrigley
       Jr. gum company designed to promote goodwill and
       lower turnover. Emphasizes employee health by pro-
       viding low-cost meals, an emergency hospital, athlet-
       ics, showers and baths, and free shampoos on company
       time. Company sponsors home economics classes and
       helps foreign employees obtain citizenship.

570 Syndenstricker, Edgar. "Existing agencies for health
       insurance in the United States." Proceedings of the
       Conference on Social Insurance. U.S. Department of
       Labor, Bureau of Labor Statistics, Bulletin 212.
       Washington, G.P.O., 1917. 430-475 p.
         Survey of health insurance in the United States,
       including discussion of employer supported sick-
       benefit funds. Based on Bureau of Labor Statistics
       studies, survey estimates the number of companies with
       funds and the number of employees covered. Discusses
       special medical services provided by some funds.

571 U.S. Council on National Defense. Advisory Commission.
       Welfare work series. Nos. 1-4. Washington, G.P.O.,
       1918.
         A series of 4 pamphlets advocating welfare in
       industry. The first pamphlet deals with industrial
       fatigue and welfare programs that can be used to
       prevent it. The second pamphlet reports rules for
       clean and healthy working conditions adopted by muni-
       tions manufacturers. Rules cover sanitation, venti-
       lation, and medical supervision. Special attention
       is paid to health care when poisonous materials are
       used in production. The third pamphlet deals with
       standards of lighting in factories and mills and the
       fourth pamphlet discusses heating and ventilation.

572 Walsh, William H. "Welfare and efficiency achieved at
         the same time." The Modern hospital, 7:2, August
         1916, 115-118.
            The welfare efforts of the United Shoe Machinery
         Company are based on the philosophy that good health
         is essential to good work. The company oversees ex-
         tensive sanitation and cleanliness practices in the
         factory. It also provides an emergency hospital and
         a variety of recreational facilities.

573 "Welfare work - stories from the various industries."
         The Modern hospital, 7:2, August 1916, 133-166.
            Focusing on health and medical benefits, article
         describes the industrial welfare programs of 27
         American companies. Primary attention is given to
         efforts in the areas of medical services, sanitation
         and hygiene, and sickness, accident, and death bene-
         fits. Non-health related programs are also outlined
         for several of the companies.

574 Whitney Anice L. Health and recreation activities in
         industrial establishments, 1926. U.S. Department of
         Labor, Bureau of Labor Statistics, Bulletin 458.
         Washington, G.P.O., 1928. 94 p.
            A survey of health and recreation benefits of 430
         companies. Results of the survey are compared to a
         similar study conducted 10 years previously. Presents
         statistics on improvements in hospital and medical
         services and surveys various types of programs. Dis-
         cusses the incidence and benefits of paid sick leave
         and vacations, disability funds, insurance, education,
         and savings plans. Estimates the number of companies
         with lunch room service, describes variations in
         services provided, and discusses costs to companies
         and workers. Surveys the incidence of such benefits
         as recreation rooms and club houses, athletic facili-
         ties, and cultural programs.

575 Whitney, Anice L. "Medical, hospital, and surgical treat-
         ment for employees." Monthly labor review, 5:3, Sep-
         tember 1917, 59-67.
            Survey of 431 companies, 375 of which had medical
         programs. Describes a variety of programs, ranging
         from first aid to hospitals with full medical staffs,
         and estimates the number of companies with each type

of program. Employer medical programs increased because of the safety movement.

PROFIT-SHARING

576 "Application of the Golden Rule in business." Monthly
       labor review, 11:6, December 1920, 102-103.
          Describes a retail tailoring company which operated
       under the Golden Rule. A profit-sharing plan was re-
       jected by workers the first time it was proposed
       because workers were content to let management deter-
       mine wages. The plan was later accepted when manage-
       ment reintroduced it. Wages, productivity, and pro-
       fits were high, even when the rest of the industry
       was in a slump.

577 Blackmar, F.W. "Two examples of successful profit-shar-
       ing." Forum, 19, March 1895, 57-67.
          Describes the successful profit-sharing plans of
       Procter and Gamble and the N.O. Nelson Manufacturing
       Company. Procter and Gamble paid employees the same
       rate of dividend on wages as was paid in common stock.
       The plan included pensions funded jointly by the com-
       pany and profit-sharing dividends. N.O. Nelson
       gave employees 35 to 40 percent of profits, payable
       in company stock. Stock could be cashed in at par
       when workers left the company.

578 Bloomfield, Daniel (ed.) Problems of labor. New York,
       H.W. Wilson Company, 1920. 436 p.
          A collection of reprinted periodical articles on
       labor issues. Pages 111-134 reprint the following
       articles on profit-sharing:

              1) Perkins, George W. "Profit-sharing." Cur-
                  rent affairs, 10:3-5, September 22, 1919,
                  23-24.
                     The chairman of the National Civic Feder-
                  ation profit-sharing committee suggests
                  profit-sharing should be introduced to
                  make employees partners. Outlines an ideal
                  profit-sharing plan and discusses reasons
                  some plans fail.

2) Dennison, Henry S. "Why I believe in profit-
   sharing." Factory, 20:424, March 1918.
        Advocates profit-sharing as a means of
        equitably distributing surplus among fac-
        tors of production. Profit-sharing can
        be used to control absenteeism.

3) Eliot, Charles W. "Road toward industrial
   peace." New York Times, September 21, 1919.
        Examines profit-sharing as a means of
        avoiding labor trouble and developing a
        genuine partnership between labor and
        capital. Discusses problems of insti-
        tuting and maintaining profit-sharing.

4) "The profit-sharing fallacy." International
   steam engineer.
        Presents organized labor's view that pro-
        fit-sharing is a tool to force workers
        to speed-up production. This would "low-
        er the status of workers and confirm their
        servitude." Profit-sharing would destroy
        unionism because workers would become
        rivals or workers in other companies.

579 Burritt, Arthur W. et al. Profit-sharing: its principles
        and practice. New York, Harper and Brothers, 1918.
        328 p.
            A comprehensive study of profit-sharing. Traces
        the history of profit-sharing and describes various
        types of plans. Profit-sharing was used to promote
        efficiency, to prevent waste, to promote stability
        of labor, to promote industrial peace, and to foster
        a spirit of cooperation. Suggests it should not be
        used as an excuse to depress wages and benefits must
        be substantial enough to be taken seriously. Dis-
        cusses problems of requiring employee to share losses
        as well as profits and considers the dangers of stock
        ownership as a form of profit-sharing. Examines or-
        ganized labor's views of profit-sharing.

580 Carnegie, Andrew. "Capital and labour harmony: partner-
        ship and profit-sharing plans." Cassier's magazine,
        34:3, July 1903.

581 Cleveland Chamber of Commerce. Committee on Industrial
     Welfare. <u>Industrial profit-sharing and welfare work</u>.
     Cleveland, 1916. 85 p.
         Describes welfare programs of a variety of com-
     panies. Lists each program by company and topic and
     provides a brief synopsis of each program. Emphasizes
     profit-sharing and describes profit-sharing plans of
     27 companies. Other welfare programs discussed are
     athletics, baths and showers, bonuses, cafeterias and
     lunches, club houses, medical care, insurance, librar-
     ies, pensions, savings and loan programs, sickness
     and disability benefits and stock purchase plans.

582 Emmet, Boris. <u>Profit-sharing in the United States</u>. De-
     partment of Labor, Bureau of Labor Statistics, Bulle-
     tin 208. Washington, G.P.O., 1917. 188 p.
         Examines all known profit-sharing plans in the
     United States in 1916. Includes a list of firms with
     profit-sharing plans. Analyzes the proportion of
     profits shared with employees, methods of computing
     benefits, and costs to companies. Outlines terms
     of typical plans and compares full profit-sharing
     plans to plans which distribute profits unequally
     among various classes of employees. Describes bonus
     and stock ownership plans and explains how they dif-
     fer from profit-sharing. Concludes that profit-shar-
     ing and related plans have helped stabilize the work
     force and improve labor relations but reports mixed
     results in their success in increasing efficiency.

583 "Employees' participation and investment plan of Kansas
     City Public Service Company." <u>Monthly labor review</u>,
     32:5, May 1931, 37-38.
         Outlines profit-sharing plan of Kansas City Public
     Service Company. Employees divide 25 percent of the
     company's net income and are paid in the form of
     securities in the company.

584 Fitch, John A. "For value received: a discussion of in-
     dustrial pensions." <u>Survey</u>, 40, May 25, 1918, 221-224.
         Describes the savings and profit-sharing fund of
     Sears, Roebuck and Company. Employees receive a
     share of profits in proportion to their savings. This
     combination of savings and profit-sharing is intended

to be used as a pension when an employee retires.
Low turnover is encouraged since an employee's share
of profits cannot be withdrawn until ten years service. However, most pension plans require at least
twenty years service so the Sears plan is much less
restricting on workers' freedom to leave the company.

585 Gilman, Nicholas Paine. A Dividend to labor: a study
     of employers' welfare institutions. Boston, Houghton,
     Mifflin and Company, 1899. 400 p.
         Chapters 9 and 10 outline profit-sharing plans,
     focusing on plans of Bourne Cotton Mills, Procter and
     Gamble Company, and Nelson Manufacturing Company.
     Pages 377-378 of Appendix II list American companies
     with profit-sharing plans. Appendix III lists sever-
     al companies that abandoned profit-sharing and dis-
     cusses reasons for abandonment.

586 Gilman, Nicholas Paine. "Model industries: a dividend
     on wages." In John Peters, Labor and capital. New
     York, G.P. Putnam's Sons, 1902. 330-343 p.
         Suggests employers should share profits either
     through direct profit-sharing or industrial better-
     ment in order to make the interests of employees and
     employers mutual. Gives examples from several com-
     panies, including the American firms, U.S. Steel Cor-
     poration and Procter and Gamble.

587 Gilman, Nicholas Paine. Profit-sharing between employer
     and employee: a study of the evolution of the wage
     system. Boston, Houghton, Mifflin and Company, 1889.
     460 p.
         A comprehensive survey of worldwide profit-sharing
     plans. Purposes of plans were to give employees a
     fair share of a company's prosperity by giving them
     an interest in the business. Discusses profit-shar-
     ing in agriculture, fishing, and mining. Chapter 7
     discusses profit-sharing in the United States. De-
     scribes various types of programs and benefits offered
     with examples from specific companies. Presents sta-
     tistical data on the success of plans. Chapter 10
     presents a theoretical analysis of the effect of pro-
     fit-sharing on the relationship among labor, manage-
     ment, and capital and discusses benefits of profit-
     sharing plans.

588 Howerth, I.W. "Profit-sharing at Ivorydale." American
     journal of sociology, 2:1, July 1896, 43-57.
          Describes welfare programs of the Procter and Gam-
     ble Company, focusing on its profit-sharing plan.
     Profit-sharing dividends were adjusted according to
     individual effort to avoid rewarding indifferent and
     industrious workers equally. Direct profit-sharing
     was replaced by a stock ownership plan when the com-
     pany was incorporated. Other welfare benefits are
     also described, including pensions, pleasant working
     conditions, community improvement, medical care, a
     lunch room, and a library.

589 James, Gorton et al. Profit-sharing and stock ownership
     for employees. New York, Harper and Brothers, 1926.
     394 p.
          Examines profit-sharing and stock ownership pro-
     grams in industry. Discusses purposes of plans and
     considers the idea that employees have a right to the
     fruits of their labor. Describes typical plans and
     programs of specific companies. Discusses dangers of
     selling stock to employees who do not understand the
     risks. Suggests profit-sharing should be combined
     with some form of management sharing. Organized
     labor attacked profit-sharing and stock ownership,
     claiming they were devices designed to weaken unions
     and are used to make employees willing to work under
     conditions they would not otherwise tolerate.

590 Kulby, Harold E. Profit-sharing at Baker Manufacturing
     Company, Evansville, Wisconsin, 1899-1958. (Wiscon-
     sin Commerce Reports, v. 5, August 1958) Madison,
     University of Wisconsin, 1958.

591 Laub, D. Kenneth. Ford Motor Company's work with profit
     sharing. Detroit Evening News reprint. November 24,
     1914. 27 p. (or see original newspaper article for
     that date)
          Analyzes the effects of the Ford Motor Company
     profit-sharing plan, which pays the largest share of
     profits to the lowest wage earners. Before profit-
     sharing could be installed, the company had to spon-
     sor English classes so employees would understand the
     program. The combination of profit-sharing and edu-
     cation led to increased savings, more employees be-

coming citizens, improved home conditions, an increase
in home ownership, increased worker productivity, and
fewer absences.

592 McNutt, George L. "Real profit sharing and the results."
     Independent, 55:2832, March 12, 1903, 619-622.
          Describes profit-sharing at A.S. Baker and Company
     as "a genuine equalizing of capital and labor."
     Claims most profit-sharing plans are "trinkets," not
     enough to really benefit workers. Workers at A.S.
     Baker received substantial dividends in the belief
     that their energies and skills were just as important
     as investors' dollars.

593 Miller, Frank B. and Mary Ann Coghill. The Historical
     sources of personnel work... Ithaca, Cornell Univer-
     sity, New York State School of Industrial and Labor
     Relations, 1961. 110 p.
          Chapter 10 is an annotated bibliography of works
     on profit-sharing. Includes brief analysis of the
     profit-sharing movement and its motivational effect
     on workers.

594 National Civic Federation. Profit-sharing by American
     employers. New York, Profit Sharing Department,
     (1916) 261 p.
          An overview of profit-sharing. Traces early devel-
     opment and describes plans of several companies. Dis-
     cusses percent of profits employees receive and methods
     of payment. Plans of the A.W. Burritt Company, Ford
     Motor Company, and the Dennison Manufacturing Company
     are outlined in detail. Organized labor opposed pro-
     fit-sharing because it was used as an excuse to keep
     wages low and it made workers obliged to employers
     so they were afraid to demand wage increases. They
     preferred a dependable fixed wage rather than a share
     of fluctuating profits.

595 National Industrial Conference Board. Practical experi-
     ence with profit-sharing in industrial establish-
     ments. Research Report #29. Boston, 1920. 86 p.
          A survey of profit-sharing and related programs,
     introduced "to secure the cooperation and loyalty of
     the working force," to reduce turnover, to avoid

labor problems, to promote thrift, and "to secure
social justice for the workers." Provides opinions
of profit-sharing by executives of specific companies
and examines reasons some companies abandoned profit-
sharing. Surveys eligibility requirements, amounts
of profits shared, and various methods of dividing
profits between capital and labor. Appendices list
companies with profit-sharing, wage bonuses, savings
sharing, and stock subscription plans.

596 National Industrial Conference Board. Profit-sharing.
     New York, 1934. 29 p.
        A survey of 231 profit-sharing plans. Examines
     ways of determining the proportion of profits to be
     shared. Management's purposes for installing profit-
     sharing are to protect employees' financial stability,
     to make wages flexible with business conditions, and
     to encourage improved work performance. Survey re-
     ports mixed success in improving work performance.
     The discontinuance of some plans during the Depres-
     sion is discussed.

597 Nelson, N.O. "The associated workers idea." In John
     Peters, Labor and capital. New York, G.P. Putnam's
     Sons, 1902. 345-352 p.
        Suggests so few employers introduce profit-sharing
     because the tendency of human nature is to be tyran-
     nical rather than benevolent. Employers need to be
     convinced that profit-sharing is not charity or throw-
     ing money away. The object of profit-sharing "should
     be to incorporate the employees into the responsible
     and coworking body." Workers should eventually be-
     come owners. Describes profit-sharing and other wel-
     fare at the N.O. Nelson Manufacturing Company.

598 Nelson, N.O. Cooperation and profit-sharing." In Samuel
     M. Jones, The New right: a plea for fair play
     through a more just social order. New York, Eastern
     Book Concern, 1899. 479 p.
        Advocates cooperation between workers and manage-
     ment in the belief that "competition is war." Sug-
     gests profit-sharing as a means of sharing prosperity
     with workers and describes profit-sharing at the N.O.
     Nelson Manufacturing Company. Describes the model
     company village of LeClaire, Illinois. Describes

businesses operated on a cooperative basis. Advocates the development of cooperative building associations so workers can own their own homes and cooperative stores to provide low cost goods to all
workers.

599 Nelson, N.O. "LeClaire, an existing city of the future."
     Independent, 77, January 19, 1914, 100.
        Describes profit-sharing and other welfare pro-
     grams of the N.O. Nelson Manufacturing Company. The
     company shared profits in the form of stock with both
     its employees and customers in the belief that busi-
     ness should be a "social trust" rather than privately
     owned. Other welfare included a model town with
     housing, a bowling alley, a club house, a recreation
     hall, and a cooperative store. Accident, sickness,
     and old age benefits were also provided.

600 Parsons, George Kingdon. "A fair basis of profit-shar-
     ing." Industrial management, 55:2, February 1918,
     140-144.
        A philosophical discussion of employee profit-
     sharing plans. Profit-sharing should be instituted
     to prevent dissatisfaction and high turnover among
     employees who see the company making large profits
     as a result of their labor. Employers should avoid
     paternalism by making employees feel profit-sharing
     is a proper reward for labor's contribution to the
     company's profits. A financial analysis is provided
     on how profits should be divided between capital and
     labor.

601 Perkins, George W. Profit-sharing: the workers' fair
     share. New York, National Civic Federation, 1919.
     39 p.
        An address before the National Civic Federation on
     workers' rights to share the success of business.
     Attacks welfare on the grounds that employees do not
     want charity but says profit-sharing is a partner-
     ship, not welfare. Outlines "correct" profit-shar-
     ing plan, including methods of dividing profits be-
     tween capital and labor and proper distribution of
     profits among employees.

602 Pomeroy, Eltweed. "Model industries: democracy versus
        profit and prosperity sharing." In John Peters,
        Labor and capital. New York, G.P. Putnam's Sons,
        1902. 353-357 p.
            Claims profit-sharing is helpful in promoting good-
        will with workers but is nothing more unless it grows
        into real cooperation. It is not democratic because
        workers have no voice in how much of profits they
        receive. It is better to have workers achieve things
        for themselves. Suggests employees are more appre-
        ciative of such benefits as Christmas and Thanks-
        giving turkeys and picnics. The real value of any
        benefits "depends on the amount of democracy diffused
        into the business."

603 "Profit-sharing in practice." Review of reviews, 34,
        December 1906, 728-730.
            Examines welfare programs of the N.O. Nelson Man-
        ufacturing Company, provided "to make life worth
        living" for both the rich and the poor. A profit-
        sharing/stock ownership program was introduced to
        bring the rich and the poor closer together. The
        company also built a model town with low cost housing,
        a school, and a library.

604 "Profit-sharing in the Pillsbury Mills." Review of re-
        views, 4:20, September 1891, 172-174.
            Details the profit-sharing plan of the Pillsbury
        flour mills in Minneapolis. To "more equitably di-
        vide the profits between capital and labor," employ-
        ees with at least two years service divide excess
        profits in proportion to their wages.

605 "Profit-sharing in the United States." Monthly review
        of the Bureau of Labor Statistics (Monthly labor re-
        view) 2:6, June 1916, 46-48.
            Summarizes a National Civic Federation report on
        profit-sharing. Report includes descriptions of spe-
        cific programs and opinions of emloyers and organized
        labor. Describes various types of plans and traces
        the history of the profit-sharing movement.

606 Rumely, Edward A. "Mr. Ford's plan to share profits."

World's work, 27:6, April 1914, 664-669.
Describes revolutionary profit-sharing plan of the Ford Motor Company. By distributing excess profits in the form of higher wages, Ford hoped to attract and maintain scarce labor supplies. A corps of 75 investigators visited homes to make sure employees were not squandering their high wages on ruinous living.

607 "Sharing profits with employees." Monthly labor review, 30:3, March 1930, 85.
Synopsis of survey of 72 firms with profit-sharing plans. Survey examines details of individual plans such as eligibility requirements, amounts of payments, and methods of disbursement.

608 Thompson, Laura A. "Profit-sharing and labor copartnership: a list of recent references." Monthly labor review, 16:4, April 1923, 167-179.
Eighty-five citations to U.S. plans, four of which have been discontinued.

609 Tipper, Harry. Human factors in industry. New York, Ronald Press, 1922. 280 p.
Chapter 19 describes profit-sharing plans and suggests general criteria for their success. Profit-sharing is designed to give workers a stake in the success of the business and motivate them to perform better. Workers should be given regular financial statements and an explanation of how the profit-sharing is computed. Frequent distribution of profits sustains motivation. If successful, profit-sharing should reduce turnover and improve work performance.

610 Wright, Carroll Davidson. "Profit-sharing." Part II of 17th annual report of the Massachusetts Bureau of Statistics of Labor. Boston, Potter Printing Company, 1886. 155-235 p.
Examines profit-sharing instead of wages in Massachusetts fisheries, profit-sharing in addition to wages nationwide, and profit-sharing through stock ownership in Massachusetts. In fishing, crews received half the value of the catch. Lists high, low, and average pay for several vessels. Surveys profit-

sharing nationwide and describes programs of several
companies. Pages 196-202 list Massachusetts companies with profit-sharing through stock ownership.
Programs of several companies are outlined.

RECREATION

611 Becker, O.M. "The square deal in works management."
     Engineering magazine, 31:1, April 1906, 38-59.
       Advocates long lunch periods with recreation to
help workers recuperate their productive capacities.
Suggests employers should provide athletic and recreational facilities and rooms for reading and re-
laxation. Companies should provide medical services,
especially on-the-job emergency care. The factory
should be as attractive and clean as possible to make
workers more content and productive.

612 Clark, W. Irving. "The place of athletics in the indus-
     trial scheme." Industrial management, 71:6, June
     1926.

613 Gilson, Mary Barnett. "Recreation of the working force."
     Industrial management, 54:1, October 1917, 52-58.
       Defends recreation in industry as a means of mak-
ing workers more productive and thereby allowing
management to shorten their hours. Recreation gives
workers a sense of belonging and cohesion which in-
creases loyalty to the company. It improves coordi-
nation of mind and hand, encourages ambition, and pro-
motes democracy since all levels of employees play.
Merits of such recreational activities as athletics,
parties, picnics, choral singing and dancing, and
reading are discussed.

614 "Indoor recreation for industrial employees." Monthly
     labor review, 25:3, September 1927, 1-14.
       A survey of indoor recreation programs of 430 com-
panies. Describes various types of facilities and
programs and estimates the number of companies providing them. Programs include sports, entertainment,
social events and cultural activities. Facilities
include recreation rooms, club houses, and gymnasiums.

Examples of model programs are provided.

615 Lord, C.B. "Athletics for the working force." *Industrial management*, 54:1, October 1917, 44-49.
　　　Advocates the establishment of industrial athletic programs on the theory that athletes are better, healthier, stronger workers. Describes the St. Louis plan, which established a system of organized teams and leagues. Industrial teams, such as the Wagner Electric Manufacturing Company, participated in such sports as baseball, soccer, and basketball.

616 "Outdoor recreation for industrial employees." *Monthly labor review*, 24:5, May 1927, 1-16.
　　　A Bureau of Labor Statistics study of outdoor recreation in 430 companies. Discusses frequency and degree of company sponsorship of a variety of sports as well as activities such as picnics, camps, and country clubs. Industrial recreation programs are becoming more difficult to organize since many workers have moved away from the immediate vicinity of the plant. Many companies support outdoor recreation by contributing to municipal programs.

617 "Report on outdoor recreation for industrial workers." *Monthly labor review*, 23:3, September 1926, 65-66.
　　　Report of the National Conference on Outdoor Recreation, suggesting that outdoor recreation should be provided for industrial workers to protect their health and stamina. Outlines standards for establishing these programs.

618 Whitney, Anice L. "Rest and recreation rooms and rest periods for employees." *Monthly labor review*, 5:4, October 1917, 151-156.
　　　Survey of 431 companies, 221 of which had rest or recreation rooms. Rest rooms and rest periods were provided to increase employees' productivity by giving them a break and change of scenery. Recreation rooms were used for a variety of social and recreational activities.

619 Whitney, Anice L. "Social and educational advantages for
       employees." Monthly labor review, 6:1, January 1918,
       206-212.
            A survey of entertainment and recreational benefits
       provided by 274 companies. Outlines the types and
       variations of such benefits as films, lectures, music
       clubs, outings, social gatherings, club houses and rec-
       reation rooms. This article is one of a series in
       the Monthly labor review, dealing with various types
       of industrial welfare programs.

STOCK OWNERSHIP

620 Baker, Helen. Statistical analysis of twenty employee
       stock purchase plans, 1925-1932. (Princeton, NJ,
       Princeton University, Industrial Relations Section)
       Ann Arbor, MI, Edward Brothers, Inc., 1932. 23 p.
            Analyzes employee stock plans of 20 companies.
       Lists type of stock offered by each company, price
       per share, dividend rates, bonuses, and terms of pur-
       chase. Examines changes in plans from 1925 to 1932
       and considers what effect the Depression had on them.

621 Davis, Eleanor. Employee stock ownership and the Depres-
       sion. Princeton, NJ, Princeton University, Indus-
       trial Relations Section, 1933. 41 p.
            A survey of 50 companies with employee stock own-
       ership plans. Plans were introduced to increase
       loyalty to the company, lower turnover, and share the
       company's prosperity. When the stock market crashed,
       nearly all stock prices fell below employee purchase
       prices. Some companies protected employees from loss
       by guaranteeing selling prices or relieving employees
       from financial obligation. Protection provisions of
       specific companies are outlined. Plans canceled or
       changed during the Depression are discussed and the
       extent of employee losses is estimated. Suggests
       companies protect employee investments to preserve
       morale and loyalty.

622 Dunn, Robert W. The Americanization of labor: the em-
       ployers' offensive against trade unions. New York,
       International Publishers, 1927. 272 p.

Chapters 7 and 8 attack employee stock ownership,
insurance and pension plans. Claims all are used to
tie workers to the company and make them less willing
to join unions. Says benefits are used to camouflage
low wages. Claims workers' share of company stock is
rarely high enough to give workers a voice in company
operations and several companies offer workers only
nonvoting shares. Organized labor calls stock plans
unsafe and unbusinesslike. Employees are often intim-
idated into subscribing to insurance plans and most
pension plans are financially unsound. Insurance and
pension benefits are not guaranteed to workers and
are often revoked if workers go on strike.

623 "Effect of stock-market crisis of 1929 on employee stock-
      purchase plans." Monthly labor review, 31:6, Decem-
      ber 1930, 49-52.
          Summarizes National Industrial Conference Board
      studies of the trend in employee stock-purchase plans
      before and after the 1929 stock market crash. Stock
      programs were expanding rapidly in 1928. After the
      crash, employee stock ownership declined only slight-
      ly. Only 11 of 150 companies reported their employ-
      ees had taken serious losses.

624 "Effect of the Depression on employee stock ownership."
      Monthly labor review, 37:2, August 1933, 279-283.
          A Princeton University study of 50 companies with
      stock ownership plans. Outlines rapid growth of such
      plans before the stock market crash. When the market
      crashed, employees suffered large losses. Layoffs
      and wage cuts forced them to sell while prices were
      low. Plans that protected employees from loss proved
      very costly to companies. A trend developed during
      the Depression to limit stock purchase to salaried
      employees.

625 "Employee stock ownership in the United States: a se-
      lected bibliography." Monthly labor review, 24:6,
      June 1927, 214-223.
          Bibliography of 107 works on employee stock owner-
      ship.

626   "Employee stock ownership plans in the United States."
      Monthly labor review, 27:2, August 1928, 99–103.
          Survey by the National Industrial Conference Board
      of 389 companies with stock ownership plans. Lists
      requirements and restrictions of various plans and
      estimated rate of employee participation. Stock
      plans were instituted to encourage employees to save,
      to make workers more efficient and interested in the
      company and to help workers build a source of income
      for old age.

627   "Employee stock participation in the Leighton Cooperative
      Industries." Monthly labor review, 27:2, August 1928,
      103–106.
          Outlines the "cooperative plan" of Leighton Coop-
      erative Industries of San Francisco. Employees own
      99 percent of the company's stock but are not allowed
      to vote unless their dividends drop below 7 percent
      for over 18 months. Results of the plan are more
      efficient workers and lower turnover. Successes and
      shortcomings of the plan are evaluated.

628   Foerster, Robert F. Employee stock ownership in the
      United States. Princeton, NJ, Princeton University,
      Industrial Relations Section, 1927. 174 p.
          A survey of employee stock ownership programs.
      Purposes of the programs were to help employees be-
      come small-scale capitalists and share in company
      profits, to lower turnover, and to create an incen-
      tive to increase productivity. Surveys eligibility
      requirements, types of stock, terms of subscription,
      and voting rights for employee stockholders. Dis-
      cusses protections to limit employees' risk and terms
      of cancellation of subscriptions. Appendix A lists
      companies with stock ownership plans and Appendix B
      describes plans of several companies.

629   Henry A. Dix and Sons Company. Description of sale and
      transfer to employees. 1923. 11 p.
          An interview with Mark H. Dix, owner of Henry A.
      Dix and Sons Company, who retired by transferring the
      company to employees through a stock purchase plan.
      Workers received extra pay so they could afford to
      buy stock. Employee stock holders were not given a
      voice in company policy. Dix said his motives for

the plan were fellowship and benevolence.

630 National Association of Corporation Schools. Bulletin,
       7, January 1920, 7-8, 26-32., July 1920, 324-327.
       (Stock ownership)

631 National Industrial Conference Board. Employee stock
       purchase plans and the stock market crisis of 1929.
       New York, 1930. 37 p.
            A survey of 150 companies with employee stock pur-
       chase plans. Found that when the stock market
       crashed, most stock prices did not fall below employ-
       ee purchase prices. Some employees took a loss be-
       cause companies would not allow them to sell their
       stock. Other companies protected employees by buying
       stock back at the purchase price regardless of cur-
       rent value. Stock plans were introduced before the
       crash to encourage thrift, to reward service, to
       stimulate interest in the company, and to raise capi-
       tal.

632 National Industrial Conference Board. Employee stock
       purchase plans in the United States. New York, 1928.
       245 p.
            An overview of employee stock purchase plans, pub-
       lished when the plans were near their peak. Describes
       types of plans, eligibility requirements, terms of
       purchase, cost to employees, and terms of cancella-
       tion. Specific company programs are outlined. Bene-
       fits of stock plans to companies are favorable public-
       ity, low turnover, employee interest and loyalty,
       fewer labor disputes, and new capital. Employees
       benefited because of the high interest paid. Dis-
       advantages to employees were the risk of loss and
       their investment often could not be cashed in.

633 "Stock ownership plans for employees." Monthly labor re-
       view, 14:6, June 1922, 17-19.
            Survey of 83 firms with stock ownership plans.
       Stock plans are considered better motivators than
       profit-sharing because employees will work harder if
       they have a chance of losing as well as winning. Con-
       cludes that most employees do not understand the risks
       of owning stock and do not take advantage of the voice

in management ownership provides.

634 Taylor, Paul S. "Leighton Co-operative Industries."
     Journal of political economy, 36:2, April 1928, 212-
     228.
          Traces the development and operation of Leighton
     Cooperative Industries, a chain of food service es-
     tablishments in which employees own 99 percent of
     the stock and receive 99 percent of the profits. Out-
     lines details of the stock purchase programs and ex-
     amines its benefits. By giving employees an interest
     in the success of the business, Leighton Industries
     attracts better and more efficient workers. Leighton
     Industries employs almost all union help and main-
     tains friendly relations with labor leaders.

635 Tead, Ordway. "The rise of employee stock ownership."
     Industrial management, 71:3, March 1926, 157-160.
          Analyzes employers' motives for introducing employ-
     ee stock purchase plans. Motives include encouraging
     thrift, preventing labor unrest, sharing the company's
     prosperity, and improving morale. Defects in stock
     purchase plans are the risk employees take when they
     invest all their savings in one company, the denial
     of voting rights to employee stockholders, and the
     requirement that employees stay with the company to
     collect benefits.

VACATIONS

636 Allen, Donna. Fringe benefits: wages or social obliga-
     tions? An analysis with historical perspectives from
     paid vacations. Ithaca, Cornell University, 1969.
     272 p.
          Chapter 3 examines employers' experiments with paid
     vacations from 1910-1935. Because of high turnover
     among production workers, they were often not included
     in original vacation plans. Employers did not want
     to pay for vacations for employees who would not stay
     with the company long enough to repay the investment
     through increased productivity. Vacation plans were
     extended to production workers during World War I when
     their increased productivity became crucial to the war
     effort. Some companies built vacation homes and rest

camps to make sure employees rested during their vacations. Many vacation plans were abandoned during
the Depression.

637 Mills, Charles M. Vacations for industrial workers. New
        York, Ronald Press Company, 1927. 328 p.
           An overview of the vacation movement. Includes a
        description of the main provisions of company plans.
        Chapter 2 summarizes terms of company vacation plans
        including length of vacations, eligibility require-
        ments, costs to companies, and management opinions on
        success of plans. Chapter 5 provides statistics on
        vacation plans in the United States. Discusses rules
        governing plans, timing of vacations, companies that
        shut down for vacations, the size of companies offer-
        ing plans, and the proportion of workers covered.
        Tables provide vacation statistics by industry and
        state, including statistics on abandoned plans.

638 National Association of Corporation Schools. Bulletin,
        6, July 1919, 305-310.
           (Annual vacation practices)

639 "Vacation policies in 1933." Monthly labor review, 37:2,
        August 1933, 283.
           American Management Association survey of vacation
        policies of 24 companies. Found vacations were most-
        ly limited to salaried employees. Eleven companies
        reported reducing benefits due to the Depression.

640 "Vacation practices and policies in New York City in
        1932." Monthly labor review, 35:3, September 1932,
        533-534.
           Survey of vacation policies of 273 members of the
        Merchant's Association of New York. Seventy-four
        companies cut benefits during the Depression. Almost
        all salaried employees and about half of hourly work-
        ers received vacations but vacations were often with-
        out pay or at reduced pay.

641 "Vacation practices for salaried workers in New York
        City." Monthly labor review, 24:5, May 1927, 35-36.

Survey of vacation policies for salaried employees
of 110 New York City businesses. One hundred firms
provided employees with two paid weeks of vacation
annually. Variations and eligibility are discussed.

642 "Vacations for factory workers." Monthly labor review,
        13:2, August 1921, 212-213.
          Survey of vacation practices of 63 firms. Thirty-
        six provided no vacations to factory workers and only
        11 gave fully paid vacations to all employees. In-
        cludes excerpts of company replies to the survey.

643 "Vacations with pay for industrial workers." Monthly
        labor review, 24:5, May 1927, 36.
          Summary of survey by "New York" magazine of com-
        nies' attitudes about paid vacations. Some companies
        said paid vacations improved labor relations and
        made workers happier and more productive while an-
        other company said vacations interfere with produc-
        tion.

644 "Vacations with pay for production workers." Monthly
        labor review, 23:1, July 1926, 35-36.
          Survey of vacation benefits in Cincinnati firms.
        One hundred eleven of the 272 firms reported giving
        paid vacations to all or part of their production
        force. Discusses duration of vacations and length of
        service requirements. Most plans were only a few
        years old and were developed to reduce turnover; to
        improve workers' morale, health and loyalty to the
        company; and to improve efficiency and the quality of
        work.

645 "Vacations with pay for wage earners." Monthly labor
        review, 22:5, May 1926, 1-7.
          Surveys changing attitudes of employers toward
        providing paid vacations. In 1916, 16 of 389 firms
        reported giving paid vacations to the general work
        force. The preliminary results of a 1926 survey
        showed 95 of 250 firms provided the same benefit.
        Study discusses length of vacations and eligibility
        requirements and examines evidence that paid vaca-
        tions contribute to lower turnover.

646 "Vacations with pay for wage earners." <u>Monthly labor
     review</u>, 40:6, June 1935, 1494-1499.
          Survey of 274 companies which in 1934 had or used
     to have paid vacation plans for hourly workers. Com-
     pares survey to data from a similar survey taken in
     1931. Discusses proportion of plans discontinued,
     suspended, or altered during the Depression and
     notes a trend toward renewing plans as the Depression
     ended. Outlines types of plans and eligibility re-
     quirements.

MISCELLANEOUS

647 "Company loan plans for unemployed workers." <u>Monthly
     labor review</u>, 35:3, September 1932, 498-500.
          Outlines typical company loan programs instituted
     during the Depression to provide relief for part-time
     and laid-off workers. Loans are either funded solely
     by the company or jointly with employees still work-
     ing. Usually no interest is charged and companies
     recognize that repayment is unlikely in many cases.

648 "Cooperative farm plan of the B.F. Goodrich Company."
     <u>Monthly labor review</u>, 36:4, April 1933, 771-774.
          Describes cooperative farming plan developed by
     the B.F. Goodrich Company to provide subsistence for
     former and part-time employees who lost employment
     due to the Depression. Workers took turns farming
     200 acres called Akron Community Gardens and the
     harvest was divided among them.

649 Eilbirt, Henry. "Twentieth century beginnings in employ-
     ee counseling." <u>Business history review</u>, 31:1,
     Autumn 1957, 310-322.
          Examines the practice of employee counseling at
     the turn of the century. Summarizes industrial bet-
     terment efforts and discusses the element of coun-
     seling involved in each program. Counseling was of-
     ten accomplished through education, medical depart-
     ments, and welfare secretaries, who were "the point
     of contact between the firm and its employees."
     Counseling generally dealt with employee welfare,
     behavior, and morals.

650   Fitch, John A. "Making the job worthwhile." Survey, 40,
         April 27, 1918, 87-89. (Reprinted in D. Bloomfield's
         Employment management. New York, Wilson, 1919. 435-
         440 p.)
              Considers methods of reducing turnover and absen-
         teeism, partially through control of welfare benefits.
         For instance, threat of loss of vacation pay may be
         used to encourage regular attendance. The Ford Motor
         Company controlled absenteeism by withholding profit-
         sharing benefits. Visiting nurses may also be used
         to discourage illegitimate absences.

650a Golden book of the Wanamaker stores...jubilee year, 1861-
         1911. (Philadelphia, John Wanamaker?) 1911. 318 p.
              Pages 229 to 237 deal with John Wanamaker's effort
         to provide technical education for the younger mem-
         bers of his work force. They were taught arithmetic,
         spelling, penmanship, bookkeeping, English composi-
         tion, commercial geography, stenography, elocution,
         history, grammer, banking and finance, commercial
         history, ethics, and French. In addition to these
         educational endeavors vacations were sponsored at
         Island Heights, New Jersey where the young men and
         women could spend a few weeks in the summer for a
         nominal cost.

651   "Industrial welfare work boiled down." The Modern hospi-
         tal, 7:2, August 1916, 129-132.
              General description of the most common industrial
         welfare practices, including medical care, cafete-
         rias, pensions, and social and recreational activities.

652   National Industrial Conference Board. Rest periods for
         industrial workers. Research Report #13. Boston,
         1919. 55 p.
              Examines rest periods as a means of reducing work-
         er fatigue and increasing productivity. The practice
         of rest periods developed out of scientific manage-
         ment and the need for high productivity during World
         War I. Surveys practices of 233 companies and finds
         rest periods may be especially useful for women and
         workers performing monotonous tasks. The Appendix
         lists rest period practices in various industries.

653 Princeton University. Industrial Relations Section.
     <u>Company loans to unemployed workers</u>. Ann Arbor,
     MI, Edward Brothers, Inc., 1932. 26 p.
          Surveys companies that loaned money to laid-off em-
     ployees during the Depression. Loan programs were
     either entirely company administered or jointly funded
     by the company and employees who were still working.
     Loans were usually interest-free and ranged from $50
     to $200. Companies realized repayment was unlikely
     in many cases. Programs of specific companies are
     discussed.

654 Rossy, M.S. "Cost of an employee service department."
     <u>Industrial management</u>, 70:1, July 1925.

655 VanNorman, Louis E. "Why not more beautiful factories?
     Some opinions of manufacturers as to attractive busi-
     ness plants." <u>Home and flowers</u>, 13:1, November 1902,
     24-27.
          Survey of 500 businessmen who overwhelmingly ac-
     knowledged the value of a clean and beautiful indus-
     trial setting. Some businessmen said cleanliness
     was important but saw no value on such beautification
     projects as flowers and gardens. Representative re-
     sponses to the survey are presented.

LABOR'S RESPONSE TO INDUSTRIAL WELFARE

Reactions of organized labor to employer welfare programs.
Welfare measures, especially employee representation plans,
were often considered as a weapon to keep the unions out.
Responses of William Green and Samuel Gompers can be located
through the index.

656 American Federation of Labor. Proceedings. Washington,
     1881-   .
         The convention Proceedings of the American Feder-
     ation of Labor are a good source for determining or-
     ganized labor's official attitude toward industrial
     welfare issues. Logically they were most concerned
     with company unions. Information on that subject is
     found not only under "company unions" but beginning
     in 1926 it is also under "Railway Labor Act" and
     beginning in 1933 additionally under "National Indus-
     trial Recovery Act."
         The following are selected references on company
     unions:
         1919, p. 302-303; 1920, p. 279; 1925, p. 230;
     1926, p. 286-292; 1927, p. 42-43, 318; 1928, p. 256;
     1932, p. 398-400.

657 American Federation of Labor. Report of the Proceedings
     of the forty-fifth annual convention. Atlantic City,
     NJ, 1925. 33-35 p.
         Attacks company unions for denying workers "the ad-
     vantages of national organization and the benefit to
     representative officials of that training which de-
     velops independent experts." Claims they are an at-
     tempt to crush organized labor. Says employee insur-
     ance programs are an attempt "to make employees
     'loyal' to the company, to undermine their indepen-
     dence, and to defeat efforts to secure wage increases."
     Attacks employee stock ownership plans because they
     often give employees no voting power and may not be
     safe investments.

658   "Attitude of American Federation of Labor on shop or com-
         pany unions." Industrial relations, 1:10, December
         20, 1919.

659   "Attitude of organized labor toward works councils." In
         Experience with works councils in the United States.
         New York, National Industrial Conference Board, Re-
         search Report #50, May 1922, Chapter 13, 138-147 p.
              Examines organized labor's opposition to works
         councils. The AFL called company unions "a delusion
         and a snare" established "for the express purpose of
         deluding the workers into the belief that they have
         some protection and thus have no need for trade union
         organization." But survey finds most employee repre-
         sentation plans do not discriminate against union mem-
         bers and unions are often able to work in harmony with
         works councils.

660   Burritt, Arthur W. et al. Profit-sharing: its princi-
         ples and practice. New York, Harper and Brothers,
         1918. 328 p.
              A comprehensive study of profit-sharing. Traces
         the history of profit-sharing and describes various
         types of plans. Profit-sharing was used to promote
         efficiency, to prevent waste, to promote stability of
         labor, to promote industrial peace, and to foster a
         spirit of cooperation. Suggests it should not be used
         as an excuse to depress wages and benefits must be
         substantial enough to be taken seriously. Discusses
         problems of requiring employees to share losses as well
         as profits and considers the dangers of stock owner-
         ship as a form of profit-sharing. Examines organized
         labor's views of profit-sharing.

661   Cohen, Joseph E. "Beating the company union." American
         federationist, 34:5, May 1927, 590-592.
              Attacks company unions on the grounds that they
         only allow workers "to concur in what is set before
         them by those at the top." Calls the company union
         "an instrument devised by the enemies of organized
         labor to crush it." Suggests independent, democratic
         unions are the only true means of protecting the in-
         terests of workers.

662 "Company unions." American federationist, 41:2, Feb-
     ruary 1934, 130-132.
         An editorial by William Green tracing the history
     of company unions and criticizing employers for using
     them to keep unions out. Claims company unions violate
     the spirit of Section 7(b) of the National Recovery
     Act, which encouraged workers to unionize. Criti-
     cizes the U.S. Department of Commerce for supporting
     company unions.

663 "Company unions not enough." American federationist,
     32:10, October 1925, 873-874.
         An editorial by William Green suggesting company
     unions are tributes to real trade unions because they
     show that employers recognize the need to give workers
     a voice in determining labor issues. Weaknesses of
     company unions are their lack of power and freedom,
     employer domination, and their inhibition of worker
     opposition. Suggests wage earners should capture
     company unions and turn them into real trade unions.

664 "Contented cows." American federationist, 30:9, Septem-
     ber 1923, 760-762.
         Samuel Gompers criticizes welfare as an attempt by
     the employer "to have his workmen perform like cows
     that resignedly chew their cud and submissively give
     sweet milk." Believes welfare programs will fail be-
     cause workers do not want to be "contented cows."
     Says welfare will not solve the labor problem and sug-
     gests workers should be given high enough wages so
     they can purchase their own benefits.

665 Derber, Milton. The American idea of industrial democ-
     racy, 1865-1965. Urbana, University of Illinois
     Press, 1970. 553 p.
         Chapter 9 examines the role of trade unions in in-
     dustrial democracy. Describes the development of a
     willingness by trade unions to cooperate with manage-
     ment to increase efficiency and productivity in ex-
     change for management recognition of unions and higher
     wages for workers. Outlines reasons for the shift
     away from antagonism and discusses views of various
     labor leaders, some of whom wanted cooperation and
     others who opposed management. The AFL endorsed
     scientific management in an effort to get management

to allow trade unions to take over employee representation plans. Discusses the struggle in the railroad
industry to integrate brotherhood unions with employee
representation plans.

666 Derber, Milton. "The idea of industrial democracy in
     America, 1898-1915." Labor history, 7:3, Fall 1966,
     259-286.
        An analysis of industrial democracy as studied by
     the two Industrial Commissions of 1898-1902 and 1913-
     1915. The hearings detail the divergent views toward
     industrial democracy of three labor groups: AFL, In-
     dustrial Workers of the World, and the Socialists, as
     well as those of the employer and of scholars. Three
     journals in particular reflect the changing attitude
     toward industrial democracy during this period: the
     Monthly review of the National Civic Federation, the
     Outlook, and the Survey.

667 Dunn, Robert W. The Americanization of labor: the em-
     ployers' offensive against trade unions. New York,
     International Publishers, 1927. 272 p.
        Chapter 12 presents organized labor's criticisms of
     welfare programs and proposed remedies. Samuel Gom-
     pers called welfare "hell-fare" and attacked it as a
     means of weakening unions. Claims welfare is no sub-
     stitute for fair wages. Suggests unions should form
     their own associations to provide a variety of bene-
     fits for workers and advocates the passage of legis-
     lative relief plans. Suggests the need for a labor
     party to represent the interests of workers. Other
     chapters attack company unions, employee stock owner-
     ship, group insurance, pension, and other programs;
     claiming they were introduced primarily to keep work-
     ers passive, and to keep unions out.

668 Dunn, Robert W. Company unions: employers' "industrial
     democracy." New York, Vanguard Press, 1927. 206 p.
        Examines the significance, purpose, and practice
     of company unions from organized labor's point of
     view. Stresses that company unions do not allow gen-
     uine collective bargaining. Traces their development
     in various industries and describes several types of
     plans. Employers introduced employee representation
     to encourage cooperation with management, to ease

ill-will and friction, and to defeat trade unions.
Describes plans of several companies with particular
emphasis on plans in the railroad industry. Considers
various methods of "selling" company unions to workers; including through threats and undercover operations of detective agencies. Chapters 12 and 13 sum-
marize organized labor's case against company unions
and tactics for replacing them with independent
unions.

669   Experience with works councils in the United States.
      New York, National Industrial Conference Board, Re-
      search Report #50, May 1922. 191 p.
          A survey of all known employee representation plans
      in the United States in 1922. Part of study examines
      the opposition of organized labor to company unions
      and considers the ability of some trade unions to work
      in harmony with company unions.

670   "Ford's 'ideal community'." American federationist,
      44:4, April 1937, 357-358.
          William Green discusses Henry Ford's plan to build
      an ideal community in Georgia. Criticizes the idea on
      the grounds that "because a man has been able to oper-
      ate a production plant successfully so that he has the
      money resources to build such a community does not
      prove that he has the qualities that fit one for con-
      trol over other people's lives." Claims the plan
      threatens the democracy and freedom of workers and
      suggests the need for cooperative joint control.

671   Furseth, Andrew. "Company unions." American federation-
      ist, 35:5, May 1928, 541-545.
          Compares company unions to the legendary Upas tree
      which lures men under the deceptive protection of its
      leaves, lulls them to sleep, and kills them with its
      poisonous fumes. Says workers are lured into joining
      company unions because they are tired of struggling.
      They are unwittingly lulled into relinquishing their
      freedom when they join company unions. Freedom and
      independence soon cease to exist as companies take
      feudal control over workers' lives.

672   Gompers, Samuel. "The company union fraud." <u>American</u>
        <u>federationist</u>, 29:12, December 1922, 888-889.
            Attacks company unions on the railroads as an ef-
        fort to displace real trade unions. Claims "labor
        organizations can be effective on behalf of the work-
        ers only when they are under the complete control of
        the workers." Says employers seek to dominate unions
        in order to minimize their effectiveness. Warns work-
        ers not to be deceived by "counterfeit" unions.

673   Gompers, Samuel. "The good and bad of welfare work."
        <u>American federationist</u>, 20:12, December 1913, 1041-
        1043.
            Comments on a Bureau of Labor Statistics survey of
        employer welfare. Suggests some of the programs for
        which companies take so much credit are no more than
        commonplace duties employers should be expected to
        perform as a matter of conscience. Many types of wel-
        fare are provided to benefit companies more than em-
        ployees.

674   Green, Marguerite. <u>The National Civic Federation and the</u>
        <u>American labor movement, 1900-1925</u>. Washington, Cath-
        olic University of America Press, 1956. 537 p.
            Chapter 6 examines the relationship between organ-
        ized labor and the Welfare Department of the National
        Civic Federation. A dichotomy existed between the
        official attitude of the Federation's labor members
        and labor leaders in general. The Welfare Depart-
        ment's initial goal was the establishment of workers'
        compensation laws. It also tried to educate employers
        in the benefits of welfare activities. The Federa-
        tion's Woman's Department and Department of Pensions
        and Social Insurance also pushed for welfare advances.

675   Green, William. "The challenge of the union." <u>American</u>
        <u>federationist</u>, 32:3, March 1925, 161-164.
            Explains why company unions are merely substitutes
        for trade unions. Traces the history of employee rep-
        resentation and describes various types of plans.
        Claims company unions do not give workers economic
        power or a voice in company operations. Calls the
        company union of the Colorado Fuel and Iron Company
        "an anaemic organization without funds and without
        experienced and self-directed officials" and summa-

rizes a report on its effectiveness. Says experimenta-
tion with employee representation only delays progress
toward unionization.

676 Green, William. <u>The Superiority of trade unions over
      company unions</u>. Washington, American Federation of
      Labor, 1926. 11 p.
          A speech to the Trades and Labor Assembly attacking
      company unions. Green said, "Company unions are ar-
      tificial in origin, growth, and development because
      they lack the elements of fraternity, brotherhood,
      and mutuality of interest." Claims workers are given
      no voice in the organization of company unions, and
      lack solidarity because company unions are not affil-
      iated with a national union. Says trade unions are
      better because they are independent, democratic, and
      more powerful in protecting employees' rights.

677 "Industrial and international peace." <u>American federa-
      tionist</u>, 11:11, November 1904, 988-989.
          Text of a speech by Samuel Gompers at a National
      Civic Federation luncheon. Praises the NCF for trying
      to bring about better relations between workers and
      employers. Says owners and laborers must work to-
      gether to achieve industrial and international peace.

678 "Industrial democracy." <u>American federationist</u>, 37:4,
      April 1930, 402-403.
          William Green criticizes the Dan River Mill employ-
      ee representation plan as "the kind of industrial de-
      mocracy whose backbone management could break at
      will." Denounces the Bemberg Glantzstoff Company for
      firing union members in violation of its agreement
      not to discriminate against them. Calls employee rep-
      resentation an extension of management and a repudia-
      tion of democracy.

679 "Labor investments." <u>American federationist</u>, 33:10,
      October 1926, 1191-1199.
          Reactions of labor leaders and students of labor to
      an <u>American federationist</u> article on company stock
      investment plans for workers. The author of the ar-
      ticle, William Z. Ripley, advocated stock investment
      programs only if employers have the same voting rights

and freedom to buy and sell stock as any other stockholder. Reactions generally agree with Ripley's conclusions and add the following arguments against stock
plans: 1) they are used as a tool to tie workers to
their jobs and the company, 2) employee stock may
sometimes be revoked by the company, 3) stock ownership may be used as an excuse to keep wages and other
benefits low, 4) employees are not advised as to the
best time to buy stock and often buy when the price
is high.

680 McKelvey, Jean Trepp. AFL attitudes toward production,
     1900-1932. Ithaca, NY, Cornell University, 1952.
     148 p. (Cornell Studies in Industrial and Labor
     Relations, v. 2)
          Chapter 4 describes welfare work as an attempt to
     furnish workers all that unions could promise and thus
     diminish the organizer's appeals. Examines the growth
     of employee representation plans as substitutes for
     unions. The AFL called the protection of workers'
     rights by company unions "superficial," no substitute
     for trade unions. Companies also fought unions by en-
     couraging employees to save, invest, and buy homes so
     they would have more to lose in case of a strike and
     would be less likely to support union organizers.

681 "A mistaken prophet." American federationist, 35:5, May
     1928, 530-531.
          William Green disputes the notion that company
     unions are a viable alternative to trade unions. Says
     company unions are organizations of management, not of
     workers and cannot possibly be as powerful and aggres-
     sive as independent unions. Claims "a constructive,
     free organization that looks to progress by affording
     men opportunity for growth is the only sure way to
     self-development and self-expression for workers."

682 "More sophisticated methods." American federationist,
     42:5, May 1935, 469-471.
          William Green attacks company unions as a "sophis-
     ticated method of opposing real unions." Traces the
     history of company unions and claims they are an at-
     tempt to circumvent the National Recovery Act, which
     gave employees the right to unionize.

683 "Mr. Mitchell's letter of resignation." American federa-
     tionist, 18:4, April 1911, 308-309.
          Text of a letter of resignation by John Mitchell
     as chairman of the Trade Agreement Department of the
     National Civic Federation and a reply to the letter
     by NCF President, Seth Low. Mitchell resigned because
     his union, the United Mine Workers, amended its con-
     stitution to forbid its members from belonging to the
     National Civic Federation. Reprints editorial from
     the Washington Trades Unionist attacking the UMW for
     its action, calling it a petty act of internal poli-
     tics.

684 National Civic Federation. Profit-sharing by American
     employers. New York, Profit-sharing Department,
     1926. 261 p.
          Pages 233-243 discuss organized labor's opposition
     to profit-sharing plans. Unions claimed profit-shar-
     ing was used as an excuse to keep wages low. It made
     workers feel obligated to employers so they were a-
     fraid to demand wage increases. Unions preferred de-
     pendable, fixed wages rather than a share of fluctu-
     ating profits. Comments by Samuel Gompers and other
     union leaders are presented.

685 "No substitute for the union." American federationist,
     34:8, August 1927, 915-916.
          An editorial by William Green claiming that if
     there had been no trade unions, companies would never
     have introduced employee representation plans, stock
     ownership plans, pensions, or insurance. Benefits were
     provided to keep workers satisfied so they wouldn't
     join unions.

686 "Outsiders." American federationist, 41:7, July 1934,
     691-694.
          A William Green editorial which calls company
     unions a refined type of warfare against labor unions'
     organizing efforts. Company unions were used to cir-
     cumvent the right to organize guaranteed by the Na-
     tional Recovery Act by substituting company-controlled
     unions for true representation. Describes the steel
     industry's efforts to substitute employee representa-
     tion for unions in spite of workers' opposition to the
     company union concept.

687 "Rockefeller organizes and recognizes a 'union'." Amer-
       ican federationist, 22:11, November 1915, 975-977.
          Samuel Gompers mocks John D. Rockefeller Jr.'s at-
       tempts to understand the lives of his employees at
       the Colorado Fuel and Iron Company. Attacks Rocke-
       feller's proposal for a company union as a pretext to
       keep the United Mine Workers out. Contends company
       unions will give employees no opportunity to push for
       meaningful demands. Rockefeller should give workers
       higher wages to spend as they wish rather than using
       the money to unilaterally introduce welfare programs.

688 "The Stetson Strike and profit-sharing." American fed-
       erationist, 23:5, May 1916, 383-385.
          An editorial by Samuel Gompers criticizing the
       "philanthropic paternalism" of the John B. Stetson
       Company, where welfare was used "to generate a spirit
       of feudalism and to drive out the spirit of independ-
       ence and liberty." Claims company dominance fostered
       a deep-seated workers' discontent that finally erupted
       in a strike. Suggests employees would have revolted
       sooner if they had not felt bound to the company by a
       deceptive stock ownership/profit-sharing plan. Says
       if employers introduce profit-sharing it should be in
       addition to, not instead of decent wages.

689 Sullivan, James W. The Trade unions' attitude toward
       welfare work. New York, National Civic Federation,
       Welfare Department, 1907. 8 p.
          Expresses the attitude of organized labor toward
       welfare work of the National Civic Federation. Labor
       leaders who were NCF members supported the Federa-
       tion's efforts to help them improve working condi-
       tions. Viewed the NCF Welfare Department as a means
       of educating employers on the needs of workers.

690 Taylor, Elva M. "Employee representation on American
       railroads." American federationist, 33:9 and 10, Sep-
       tember and October 1926, 1103-1108 and 1201-1217.
          Traces the history of employee representation plans
       in the railroad industry, introduced in an atmosphere
       of volatile relations between companies and the many
       trade unions that represented railroad employees.
       Union leaders attacked the plans, claiming they were
       attempts to weaken unions. The plans, which focused

on grievance settlement, were controlled by the companies and gave no real power or representation to
workers. Unions rebelled against company attempts to
bar union members from employee representation councils.

691   Todd, Arthur J. "The organization and promotion of in-
      dustrial welfare through voluntary efforts." <u>Annals
      of the American Academy of Political and Social Sci-
      ence</u>, 105, January 1923, 76-82.
         Examines motives and merits of industrial welfare.
      Estimates the prevalence, cost, and ease of adminis-
      tering various programs. Examines various views on
      the employers' responsibility to provide for the wel-
      fare of workers and discusses the hostility of organ-
      ized labor toward the motives and methods of welfare.
      Unions opposed welfare because it was paternalistic
      and made workers dependent on the employer. Presents
      various opinions on whether welfare is compatible
      with collective bargaining. Concludes that wages are
      not lower when welfare is provided and welfare will
      not prevent labor trouble.

692   "Vanishing of capitalist 'unionism'." <u>American federa-
      tionist</u>, 21:8, August 1914, 640-642.
         Samuel Gompers' editorial attacking employers who
      manipulate the lives and conduct of their employees.
      Considers employee representation plans weapons to
      keep unions out by giving workers "harmless imita-
      tions." Claims the company union of C.W. Post failed
      because it was artificial and useless. Attacks the
      National Association of Manufacturers' efforts to use
      company unions as a weapon against outside unions.

BIOGRAPHIES

Biographies of leaders in the welfare movement, focusing on their welfare philosophies, programs, successes and failures. Individual names can be located through the index. This section is highly selective.

693 Boettiger, Louis A. Employer welfare work. New York, Ronald Press Company, 1923. 301 p.
     Chapter 9 outlines paternalistic welfare efforts of Francis Cabot Lowell and Nathan Appleton in textile mills of Lowell, Massachusetts. Lowell Mills strictly controlled workers' lives by providing supervised housing, meals, schools, a library, a hospital, a savings bank, and a newspaper. Employees who did not follow moral codes were discharged.

694 Collier, Peter and David Horowitz. The Rockefellers: an American dynasty. New York, Holt, Rinehart and Winston, 1976. 746 p.
     Traces the history of the Rockefeller family, including John D. Rockefeller Jr., a major stockholder in the Colorado Fuel and Iron Company. Chapter 8 describes Rockefeller selling the idea of an employee representation plan to workers of the company in the wake of a bitter, violent strike and public outcry against the company. Under the plan, employee representatives and management would decide issues concerning working and living conditions, safety, sanitation, housing, and education.

695 Crowther, Samuel. John H. Patterson: pioneer in industrial welfare. New York, Doubleday, Page and Company, 1924. 364 p.
     A biography of the president of the National Cash Register Company, a leader in welfare work. Traces the development of his philosophy that "the basis of

a good product is labor" so labor should be treated
well. He believed, "Men and women work better when
they have self-respect; the first step toward self-
respect is decent living and working conditions."
Welfare began with gardening projects with neighbor-
hood boys in order to renovate the area around the
factory. Gradually a variety of programs were added,
including a dining hall with low-cost meals, schools,
movies, a library, the NCR country club, and profit-
sharing. He especially emphasized health because the
human body cannot be efficient without it.

696 Dawson, R. MacGregor. William Lyon Mackenzie King: a
     political biography, 1874-1923. Toronto, University
     of Toronto Press, 1958. 521 p.
     A biography of Mackenzie King, former prime minis-
ter of Canada, who helped formulate the employee representation plan of the Colorado Fuel and Iron Company. Chapters 8 and 9 describe King's role in helping John D. Rockefeller Jr. institute a program of
industrial relations in the Colorado coal mines. King
was put in charge of developing labor relations in an
atmosphere of hostility following a long and violent
strike. Describes details of the employee representation plan and other welfare improvements; including
housing improvements, wash houses, schools, and recreation centers. The company abandoned its policy of re-
quiring employees to shop at the company store.

697 Dorn, Jacob Henry. Washington Gladden, prophet of the
     social gospel. Columbus, Ohio State University Press,
     1966. 489 p.
     Chapter 8 discusses Washington Gladden's views on
the status of the working class. He believed employers should apply the Golden Rule to business by providing for "the health, comfort, intellectual improvement, and moral and religious welfare of his workers."
He suggested employers should even rent pews in church
for their workers. Believed capital and labor should
share ownership of business through profit-sharing and
cooperatives. Industry should be geared to human welfare rather than profit.

698 Ferns, H.S. and B. Ostry. The Age of Mackenzie King:
     the rise of the leader. London, William Heineman,

Ltd., 1955. 356 p.
     A biography of W.L. Mackenzie King, former Canadian
prime minister and industrial relations adviser to
John D. Rockefeller Jr. King helped Rockefeller set
up an employee representation plan in the Colorado
Fuel and Iron Company following a long and violent
strike. Chapter 7 describes King's association with
the Rockefellers and subsequent involvement in the
company's labor relations. Describes the intolerable
working conditions in the mines and the company's
absolute control over miners through control of the
company store, housing, and law enforcement. Examines
violence caused by opposition to the United Mine
Workers.

699 Filene, A. Lincoln, _A Merchant's horizon_. Boston, Hough-
     ton Mifflin Company, 1924. 266 p.
     An autobiographical account of the philosophies and
programs of the Filene family, founders of Filene's
Department Store in Boston. The Filenes believed humanitarianism and profitability must go hand in hand.
Combining industrial welfare and democracy, the family
gave employees partial control over the business and
allowed them to institute and manage several welfare
programs.

700 Fosdick, Raymond B. _John D. Rockefeller, Jr.: a por-
     trait_. New York, Harper and Brothers, 1956. 477 p.
     A biography of John D. Rockefeller Jr., a major
stockholder in the Colorado Fuel and Iron Company.
Chapter 8 describes his employee representation plan,
introduced to ease labor unrest following a bitter
strike. Samuel Gompers attacked the plan, claiming
it gave workers no real power. Chapter 9 discusses
Rockefeller's advocacy of employee representation as
a substitute for unionism and describes the spread of
the plan throughout the country.

701 Hicks, Clarence J. _My life in industrial relations:
     fifty years of the growth of a profession_. New York,
     Harper and Brothers, 1941. 180 p.
     The autobiography of Clarence J. Hicks, one of the
earliest practitioners in the developing profession
of industrial relations. He saw welfare work as a

joint business venture between employees and management because he believed paternalism was not the way
to care for workers. Describes his role in the International Harvester Company, the Colorado Fuel and Iron
Company, and Standard Oil Company of New Jersey, where
he helped introduce employee representation plans and
administer other welfare benefits. Traces the development of the philosophy of the unity of interests
between employees and management which is the basis
of employee representation.

702 Johnson, Gerald W. The Making of a Southern industrial-
     ist: a biographical study of Simpson Bobo Tanner.
     Chapel Hill, University of North Carolina Press,
     1952. 84 p.
         Describes the contribution of Simpson Bobo Tanner
     toward the industrialization of North Carolina. The
     labor policy of his cotton mill was "paternalistic to
     the last degree" but he believed mill workers were
     as good as anybody else. He regulated both working
     conditions and private lives by forbidding drinking,
     profanity, gambling, and promiscuity on company prop-
     erty, including in the company-owned mill village.

703 Lander, Ernest McPherson, Jr. The Textile industry in
     antebellum South Carolina. Baton Rouge, Louisiana
     State University Press, 1968. 122 p.
         Chapter 4 presents a biography of William Gregg
     who believed cotton mills could be profitable in South
     Carolina and became a textile magnate. He built the
     Graniteville Manufacturing Company and developed an
     extensive welfare program, including housing, churches,
     a school, and pleasant working conditions.

704 McGregor, F.A. The Fall and rise of Mackenzie King:
     1911-1919. Toronto, University of Toronto Press,
     1962. 358 p.
         A biography of former Canadian Prime Minister
     William Lyon Mackenzie King, who spent several years
     studying the U.S. and Canadian labor movement. He
     advised John D. Rockefeller Jr. on handling labor
     problems at the Colorado Fuel and Iron Company.
     Following a violent strike, King and Rockefeller in-
     troduced an employee representation plan to give

workers a voice in determining wages and working
conditions. Chapter 9 describes King and Rockefeller
selling the plan to company leaders, workers, and
organized labor and discusses features and problems of
the plan.

705 McQuaid, Kim. "An American Owenite: Edward A. Filene
     and the parameters of industrial reform, 1890-1937."
     American journal of economics and sociology, 35:1,
     January 1976, 77-94.
          Biography of Edward A. Filene, one of the earliest
     American proponents of industrial welfare. Examines
     Filene's incorporation of welfare programs and in-
     dustrial democracy in his Boston department store.
     Article also outlines Filene's community service and
     social reform activities.

706 McQuaid, Kim. "The businessman as reformer: N.O. Nelson
     and late 19th Century social movements in America."
     American journal of economics and sociology, 33,
     October 1974, 423-435.
          Traces the career of Nelson O. Nelson as a social
     reformer and model employer at the N.O. Nelson Manu-
     facturing Company. Nelson's activities included in-
     troducing such welfare programs as a Christmas bonus
     plan, profit-sharing, and sickness, death, and retire-
     ment benefits. He built the model company town of
     LeClaire, Illinois. His struggle to keep programs
     alive during the Depression of the 1890's and his un-
     successful attempt to form a producers' cooperative
     are examined.

707 McQuaid, Kim. "The businessman as social innovator:
     N.O. Nelson..." American journal of economics and
     sociology, 34, October 1975, 411-422.
          Discusses the activities of social reformer and
     welfare leader Nelson O. Nelson who promoted "garden
     cities" and the consumer cooperative movement. His
     welfare efforts included profit-sharing for both em-
     ployees and customers. Employees received a third of
     the company's profits. They were paid in stock so
     they would eventually take over ownership of the com-
     pany. Nelson opposed craft unions because they tried
     to take excessive profits for themselves at the ex-
     pense of nonunionized employees and customers. He

became disillusioned near the end of his life when his
profit-sharing and cooperative experiments failed and
were phased out.

708 McQuaid, Kim. "Henry S. Dennison and the 'science' of
     industrial reform, 1900-1950." American journal of
     economics and sociology, 36, January 1977, 79-98.
          A biography of Henry S. Dennison, president of the
     Dennison Manufacturing Company and a leader in indus-
     trial welfare. He believed welfare was the best ave-
     nue toward the betterment of American industrial so-
     ciety. He instituted a program of stock ownership
     for managers and provided a variety of welfare bene-
     fits to workers. Dennison served as an industrial
     adviser to government and lobbied for various types
     of labor legislation.

709 McQuaid, Kim. "Industry and the cooperative common-
     wealth: William P. Hapgood and the Columbia Con-
     serve Company, 1917-1943." Labor history, 17:4,
     Fall 1976, 510-529.
          Traces the career of William Powers Hapgood,
     founder of the Columbia Conserve Company. Hapgood
     transformed the company into a cooperative experiment
     in industrial democracy. A joint worker/management
     council decided issues concerning wages, working con-
     ditions, and problems of management. Hapgood held
     veto power but his veto could be overridden by a
     two-thirds vote. Furthermore, the council had the
     power to fire Hapgood. The council was open to all
     employees who wanted to join. Workers were made part
     owners in the company through profit-sharing and stock
     ownership. The cooperative did not survive the fi-
     nancial pressure of the Depression.

710 Mitchell, Broadus. William Gregg: factory master of the
     Old South. New York, Octagon Books, 1966. 331 p.
          A biography of William Gregg, a leader in the tex-
     tile industry and industrial welfare in South Caro-
     lina. Analyzes his development of cotton mills into
     a profitable industry. Mills provided employment for
     poor whites and brought them out of "degradation and
     poverty" by feeding, clothing, and housing them. De-
     scribes sturdy, comfortable, and clean houses, churches,
     and schools. Chapter 4 defends paternalism as

necessary to bring the people out of their poverty.
Chapter 5 describes Gregg's goal of eliminating il-
literacy among his workers. He enforced compulsory
education in mill schools for all children under age
12. Supervision of workers' morals was included in
his welfare programs.

711 Tarbell, Ida M. Owen D. Young: a new type of industrial
     leader. New York, Macmillan Company, 1932. 353 p.
       A biography of Owen D. Young, who helped move the
     General Electric Company from antagonistic labor re-
     lations aimed at keeping unions out, to a policy of
     cooperation and conciliation with workers. He be-
     lieved employees would be better, more loyal workers
     if they were given an interest in the success of the
     company. He introduced a plan of employee represen-
     tation which led to the adoption of investment, pen-
     sion, and unemployment protection plans. He helped
     develop the "Swope Plan" for stabilizing employment
     in the industry. His wide range of political activ-
     ities and public services are also discussed.

712 Winston, George T. A Builder of the New South, being
     the story of the life work of Daniel Augustus
     Tompkins. Garden City, NY, Doubleday, Page and
     Company, 1920. 403 p.
       A biography of Daniel Tompkins who helped build the
     textile industry in the South. He built mills, mill
     villages, and textile schools and advocated compulsory
     education for all children. Pages 262-273 describe
     his welfare activities including building and support-
     ing houses, churches, and schools. Describes workers'
     aversion to paternalism and suggests the need to
     help workers help themselves. Chapter 18 describes
     his efforts to promote thrift among workers by intro-
     ducing building and loan associations to provide "home
     money for home people."

COMPANY INDEX

This index is in two parts: Company and Miscellaneous. For
information on industries not listed separately (i.e. mining,
railroads, steel, and textiles) see names of major companies
in the field. For instance if information is wanted on retail
trade see Filene's Department Store, Wanamaker's Department
Store, etc. or on the petroleum industry see Standard Oil
Company.

Brown (J. Morton) & Company: 587
Brown Paper Mill Company: 78
Brownel (F.A.): 158
Browning Company: 73, 149
Buckeye Steel Castings Company: 336
Bucyrus Company: 628
Bucyrus, Ohio, Foundry & Manufacturing Company: 587
Budd (Edward G.) Manufacturing Company: 628
Buffalo Smelting Works: 177, 531
Bullock Electric Manufacturing Company: 158
Burritt (A.W.) Company: 579, 581, 594, 628, 660

Cadillac Motor Car Company: 204
California & Hawaiian Sugar Refining Corporation, Ltd.: 152,
    206, 222
California Packing Corporation: 628
California Petroleum Corporation: 628
Callaway Mills: 378
Callender, McAuslan and Troup Company: 175
Calumet & Hecla Company: 283, 285
Cambria Steel Company: 73, 149, 158
Cameron (A.S.) & Company: 587, 610
Canadian National Railways Company: 327
Carnegie Steel Corporation: 158
Carpenter (G.B.) & Company: 531
Case (J.I.) Company: 513, 522
Cassidy & Son Manufacturing Company: 177
Catoir Silk Company: 177
Celluloid Company: 171, 244
Century Company: 587
Cheney Brothers: 74, 158, 239, 405
Chesebrough Manufacturing Company: 177
Chicago & Alton Railroad Company: 531
Chicago & Eastern Illinois Railroad Company: 531
Chicago & North Western Railway Company: 327, 331
Chicago, Burlington & Quincy Railroad Company: 158, 319, 531
Chicago Great Western Railway Company: 158
Chicago, Milwaukee, & St. Paul Railway Company: 327
Chicago, Milwaukee, St. Paul & Pacific Railroad Company: 331
Chicago Rapid Transit Company: 589
Chicago, Rock Island & Pacific Railway Company: 628, 653
Chicago Telephone Company: 158, 173, 218, 573
Chrysler Corporation: 110
Cincinnati & Muskingum Valley Railroad Company: 328
Cincinnati, Hamilton & Dayton Railroad Company: 531
Cincinnati, Lebanon & Northern Railway Company: 328
Cincinnati Milling Company: 573

Dean River Power & Manufacturing Company: 403
Deere & Company: 653
Delaware & Hudson Canal Company: 158
Delaware & Hudson Railroad Company: 520
Demountable Typewriter Company: 513, 522
Demuth (William) & Company: 107, 149
Dennison Manufacturing Company: 74, 77, 116, 219, 508, 510,
    513, 518, 520, 532, 535, 579, 581, 589, 594, 628. 660, 708
Devlin (Thomas) Manufacturing Company: 579, 660
Diamond Saw & Stamping Works: 177
Dix (Henry A.) & Sons Corporation: 628, 629
Dodge (Alfred) & Sons: 501, 531, 587
Dodge Manufacturing Company: 472
Doherty (Henry L.) & Company: 628
Dold (Jacob) Packing Company: 177, 579, 581, 660
Draper Company: 158, 442
Droste (George F.) Bakery: 177
Dunn (T.B.) Company: 177
Dupont (E.I.) De Nemours & Company, Inc.: 152, 581, 620, 628
Durham Hosiery Mills: 424
Dutchess Bleachery, Inc.: 74, 120, 416, 429, 510, 513, 518, 520
    522, 535
Dutchess Manufacturing Company: 149
Dwight Manufacturing Company: 403

Eastern Manufacturing Company: 553
Eastman Kodak Company: 74, 86, 152, 177, 203, 589, 628
Eaton, Crane & Pike Company: 628
Edison Electric Illuminating Company of Boston: 152, 158,
    173, 581
Edison General Electric Company: 177
Edison (Thomas A.) Interests: 556
Electric Storage Battery Company: 628
Elgin Watch Company: 158
Endicott-Johnson Company: 177, 449, 559, 589
Equitable Life Assurance Company: 573
Equitable Trust Company: 496
Everlastik, Inc.: 149

Fairbanks (E.&T.) Company: 158
Falk Corporation: 78
Famous Players-Lasky Corporation: 628
Farr Alpaca Company: 579, 589, 660
Fels & Company: 158
Ferris Brothers Company: 158, 171, 244
Field (Marshall) & Company: 165, 173, 573

MISCELLANEOUS INDEX

Items in this section were arbitrarily included. Not all
associations, names of persons, or organizations are listed
below. They generally were included only if the person,
association or organization made a major impact on the industrial welfare scene.

American Federation of Labor: 83, 146, 149
    See also: Section VIII. Labor's Response
American Management Association: 639
Appleton, Nathan: 5, 192, 693

Beeks, Gertrude: 1, 154, 247
Bloomingdale Brothers Employees' Mutual Aid Society: 173

Callaway, Fuller E.: 379
Carnegie, Andrew: 181, 341, 348, 354, 580
Colorado Coal Commission: 287, 296

Dennison, Henry S.: 3, 508, 578, 708

Filene, A. Lincoln: 22, 699
Filene, Edward A.: 3, 23, 40, 95, 112, 699, 705
Firestone, Harvey: 230, 231
Ford, Henry: 606, 670

Gantt, Henry Laurence: 46, 404
Gladden, Washington: 697
Gompers, Samuel: 67, 303, 664, 667, 672, 673, 677, 684, 687,
    688, 692, 700
Green, William: 79, 101, 119, 391, 662, 663, 670, 675, 676,
    678, 681, 682, 685, 686
Gregg, William: 402, 703, 710
    See also: Graniteville Manufacturing Company in Company
    Index

228

Hapgood, William Powers: 99, 113, 709
    See also: Columbia Conserve Company in Company Index
Hicks, Clarence J.: 701

Jones, Samuel M. (Golden Rule Jones): 225

King, William Lyon MacKenzie: 302, 696, 698, 704

Lake Carriers' Association: 194
Lenin, Vladimir I.: 40
Loggers and Lumbermen; Loyal Legion of: 122
Lowell, Francis Cabot: 5, 192, 693

Mitchell, John: 683

National Association of Corporation Schools: 467, 476, 512
    630, 638
National Association of Manufacturers: 59, 692
National Civic Federation: 1, 6, 27, 34, 43, 62, 153, 154,
    165-167, 183, 264, 320, 403, 494-496, 532, 540, 578, 594,
    601, 605, 674, 677, 683, 684, 689
National Industrial Conference Board: 44, 92, 122-124, 168-
    170, 239, 458, 477-479, 497, 533, 562-564, 595, 596, 623,
    626, 631, 632, 652, 659, 669
National Industrial Recovery Act: 79, 82, 119, 122, 129, 656,
    662, 682, 686
National Labor Relations Act: 78, 82, 94
National Labor Relations Board: 78, 96
National Metal Trades Association: 265
National War Labor Board: 72, 82, 92, 108, 123, 124, 136
Nelson, Nelson O.: 3, 202, 242, 597-599, 706, 707

Patterson, John H.: 200, 248, 695
    See also: National Cash Register Company in Company Index
Pullman, George: 436, 450

Railway Labor Act: 310, 321, 656
Randolph, A. Philip: 326
Rockefeller, John D. Jr.: 273, 275, 300-303, 687, 694, 696,
    698, 700, 704